Infinite Quest

Infinite Quest

Develop Your Psychic Intuition to Take Charge of Your Life

John Edward

STERLING ETHOS
New York

CAROL

STERLING ETHOS
New York

An Imprint of Sterling Publishing
387 Park Avenue South
New York, NY 10016

STERLING ETHOS and the distinctive Sterling logo are registered trademarks of
Sterling Publishing Co., Inc.

© 2010 by John Edward

Book design and layout: Creative Media Applications, Inc.

ISBN 978-1-4027-7893-3 (hardcover)
ISBN 978-1-4027-9779-8 (paperback)

Library of Congress Cataloging-in-Publication Data

Edward, John (John J.)
   Infinite quest : develop your psychic intuition to take charge of your life / by John Edward.
     p. cm.
   Includes index.
   ISBN 978–1–4027–7893–3
1. Psychic ability. I. Title.
   BF1031.E44 2010
   133.8—dc22
               2010021141

Distributed in Canada by Sterling Publishing
^c/o Canadian Manda Group, 165 Dufferin Street
Toronto, Ontario, Canada M6K 3H6
Distributed in the United Kingdom by GMC Distribution Services
Castle Place, 166 High Street, Lewes, East Sussex, England BN7 1XU
Distributed in Australia by Capricorn Link (Australia) Pty. Ltd.
P.O. Box 704, Windsor, NSW 2756, Australia

For information about custom editions, special sales, and premium and corporate purchases,
please contact Sterling Special Sales at 800-805-5489 or specialsales@sterlingpublishing.com.

Manufactured in the United States of America

10 9 8 7 6 5 4 3 2 1

www.sterlingpublishing.com

This Book is dedicated to Sandy Anastasi
for helping me harness and train my ability, and
shape and develop my teaching.

And in loving memory of my amazing friend Shelley Peck,
who will always make me smile when I think of
the many adventures we have shared in this lifetime.
You are missed, my Scorpio friend.

CONTENTS

LETTER TO READER FROM JOHN EDWARD

Dear Friend,

This book has been twenty-five years in the making; actually, it's really more like forty. Why such a discrepancy in the years? Well, it's simple. I turned forty last year, and it is my twenty-fifth anniversary of being a psychic medium. I won't go into detail about how I started in this profession, because I covered that in my first book, *One Last Time*. Instead, I want this book to be all about YOU, not me. Well, technically, it's about me and my experiences, but I am sharing the lessons I learned to empower and enhance your existence in this lifetime as YOU.

If you are browsing through a bookstore or shopping around online and happen to be reading this, you're supposed to be. You may often hear that everything happens for a reason, but now ask yourself the question "Why?" Did you get the answer? If so, do you know *HOW* you got your answer or even if you were the one who thought it? Confused? Stay with me.

Think of this entire book as an experience designed to be an earthly guide to a spiritually energetic Divine process. That process is YOU. Questions will be posed to you throughout our voyage together and new ones will be formed by you along the way. I am going to take you on a metaphysical excursion, teaching you through my life's lessons and experiences and by using metaphor and anecdotes from movies, television, and literature, all to help you evolve in your own QUEST of the INFINITE.

So set some time aside for us and we will journey into aspects of yourself and your own process of psychic evolution. And even though this book is designed to be about psychic development, I am hoping that you get the bigger picture . . . it's really about evolving into being the best YOU possible.

Are you ready to join me on an adventure? If so, read on.

—JOHN EDWARD

PROLOGUE

"Can you write a book on psychic development?"
*"How about writing a book about the Afterlife and
what the Other Side is like?"*

Those are some of the questions that I often have been asked when dealing with the publishing world. I have always declined to cover these topics in a book for a variety of reasons. Maybe it's my seventh-grade math teacher's fault.

"Never put into writing what you don't want someone else to read," Ms. Gordon would say with an all-knowing smile.

Usually she was speaking about the kids passing notes during her class. I'm happy to report that I was NOT one of those kids writing my secrets down for a friend, only to cringe as I heard them read out loud by my teacher. I was too busy daydreaming and staring at the energy I could see around people, which I didn't have a name or explanation for yet. Later I would learn that I was looking at people's *auras*.

I guess the main reason I didn't want to write this particular book before was that I worried that it would only teach people how to do a psychic reading. You see, ethics and responsibility are essential elements in giving a reading and can't be taken lightly by anyone. And I admit that I was not quite sure that I would be able to sufficiently get that message across. I will stress it again to make sure that right from the beginning you are hearing me loud and clear: *THE ETHICAL RESPONSIBILITY THAT GOES INTO DOING A READING FOR SOMEONE IS ENORMOUSLY HUGE!*

I promise we will go over this critical point ad nauseam before you finish this book. Why? Because I want you to understand that this intuitive work and world of energy that you are a part of is special, magical even. And unfortunately, it's not uncommon for people to inflate their own greatness and to feed their insecurities by stroking their own "Inner Monster," otherwise known as their EGO. Folks, let me tell you right here and now: EGO SUCKS and is *not* your friend when you are trying to develop into the type of spiritual person you viscerally know you truly want to be. If you are not vigilant, your ego can easily be your biggest downfall to your practice. My Guides once came through me during a deep channeling session that I did in a controlled environment, and they told one of my students (now a successful professional psychic medium) that he should be patient with me as his mentor because I can be **"harsh."**

I did not remember this session even though I was the instrument for it. And when it was recounted to me, I will personally admit that I was slightly offended by the message and thought maybe my student was embellishing so I would go easier on him.

"I am not harsh!" was my first reaction. *"Harsh? Really?"* was all I kept saying for the next twenty-four hours after that . . . and then the truth hit me. I am harsh. I am like a militant drill sergeant who is willing to do whatever it takes to bring out the best from his troops. I will be that same way here with you to the utmost of my ability, but your free will has to choose to let my voice speak to you through the pages of this book.

So in keeping with my promise, I want to be very clear now and throughout this work. I am not writing this book so that you can have a new occupation of doing psychic readings for people. If that is your primary goal, return the book immediately, put it on your shelf, or give it away. This book is *not* meant for you.

If you are expecting to find within the confines of this book the ammunition to support your Inner Monster and to celebrate how special and "gifted" you are in your psychic ability, this book is **clearly** not for you.

However, if you are excited to discover more about yourself, your spirituality, and your intuition; about connecting with your Higher Self and your Spirit Guides, learning how to make more empowered choices, and manifesting the future that you want, please read on.

Why have I always declined writing this type of book in the past? The reason was simple. FEAR! I was afraid to and have struggled with my fear internally over the last fifteen years. Of course, I have discussed psychic development in my other publications and even recorded a set of audiotapes on my teachings, but never written a book on the subject. A book is like a textbook to me, a how-to manual of sorts. I wasn't ready to do that for fear that it would fall into the wrong hands. I was worried that people would absorb the development content and launch into doing readings based on my teachings and miss the most important part of the message. Now, I don't want to sound all top-secret paranoid, but I feel that the skills that I'm disseminating in the pages of this book are powerful tools that will enhance your experience as YOU, if you pay close attention to them.

I know that my path and purpose in this incarnation (lifetime) is to raise people's awareness to the world of energy around them and to help them recognize how they can work with it, not against it. "Mission Accomplished" in my personal scorebook. After close to a thousand hours of television aired internationally of both *Crossing Over with John Edward* and *John Edward Cross Country,* and six best-selling books that all deal with metaphysics, I really feel that I have been instrumental in getting people to begin a dialogue with themselves on their own beliefs about an Afterlife, their loved ones on the Other Side, and all the potential that these concepts bring.

But when editors, publishers, and clients alike were clamoring for me to write the quintessential book on what the Other Side is like or a book on psychic development, I continued to politely decline. I live here on this plane of existence known as EARTH, and I know that there *is* something else beyond this since I've been conversing with

IT for decades. But because I know that there is a subjective element at work here for me as well, I didn't want to fall into the category of making umbrella statements. I really dislike when someone in a position like mine makes these grandiose and overly simplified statements that end up doing a disservice to the field as a whole.

It comes down to the word *responsibility*. I didn't want to take it on; I was fearful of being karmically responsible for instructing others how to do a reading and their words then being tied to me. Even though that would NOT actually be the case, I still like to make sure that I approach my teaching as if it were. But it is that very same feeling of responsibility and dedication that I have for my work that now has me sitting at my desk writing this book. There is an ever-growing amount of material regarding psychic powers available, which concerns me because it rarely includes the ethical component that is absolutely essential for novices to understand.

I have taught only a handful of psychic development workshops and classes over the years and during the last one I had the attendees all sign a legal waiver stating that they would not use my name in conjunction with any readings that they might give later. Why did I have such a deep internal struggle? You guessed it: the likelihood of egos running around totally out of control.

THE INNER MONSTER NAMED EGO

One of the things that I want to clarify now is that we will be addressing the concept of *EGO* and how to balance it like walking a tightrope between two skyscrapers. One false move and—well, the conversation is a séance. When I speak to people, both professionals and novices, about psychic development, I say that I need to have just enough "ego" to allow me to do this work, but anything more than that gets in the way. Managing your ego as well as juggling your thoughts, feelings, and impressions and then having to be logical and self-aware at the same time is not an easy thing to accomplish.

But before we go down the rabbit hole and view life through the looking glass and all the other metaphysical anecdotal examples I'll probably list as we embark on our adventure, I want to repeat once more exactly what this book is and isn't about. As I am writing this, I am wondering if the publisher is going to have a "cow" and ask me to remove it. Let's face it: the publisher is in the business of selling books. But I want you to really know what you are in for if you buy this project. YES, you read that correctly. This is a *project* and what we are building is YOU.

This project of YOU, your *Infinite Quest*, is an amalgamation of my last twenty-five years of doing metaphysical work. Please think of me like yourself, a student of the process and these teachings. I am still learning and evolving in my own project. Shifts and changes happen over time, but sometimes the impetus is just a thought or simple moment. What if standing in the bookstore or sitting at your desk is that moment for you right now? What if someone handed you this book for a reason? And I know it's not because you saw my handsome face with my amber eyes and felt my charismatic personality jump out at you from the cover! (Don't worry . . . ego in check.)

There is a REASON why you are now reading this book. I believe it's because your Higher Self, your Spirit Guides (YES, you have them), and even some of your dead relatives (they care about education on the Other Side, too) have led you to participate in what we are going to address in this book: how to create the very best YOU.

So again, to be overwhelmingly clear: If you're buying this book to learn how to do psychic readings professionally or to be able to say that you studied my work and now you can give readings just like me . . . well, to borrow from one of my favorite movies, *Young Frankenstein:* **"Listen to me very carefully. PUT DA BOOK BACK!"** Okay, I know Gene Wilder actually said "candle," but it made me laugh as I was writing this and I hope some of you chuckled as well.

SPOILER ALERT: Reading this book is going to be like taking a long car ride with your annoying brother in the backseat on a hot summer day. I will be pointing out all the road signs on our metaphysical trip, announcing we are NOT there yet, and also poking you while you're trying to just "be" on your journey. My Italian grandmother used to tease me, calling me a pain in the ass. And I guess I still am, especially when it comes to my dedication to my work and the code of ethics I expect to be followed. But don't worry, we will enjoy our time together. We will learn and evolve. We WILL develop our abilities. But ultimately, your goal should far exceed whether you can do a reading for another person and get the "Oh my God, how did you know that?" reaction. The goal for me is to share with you how in the last twenty-five years I have lived by these metaphysical principles and how they can create positive change in your life, too.

WARNING! WARNING!

If you proceed further, you are doing so by your own volition and free will. You are deputizing yourself as a STUDENT of the UNIVERSE (not John Edward) and are acknowledging to the Universe that you are willing to take responsibility for learning from the experiences in your life, as well as mine. And like in the movie *The Matrix*—here's your blue pill or red pill moment . . .

THE
JOURNEY
Until Now

SECRET TO LIVING A PSYCHIC LIFE:
It's a common mistake to think that when you develop your
psychic abilities you are doing so just to give readings. That
is actually a small part of the bigger energetic picture that
is potentially available for you. The ultimate goal is to live a
psychic life *every day* and to use that newfound recognition to
take chances and make choices with confidence.

In order to move forward, we need to understand the past. This is a simple idea but will be one of the more difficult things we will learn together. I am going to teach you many different ways to develop your intuition and raise your spiritual awareness. But none of it will mean anything if you don't understand your life's path to how you got to here, right now, today. This includes being able to examine as objectively as possible the preset messages you carry around with you as you walk through life. We will use physical fitness as an example of what I mean.

Are you overweight?

If you answered the question "Yes," then the next question is:

Do you want to be?

If you answered the question "No," then my response is simple:

CHANGE IT!

If your response is **"I CAN'T CHANGE IT!"** . . . then we have our first obstacle to overcome. Until you move beyond this type of negative mental roadblock, I can't help you with another damn lesson in this book. The whole thing will be words and stories on a page, experiences that I relate to you from my life that you can read about but will feel removed from. *"How nice for him but I can't do that!"* will be your answer to my questions and suggestions. Listen, I get it. I really do. I want you to know that I am sympathetic to having to make major changes in your thinking and programming.

A few years ago, my friend, Frank Sepe, an author, lecturer, all-around life coach, and celebrity trainer who has graced the covers of hundreds of magazines, was putting me through a series of workouts. He has a model body and is amazingly fit, very good-looking, and as passionate about fitness, nutrition, and health as I am about metaphysics. You can definitely say he is "harsh" like me, as well as one of the wittiest and most sarcastic people I know.

We have had many great conversations about personal motivations and goal-setting, and the parallels between his work ethic and mine are really quite similar. One day as I was ready to pass out after one of his workouts, he asked me if I would write the foreword to his next book on abs. I laughed, thinking he was being sarcastic. If the foreword was about chocolate chip cookies and the abs were the Pillsbury Doughboy's, maybe I would've taken him seriously. But I honestly thought he was kidding.

A few weeks later, he asked again and this time I thought, *"Why is he messing around with me?"* Perhaps this was some sort of psychological warfare he was launching. If I had to write a foreword for a book about abdominal muscles, maybe I would use that as the impetus to actually "find" a set of abs to write about!

At that point, I wanted to take a poll of all his clients and see if he was asking them to write for his new book . . . he was not. Finally, a month later Frank told me that if I was going to write the foreword I would have to do it within a week. The reality that he was serious hit me like a ton of bricks. My first thought was maybe he wanted a pseudo-celebrity's name on the cover, but with the long list of celebrities that he has on speed dial I quickly realized that my name was *not* the reason. So I asked him, *"Why are you asking me, someone who clearly does not have a six-pack set of abs, to write the foreword to your book?"*

Frank's reply was simple: *"You get it."*

I get it. I get that the work is first done in the mind, not the body. That a person has to truly want to make the change before it can begin to happen.

Standing there in the middle of the gym, those three words rocked me to my core: *I get it.* Did you ever just hate someone for pointing out the truth? In that moment I couldn't blame anyone else on the planet—not my genetics, not my schedule, not anything else but me for WHY I didn't have six-pack abs.

I had to own that I knew how to get them. I knew what goes into developing them, and the fact that I didn't have those abs—well, it means I had to own that and be responsible for that fact. OUCH! Being self-aware can be shitty sometimes. Enlightenment was starting to feel like a carb-free diet to me at that moment.

I had been yo-yo dieting and working with trainers in the belief that I did want the beach body physique. Frank pointed out that I was smart enough to know how to make it happen and that nobody else could do it for me . . . no supplement, no machine, no trainer . . . just me. Now I had to sit with the knowledge that maybe I just didn't want to put the necessary time and energy into that result, even though I thought I truly did. But if I *really* wanted that six-pack body, I would've already had it.

I am here to be your personal trainer for your spiritual development. So even though this is a book about developing your psychic abilities, we need to address other areas of your life as well, things that you will probably not find in any other ESP how-to manuals. This is a life project that will force you to address questions that you might not ever have thought of if you were not experiencing this book.

I want you to take the time to consider these questions so that you enjoy the revelations along the way and you aren't just focused on the destination of *"being psychic,"* but really enjoying your personal journey on the highway of your life.

So there will be no "step one, do this; step two, do that; and when done with all the steps, go do a reading" to be found in this book. I'm actually hoping that by the time you have finished this book, you will have gained a self-discovery and an awareness that lead to a more fulfilling life experience.

Now don't think I forgot about my earlier question when I asked if you are overweight. It doesn't really matter to me if you are or aren't, but it does matter to me how you answered the question to yourself and if you can allow yourself to say that you are the only one responsible for why. The same concept is applicable to whether you are an avid smoker, heavy drinker, endless procrastinator, or compulsive gambler. **It's not anyone else's fault.**

You will not be able to raise your vibration of self-discovery if you can't own who you are today and, more importantly, reflect back on the decisions, choices, and situations that created YOU. Those aspects that help to shape you and your life, your beliefs and thoughts, are part of your energetic programming. We will be challenging a lot of that preexisting programming. Some of those challenges will turn into the "AHA" moments where you are in total alignment with yourself and the Universe, and others—well, they may take a little more time to change.

When I was nineteen, I was confronted with life in a very profound way when my mother lost her battle with lung cancer. She was and still remains a cornerstone in the foundation of my life and Project ME. The morning that she crossed over I had to go pick up a tuxedo for my cousin's wedding. The ceremony was two days later and I was in the bridal party. My mom wanted to make sure that the wedding was going to happen regardless of her condition and made everyone promise that they would attend if she didn't make it there "physically." By the way, you will notice that I do not use the words *died, death, dying,* or my least favorite term for all you medical folks out there, *expired.* As a society we tend to differentiate between death and life when mortality is actually a part of LIFE.

I sat in my car staring up at her bedroom windows as the reality of her absence was becoming more like the Grand Canyon in my life with each passing minute, and I had the following thought: *"Nobody will ever care what time I come home again."* My parents were divorced, and my mother and I lived upstairs in my maternal grandmother's house. I felt totally alone. I felt like I was spiraling into an instantaneous deep pit of despair and I remember thinking, or "hearing," that I had two choices:

OPTION #1: BE A VICTIM
and
spiral further into negativity and use this as the excuse.

OPTION #2: MAKE IT AN ADVENTURE
and
turn life into whatever good you can manifest.

Thankfully, I chose Option #2 and my life has been an active adventure ever since. *I am here to tell you that you cannot expect anyone to do anything for you, nor should they.* You have up until now unconsciously created the opportunities in your life and you attracted the people who assisted in being the catalyst for the experiences you have had . . . both positively and negatively. Let's not start arguing so early on our journey together. If this material is already challenging your programming because of *where* you feel you are at in your life, and you are blaming other people, their actions, your lot in life, or the dog …well, it is sounding like you might have chosen Option #1. Travel on with me and learn how to change your framework over to Option #2 and plant seeds for what you want to grow in your spiritual garden.

Don't look outside yourself for what you already have. Allow yourself to turn your life into an adventure today and every day.

DETOURS AND TRAFFIC

There will be many detours along this highway. There will be a lot of traffic blocking your progress and getting in your way. Please remember that you have created and attracted all of it. So instead of being angry or frustrated, try to understand it. Seek out the meaning in every experience you have. Just like in school, once you graduate from a grade, you move on to the next level. However, if you fail the lesson, you repeat it over again until you learn what you need to know. Life is not so different and the school is the UNIVERSE.

YOU AND YOUR TEAM

There's no easy way to say this: **There are "Invisible Forces" helping you all the time.** Call them your angels, your Guides, or your relatives; call them Frank, Bob, or Mary if you like; let's just start acknowledging them and then you can name them whatever you wish.

I am blessed with two beautiful children. At the time of this writing, Justin is seven and Olivia just turned three. I will be teaching you the exact same lessons I am teaching my kids on their journeys.

One day, Justin told me that he "heard" someone calling his name at home and after he walked around the house asking his grandparents and his mom what they wanted, they simply replied that they hadn't called him. I remember seeing a look of puzzlement on his face. I didn't address it at that moment. A couple of days later as I started getting him ready for school, he was sitting up in his bed instead of jumping out of it, and I asked him what was going on.

"I don't understand why that happens so much," he said, with that same puzzled look on his face.

"Why what happens, Justin?"

"Why I hear someone say, 'JUSTIN! JUSTIN!' and there's nobody there . . . who is saying that? How is that possible, Daddy?"

I was rendered speechless for a few seconds as he looked at me with great intensity. I think I would rather have had to explain where babies come from at that moment than have this particular talk with him. It is hard enough having discussions with adults who I don't think fully get it, and now here I was breaking it down for someone who thinks it's hilarious that when he laughs too hard when drinking milk it flies out of his nose.

I am not going to address our conversations in detail at this point, because I will talk about children and psychic development later in the book, but here is what Justin walked away knowing. **He has a TEAM of people that God put in his path to help him live the best life**

possible . . . and now you know it as well. A Team that consists of the family that loves him here in the physical world, as well as those that are still his family and love him but are basically invisible. A Team that can't do things completely for him, but if he *"listens"* and learns how they communicate with him, he will gain incredible insights.

His innocent response was, *"Cool, I have a Team. Daddy, can they help me with my homework?"*

You have a Team as well. Some of them might have been with you from other incarnations, and some might have been assigned to you specifically for this lifetime. Some Spirit Guides come and go, and sometimes they may even be family members. And, yes, they can help you with your homework, too.

Now there are a number of questions that are probably pouring through your mind as you are reading this information. This is one of the rest stops on our journey. We are going to pull over for a moment in our process, and you are going to think about your Team. You don't need to do this out loud, but I want you to acknowledge the fact that *THEY* are there. You may want to say a prayer of thanks for their years of service of invisibly assisting you, watching you make some choices that—if they HAD a physical body—would have made them try to shake some sense into you and other choices that would have made them stand up and cheer.

Right now, I want you to put the book down and close your eyes. I want you to just allow your Team to show you in some way a memory of an experience where they might have been present. Once you think of at least one, start reading again.

Okay, so if you either ignored me and kept on reading because you are one of those people who like to read the last chapter of the book to see if all the characters are still alive and present, or, perhaps, you want to continue to ignore your Team even after I am establishing the fact that you have one at your disposal, **STOP** reading this instant. Please just do the exercise now since we can't go any further until you do! Good. I am going to have to take you at your word here and hope that you did attempt the exercise. There will be many more like it. If you want to write down in the book what you saw, that's fine. It's even better if you want to write it down in a journal. Whatever memory or experience you had, I want you to know that there's always a different perspective to it. Many times that is all your Guides do. They give us their unique perspective to assist us in making more informed choices. But we still have our *Free Will* to do what we want. We will discuss more about that further down the road on our journey.

Think about what you were feeling as you saw that past situation. Remember it and write it down. Try to be present in the memory and see if you were experiencing that memory or situation in a spectator-like manner or if it felt the exact same way as when it initially happened. The reason why I need you to do this type of examination is to learn how you *"see"* or *"feel"* things. I want you to become a reporter of your own life's experiences from this point on . . . like you have to be that set of eyes and ears for someone who can't actually be there.

Can you recall any experience as a child where you had this strong *"feeling"* not to do something? Can you remember the result of listening to it or not listening to it? It is very important to take some time now to ask your Team to give you more of their guidance because you are now going to really listen to them when they do.

Team Awareness Exercise

I want you to take the time to reflect back consciously on your past to be aware of more moments or situations when you think you might have had assistance from your Team, but because you were in the experience you weren't paying close attention to how things were "feeling."

Ask your Spirit Guides to show you examples of various times in your life when they were helping you and how they did

**it. Observe how you experience the answers. Yes, you might think
you are making it up . . . just keep going. Write it all down without
any judgment.**

I wouldn't be surprised if in less than thirty minutes you had two
pages of information and experiences. I like to refer to my Team as
"the boys." I have done so since I first began developing my abilities.
I believe my Guides were the ones who suggested that I call them
"the boys" because I was starting to feel like I was part of the TV
family *The Waltons* when I was going to sleep at night whenever I
was doing a meditation or preparing for a reading. For my younger
readers who may not be familiar with the show, at the end of each
episode all the members of the large Walton family (including seven
children) would call out "goodnight" to each other from their beds as
the credits rolled. And in the same way, I would call out to each of my
Guides until the list became a bit lengthy, and I was told "the boys"
would work just as well.

IMPORTANT NOTE: I am going to refer to "God" a lot, and
I am going to talk about Divine Guidance and Wisdom, but I
am NOT going to write about religious organizations. When
I began doing this work, I made a conscious decision to not
discuss God in any denomination, especially in dealing with the
media. I feel that I am painting a portrait of energy, and how
people choose to frame that portrait is up to them. Some people
might have no frame and others a thick one. Don't get hung up
on the semantics; wherever I mention "God," understand that
I am using it as a concept. If it makes you uncomfortable, just
substitute whatever higher power or source that resonates the
most with you.

At this point I am so excited for you and your realization (maybe for the first time) that you're not alone and never have been. Isn't it a great feeling to know that God loves you enough to give you a lifelong Team of spiritual sitters in a way to help you be the best YOU possible?

Some of you might be nodding now and saying, "Wait . . . I already know that I have Spirit Guides because I have been reading and learning about metaphysics for thirty years!" My response is "Good for you." Now, please keep reading.

What We Know Now

Okay, so we all have Spirit Guides that are working with us. We will call them your Team. We all know that they have been working with us since we arrived into this lifetime, and we know that they can't *do* things for us, but can *assist us* in making our choices by inspiring us in many different ways.

How can I get more in touch with my team?

That is the most obvious question and it has a simple answer: **Meditation and Prayer.**

Wait, before you start chanting like a monk or breathing like a yogi, I need to address one of the most critical aspects of your development.

PSYCHIC SELF-DEFENSE

I know that every time I bring up the subject of psychic self-defense, people get all these visual images in their minds. Some laugh at the concept, and others take the idea to a place of fear and that unfortunately stops them from being able to move forward.

What is it and why is it so important?

When you are opening yourself up to something new, regardless of the concept, there are elements of it that you need to be aware of, precautions and things to *respect* for your personal well-being. For example, if you were to take up being an equestrian, you would need to develop an understanding of how to treat the horse with respect, as you would not want to be injured. You learn how to control the energy of the horse, and how to become one with it, and how to recognize if it is not in a good mood or place to ride or jump. Otherwise, the results could be catastrophic.

The same holds true if you were to take up flying planes. Clearly, you get the need for precautions and personal protection here…point made. But what about an example that is less obvious but equally as dangerous in a different manner, such as cooking?

With cooking, there is the obvious need of taking precautions when working with sharp utensils and the heat of the stove or oven, but other risks are also lurking. Dangerous bacteria like E. coli and salmonella can be lethal to your health. You should always take special precautions when handling and preparing certain foods to make sure that these health issues never arise. You need to do the same with psychic energy as well.

Sex is another example that I like to use in regard to energetic protection, or more specifically, unprotected sex. It is the closest analogy to working with psychic energy that most people can understand. You are opening yourself up to the energetic experience and the world of energy around you. Quite honestly, you never know what you may pick up; if you are not careful, the results could be long-lasting and quite negative.

If you attempt to do readings for people, you are now a target or a receptacle for energy, both positive and negative, from their lives. This is true for anyone, by the way, whether you are reading a family member you love or a complete stranger. You may have an experience on one level and not realize what you "pick up" until much later. You might never know that you took on this person's energy and it could definitely be detrimental.

Yes, of course there are negative elements and dark forces in the Universe. And, yes, there are energies that want to do terrible things, damaging things, to other people. If you don't believe me, just turn on the news. If this is happening with people in the physical world, of course it will happen in the other worlds we reflect. The Other Side or the other dimensions I am speaking of have many levels, with energies both evolved and not. We want to protect ourselves from that obvious predatory energy (meant to be read with an "oh shit" feeling), but we also want to protect ourselves from the energies of the people in our everyday lives just as much.

I want to congratulate you on the fact that you are embarking on this journey of self-discovery. Just know that by doing so, you are opening yourself up, and you need to be aware of what's in your life currently and who and what is around you at all times. There will be measurable differences in your life because in some ways you are removing *shields of protection*, natural barriers, like energetic calluses that formed over time. And now, in their place, you are more exposed, unshielded, and vulnerable to energetic attack.

Psychic self-defense is the energetic "condom" that allows you to engage in what you need to experience in life, but protects you from taking on the ill effects.

Psychic Self-Defense Exercise

Just so we can continue on our journey, I want you to imagine an icon or symbol that you feel is a "power symbol" for you. It can be religious, or something like the Superman logo, or it could even be an animal—whatever YOU feel can be a representation of protection. Know that when you imagine connecting with that symbol you are protected and safe from harm. You are giving yourself permission to be protected as well.

You also want to consciously call upon your Team to assist you in fortifying your spiritual energy of protection. Be diligent about this, PLEASE. I will reaffirm many things throughout this book—especially balancing EGO and AWARENESS and always protecting yourself energetically.

Most importantly, you will hear me and many others talk about the *WHITE LIGHT.* This is an essential ingredient to carry with you on your journey. It is considered to be the *"White Light of God."* Please memorize the following and say it as often as you like or feel necessary:

> "I ENCIRCLE MYSELF IN THE WHITE LIGHT OF
> GOD'S LOVE AND DIVINE PROTECTION."

While you are repeating this to yourself over and over, becoming one with the thought and weaving it into the very heart and soul of who you are, your cellular as well as "soul-ular" self, imagine this pure brilliant white bright light coming from above you, maybe through the clouds or directly from the sun. Allow yourself to bathe in that light, allow it to warm you and permeate every cell in your body . . . down to your core. THIS IS SO IMPORTANT, I can't stress it enough. I want you to get used to doing this a lot. You want to build up your ability to call upon this light at all times, almost like you are always basking in it.

There will be additional PSD techniques in the latter part of this book, but now we can build upon Project YOU with a strong foundation of understanding.

Don't forget—whenever you are going to address your Team, you are going to make sure that you are practicing psychic self-defense at all times.

COMMUNICATION WITH YOUR TEAM

I have just informed you that you have a Team of Guides that are working with you on your journey. Now we need to move forward, while using the PSD technique of the white light and saying your prayer, in learning how to recognize how your Team communicates with you.

The Five Psychic Senses

You are going to think that I like to complain a lot in this book. I assure you that is not the case at all. I get the same questions everywhere I go. The cities, states, and countries may change, but the questions that people ask do not. Some of them are clearly written by the Inner Monster, but others are born from not being informed or from accepting a scripted movie or television show as the sole source of information. I am a huge fan of the movie *Ghost*, but clearly know that it is a work of fiction that is based on metaphysical fact and then dramatically embellished to tell a story. The movie is a great metaphor for life, just like the Bible. Please save your letters! I believe that the Bible was inspired by God in the hearts of human beings to capture, teach, and share a divine message about living a great human experience. I consider it to be the greatest piece of psychic material, actually—a channeled book of sorts.

Just as we have five physical senses of seeing, hearing, smelling, feeling, and tasting, we have psychic ones that correlate. I call them the "*five psychic sisters*" ... "The Five Clairs"!

Clairvoyance—*clear seeing*
Clairaudience—*clear hearing*
Clairsentience—*clear feeling*
Clairalience—*clear smelling*
Clairambience—*clear tasting*

I would like to be the first person to tell you that there is ABSO-LUTELY NOTHING CLEAR about any of the above experiences at all. I jokingly think that they should be called instead *subtle-voyance,*

THE NOTES

I will use many metaphors and analogies to help you understand these subtle yet complex concepts. The language of music is written with musical notes that create chords, rhythms, and songs. Similarly, these notes are like letters that make up words, sentences, and so on. In the same way, the energy that is coming through from your Team of Guides, or Aunt Mary, for that matter, is going to consist of various "symbols" in a way. It's all about learning your set of symbols and how your Team expresses them. Please know that it will always be in YOUR frame of reference, and that's the place you must always begin.

subtle-audience, et cetera...you get the point.

These are the abilities or faculties that psychic energy flows through and manifests as. Take a minute and think about psychic energy as being AIR. And the abilities described above as the instruments: flute, clarinet, trumpet, saxophone, and tuba. The energy flows through all those instruments and produces a sound that is unique to each. The quality of that sound depends on the musician and his or her level of natural ability or learned skill. Will it be noise? Or will it be music? Each one portrays the energy "air" differently, but they can all come together for an orchestral experience of perception.

Your Team will help to "move" the air or energy into your various instruments and play the information. One of your jobs is to recognize what instrument you are most comfortable playing.

Okay, enough of the instrument metaphors. Let's get back to YOU again.

Are you a visual person? Are you more of a word person? Are you highly emotional? Predominantly, you will find that seeing, hearing, and feeling are the most used instruments in our psychic wind section. To what degree, you will now have to start noticing on your own. I can't really tell you. However, rudimentary astrology can come into play here to get you started on finding out.

For example, if you are an AIR sun sign (Gemini, Libra, Aquarius), I would venture to guess your clairaudient ability would be the most prominent due to your affinity with words.

If you are a WATER sun sign (Cancer, Scorpio, Pisces), you are more likely a clairsentient person, because of the emotional dominance.

EARTH signs (Taurus, Virgo, Capricorn) are more comfortable with the physical senses, so seeing, smelling, or tasting work best since they need more proof to make the experience real.

And last but not least, FIRE signs (Aries, Leo, Sagittarius) are best at clairvoyance, because they tend to perceive more in visuals since they prefer a fast, spontaneous connection.

What I have described represents just a few grains of sand on a beach in regard to the depths you can go with the science of astrology.

Again, this is a quick example of what the world of energy is that you are living in and are now attempting to understand. You can't really develop Project YOU without getting into all these other modalities. That's why I try to make it crystal clear how important it is that this can't be just a book on how to do a reading or connect with a dead relative.

Please don't be alarmed if right now you are thinking, "I have no idea if I am a tuba player or a flutist." *"Patience, grasshopper"* . . . everything in due time.

2

MOTIVATIONAL ENERGY

A REFLEX is defined as an involuntary reaction to a stimulus or any automatic, unthinking, often habitual behavior or response.

When you hear the word *reflex,* you probably immediately conjure up the image of a doctor with a little hammer hitting your knee and watching it move like someone else made it happen. That Pinocchio moment of feeling like you are a marionette is clear to see and feel because of the obvious stimulus. What about the stimuli that are all around you every day that cause you to have various sorts of reflexes, or, more realistically, reactions? Some of them will infiltrate your thinking and can actually affect the way you make choices.

As I said in Chapter 1, we will be interweaving concepts and overlapping themes throughout our journey, reminiscing and building on lessons introduced and learned in previous discussions and examples. It might feel like I am digressing or covering the same material at times, but I have my rationale for doing so. For instance, the concept of *psychic self-defense* is one of the techniques that I will be talking about repeatedly since it is essential that you understand its importance in your development.

There are many reasons why you need to be on the defense psychically twenty-four hours a day. When you watch television, for example, it is often because you are looking to be somewhat mindlessly entertained. You are not watching it because you want to be accosted by someone else's issues (reality shows notwithstanding), yet you are under attack every single time you turn it on. Imagine that you are viewing your favorite television show (one of mine happens to be *Lost)* during a crucial moment in the plot, or maybe it's a comedy where you are actually laughing out loud (*Seinfeld* is a classic example), when all of a sudden a man walks into the middle of your living room and tells you that you might have a disease if your legs are restless all night, or a woman climbs through your bedroom window and begins to talk about your "whoo-whoo" and why it's itchy, or a lizard dances into your kitchen while you're pouring your morning coffee and starts spouting off about how you can save money on your car insurance.

Didn't all those scenarios seem ridiculous? Of course they are. I mean, you would never allow these random strangers to infringe on your life and barge into your home, right? You have locks on your doors and security systems to ensure your privacy and protect you from such a violation.

Would you believe me when I tell you that you often allow these intrusions to take place? Don't believe me? Well, I just did it to you. When I "told" you that I liked *Lost* and *Seinfeld,* I possibly planted a seed for you. Either you are already familiar with both, or you might have said to yourself, "Maybe I should check them out." Mentioning my favorite shows elicited a reaction and influenced you ever so slightly.

Some of you already know where I am going with this line of thinking. TV commercials in the USA typically make these types of "suggestions" twenty minutes out of every sixty-minute program that you watch. That is a fact. It is advertisers who pay for the shows that are produced and aired. That's the business side of television; someone has to pay for it. Now, let's see how you are paying for it metaphysically.

You are lying in your bed at night exhausted. You are depleted and just want to watch a little "telly" and relax. Perhaps you turn on the evening news so you can catch up on what's happening in the world. This is where the *"attack"* begins. The news is rarely positive. In a twenty-two-minute broadcast, you are bombarded by the down-turning of the economy, celebrity scandals, fighting politicians, sense-less murders, the depressing results of the latest natural disaster, and the overwhelming weight of war . . . get the picture? Why? Because bad news sells. There's nobody to blame, really; it's just how people are. We are naturally voyeuristic about other people's lives and experiences. We stop and look at the car accident. We care. We empathize. We might even feel horrified or sad. We imagine what it would be like to be in that position, and without necessarily meaning to we open ourselves up to it.

It's like inviting a vampire into your home. What happens to you during that period of time is just plain negative and then you go to sleep with that energy permeating your thoughts and infiltrating your psyche. Your dreams might be violent or uncomfortable, but that would be the least of your issues. It's in the coming days that you are most definitely under the influence, like a slow-released poison that you succumb to over time. You begin to think that you need to switch your car insurance, or you start to react in fear to some of the stories that you saw on the news as if they were happening directly to you. Remember in the movie *Ghostbusters* when the characters get "slimed"? You are being attacked in the same way, but you just didn't consciously know it. Now you do.

Now, I am not telling you to bury your head in the sand and ignore the rest of the world's troubles, but I am saying, be more aware of what you watch before you go to sleep at night. Try a comedy or a cartoon, or even better do something else. Meditate, listen to music, read a book, or make love ... whatever activity it is, create a relaxed and positive sleeping space. More importantly, start to program your own personal "network." Choose the images, thoughts, and issues that are going to positively influence the way you want to achieve change.

I know you're wondering now why I am on Chapter 2 of this book and you are not learning how to conduct séances yet, like Whoopi Goldberg's Oda Mae Brown in the movie *Ghost*. Do we need to have this conversation again? You know, the one about how this is a book about YOU developing spiritually, not just about how to speak to the dead and do readings? Still with me? I am assuming you said "*yes*," so let's move on.

We first need to address the motivational energy that is driving your development—the "*whys*" of it all. Here is a fun way to remember it. When you answer the "*why*" you become "*wise*" in the process. You discover the driving force of what you want and you then have a destination to plot out.

Ask yourself the following question and answer it honestly: **Why are you reading this book?**

As your guide on this literary journey, I will be fine with any answer except that you only want to do readings professionally. Truthfully, you will learn how to do that from this experience, but only if you start from a more personal and spiritual goal.

I believe that it's a timing issue for you. There is a *reason* why you are reading this book now. You might have picked it up for one reason, and you will see a deeper and more significant reason develop as you work with this material. Actually, I believe that there will be many reasons, but some stand out clearly more than others.

FEAR AND LOVE

I am going to tell you that in the last quarter century of working in this world of metaphysics and listening to countless self-help experts, motivational speakers, metaphysicians, et cetera, I have found there are only a couple of basic motivations we as humans can categorize: **FEAR** and **LOVE.**

I can hear and feel the rumblings from some of you while you are readings this. Settle down and explore this concept a bit. Think about it outside of your life. Think about your friends and family members whom you understand better than they sometimes know themselves. What motivates them would be the same thing, FEAR and LOVE.

Motivational Energy Exercise

Write down on a piece of paper all the goals that you have had over your lifetime. Then circle all the ones you achieved and cross out the ones you did not. The ones you reached you can more than likely attribute to LOVE and the ones you didn't usually fall under the FEAR category.

We do something for the love of it or the fear of it. Unfortunately, more people are motivated by fear than love. It is a great motivator and not always a bad one, by the way.

When I was a young child, my mom's extended family had an unspoken protective attitude toward me. Her sister, my Aunt Theresa, was and continues to be extremely close to me and now is the same way with my children. Every Sunday, she would come out from Brooklyn to visit me in Long Island and, weather permitting, we would go bike riding. We would ride our bikes up to the local deli and then ride back through the elementary school behind my grandmother's house. There was a six-foot chain-link fence that separated her backyard from that school. One Sunday, there were five adults trying to get me to climb over this fence to the schoolyard. I couldn't do it. It was like my arms and legs would not cooperate. I was paralyzed by the fear of falling, the fear of looking stupid, and the fear of my cousins laughing at me. Five of them hurled themselves over the fence with ease. I was a bit husky as a kid and self-conscious, so I quit before I even gave myself the chance to do it. I missed out on the festivities up at the field with my cousins, and all the adults had that "poor little fat kid" look on their faces. Nothing one of my granny's meatballs wouldn't cure!

Well, the following week, Aunt Theresa and I were doing our Sunday ride, but this week was different because she brought her dog, Jodi, along. Jodi was the same age as me and we grew up together. There are dogs and there are *dogs*. Jodi was one classy little black poodle and smart as a whip. She accompanied us proudly, keeping up with no problem whatsoever. When we reached the elementary school, there were two teenage boys hanging out with their big dogs. The boys started to wise off to my aunt. Jodi sensed the negativity and started to bark. Her barking alerted the two German shepherds and they went into attack mode. The situation began to get out of hand very quickly. My aunt told me to leave and go get help. The last thing I remember was her scooping Jodi up just before the ferocious dogs reached them. A moment later, and Jodi would have no doubt been mauled.

I tore off toward my grandmother's house and headed for the parking lot. One of the German shepherds decided that I was the prey instead and busted away from its owner. I knew this was *not* a good thing because the owner of the dog was screaming to the dog to come back. Hearing the panic in his voice triggered my "flight or fight" button. I flew! I started pedaling so fast that I lost control of the bicycle and wound up, you guessed it, right by that fence. Okay, what were my options? (A) Being a chew toy for the barking, teeth-baring dog, or (B) scaling that previously insurmountable fence.

Let me tell you that I got over that fence so fast I was like an Olympic gold medalist. The look of sheer astonishment on the faces of the same relatives who had pitied me the previous Sunday was unbelievable, and I would have basked in the glory of my accomplishment if I wasn't so concerned about Aunt Theresa and Jodi becoming the mean dog's lunch back at the school. The story is a juicy one, involving a number of fistfights, a few cop cars, and some funny one-liners, but thankfully, both Aunt Theresa and Jodi were safe and unharmed when all was said and done.

The point of the story is that I know FEAR isn't always a bad motivator. Its best use is when you're facing a survival type of decision. But I am going to say that most times, people utilize the FEAR motivation to STOP them from accomplishing things or reaching their goals.

There are about fifty examples that I could use to demonstrate the paralyzing effect that the downside of FEAR can bring, but none more personal than my mother's. When she was in the final stages of her lung cancer, with only weeks to live, I was standing next to her hospital bed and had a "flash" of her bureau at home, and one particular drawer. I had this overwhelming pull to see what was inside it.

I told her that I would be right back when she asked where I was going, and I drove the fifteen minutes back home. I walked right into her room and opened that drawer. Underneath her clothing was a manila envelope dated two years earlier. I opened it up and it was a mammography report detecting irregularities in both her breast and chest X-rays and stating that she needed to come in for future testing. My mother's overwhelming fear kept her from returning to the doctor for a diagnosis or any type of treatment. I very calmly returned the report to the drawer, drove back to the hospital, looked at her directly in the eye, and said, *"YOU KNEW!"* Nothing else had to be said or discussed in that moment. She gazed back at me and said, *"I was afraid. I was afraid that I was going to have cancer and die."*

She did . . . a few short weeks later.

*   *   *   *   *   *   *

WE HAVE TALKED A GREAT DEAL ABOUT THE motivations of FEAR in both a positive and negative aspect. I think it is important to address the motivating force that we need to be moving toward more in our life, and that is LOVE. One can debate both sides of each motivator and see aspects of both in each situation, just like looking at sprinkles on a scoop of vanilla ice cream. People will see what they resonate with most first.

I also think that many of the motivators about love are obvious and don't need to be discussed. They are self-sufficient gifts that are unconditionally anonymous. But some of our love motivators are not so clear-cut and can also be painful. The one in my work that I want to address here has to do with the end of someone's life.

For some, the last chapter or epilogue of their physical existence is not written. Most of the story has been told, but the last few pages are blank, and the author needs a bit of help in the telling of the finale. I will spell out bluntly the lesson to be learned here: **Get your**

affairs in order so that people don't have to wonder about what you would have wanted. Tell people what types of extraordinary measures or means you would be comfortable with and just how far you want the health care field to take you before your final exit. Too many people don't want to deal with this concept, and it's just plain laziness or foolishness. We are all going to *cross over*. There is no escape from it. We should plan for it, and clearly delineate for our loved ones remaining what we wish to happen, and be realistically loving about it.

Death brings out the "idiot" side of some people. I tell my clients all the time, "Welcome to the idiot zone" right after the loss of a loved one. Well-meaning folks will come up to you and say and do things that are grossly insensitive and insulting, all in the name of making you feel better and letting you know that you are loved. Please know that there is not a thing you can do during this time except to ride the wave of it. You can help ease your family's future journey through the idiot zone by making sure that you have your will, health care proxy, and living will all clearly in order.

When someone falls ill to the point that something has to be done to assist them in their care by either taking them off life support, withdrawing a feeding tube, ceasing treatments, and/or pulling the proverbial plug, the caregiver is left with a lifetime of grief and guilt that for many can be unbearable.

I like people to know that when we have to do such things, it is the LOVE principle that we are coming from. Because of the love we feel for that person, we are assisting them on their journey, one that they will be embarking upon with or without our help. During times like this, people often fall into the blind faith category, believing that a miracle will happen. YOU are that miracle for that person and YOU create it for them. My Guides showed me that when someone needs that kind of assistance to leave, it's like they are in the backseat of a new car with child-protective locks. They are at their destination and are ready to get out of the car, but they are locked in, dependent on others to get out. The same way we lock children in to make sure they are secure and safe, we lock in our loved ones, and we have to free them. We need to open the door and allow them to choose when they wish to leave. For them, the choice was made and we are just assisting them in a loving and supportive way.

I hope that this example of unconditional love assists in releasing you of the emotional burden you might feel if you have had to make this decision regarding someone in your circle of family and friends.

Fear or Love Exercise

Take some time to think again about some of the life-defining experiences you have had, but this time, try to examine where you were coming from emotionally. It is likely that many times your motives were multifaceted and not clear-cut. Sometimes, you will rationalize that it was one thing and NOT something else. But this is all about YOU, so remember: only you have to judge your honesty. You have nothing to prove and nothing to hide.

Sometimes it is easier to see what I am talking about when you look at motivation in regard to others. So for the purpose of this exercise, you could think of your best friend or a sibling and what has motivated them in the past.

Do you really want to do some self-exploration and grow spiritually? Allow yourself to consider what your parents' motivations were and how you fit into them. The more you can learn to understand and view your parents without judgment and blame, the more you will be able to experience a feeling of freedom and the more evolved you will become in the process.

As I am sure you are gathering from doing this, there are many more examples that tie into the FEAR model rather than the LOVE model. You will begin by thinking it's a LOVE motivation, but then,

if you're honest with yourself and you make sure the Inner Monster is in check, you will begin to see that LOVE may start off being the motivator but FEAR grabs the baton and finishes the race.

If you feel the need to throw the book down and trash me on the Internet or write me an angry e-mail, stop and think again. If you are having such a strong reaction to what I am writing, it is because I am challenging YOU. I am just trying to help you achieve the goal of developing spiritually. Because all these psychological factors are so connected, I need you to clearly understand what your current motivations actually are and what they were in your past. The reason is simple. I want to raise your awareness of the choices you have made and help you determine the processes that went into making them. Once explored, that can lead to making decisions better, quicker, or more efficiently than before. I want you to be certain the motivation is LOVE—simply, *the love of yourself.* Here is my reasoning applied specifically to doing a reading. You are in the middle of a consultation or answering a client's question. You can tell that they are stuck in some type of pattern in regard to relationships. You recognize that you are seeing that they are about to repeat the same pattern again and you want to help them explore various options.

MONEY, MONEY, MONEY

I know that right now you are thinking that love and fear are not the only motivating forces. You are screaming at me (in your mind, of course) that money is one of the biggest motivating factors out there, closely followed by ambition, greed, power, and fame. I concur. They all are motivators, but I would classify them as "sub-motivational" energies that fall under the two main categories of LOVE and FEAR.

If you are not able to understand how you're in touch with the FEAR and LOVE principles of motivation, then you will not be able to assist your clients in exploring their own. You won't be able to take them on that journey of understanding and decision-making to alter what is coming up. They will just repeat their cycle again. If you have not done the work on your personal motivations, your frame of reference of being able to empathize with your client or friend won't matter.

> **Remember:** To uphold the integrity of your own development when conveying any psychic information to clients, whether in a phone conversation or an in-person session, your job is to leave people better than you found them. The words you deliver must NEVER be used to TELL clients what to do. Instead, it is your responsibility to inspire them to use their free will and manifest their own realities.

That is the reason why I feel it's *imperative* to understand the FEAR and LOVE motivational principles of energy before we go any further.

Take a few moments now to think about this and how it affects what you are doing currently in your life. Is there something that is occurring that you need to make a decision about and you feel like you are standing at a crossroads or impassable fork?

Do you feel unhappy in a relationship and want it to change but feel stuck?

Are you contemplating leaving your job to go back to school or shift to a different career you are more passionate about?

If you can identify with these types of life-changing themes and feel stagnant and paralyzed, but are afraid of the potentials of these changes, then you know that you are operating from a fear-based motivation. Let us see how we can shift that to be more love-based.

You "know" that you are at a crossroads or an impassable fork of choice. Instead of standing still and doing nothing, you honor what you are feeling about yourself and the predicament you are in. You utilize your free will and actively choose to be proactive in the situation and make the change you want to achieve. **Create the reality and make life happen for you instead of letting it happen to you.**

Perhaps you recognize that you are in a relationship that leaves you feeling lonely or unappreciated. You have two options. One is to stay and put the energy into making it work because you truly want to, not because you have to or feel like the world will be angry at you for doing what might be unpopular. The second option is that you realize that the relationship is toxic for you and limiting your growth. You know that you deserve and desire better for yourself, your partner, and for your family and you decide to do what's in your heart. You end what you feel is wrong and start working on yourself to attract the fulfilling type of relationship you actually want.

Or perhaps it is your career path that needs a change. Maybe your whole life you have dreamed of being a professional baker. You have always enjoyed baking as a hobby. Your friends and family always ask you to make the pies, cakes, and cookies for parties and holidays, but you would never charge them because they are family, and what are a few eggs, flour, cocoa, and sugar? What about your time and energy? Not to mention all those ingredients. All this adds up to *value*, and you need to recognize that. But now you're thinking about leaving your job to go back to culinary school or to open your own bakery. You are following your passion, and soon love becomes the motivating factor ruling your choices.

* * * * * * *

LET'S REVIEW THE WHOLE PSYCHIC DEVELOPMENT aspect of motivational energy:

We need to understand *why* you have made the choices in your life up to now.

We need to understand what *motivational energy* was present.

We need to understand *what* and *why* energy has inspired you now to want to develop your psychic abilities.

What is your motivation for doing readings for another person? Hint: The only acceptable answer ever should be to help someone.

We need to understand how to change the FEAR factor into a LOVE dynamic.

3

PSYCHIC ENERGY

THE FORCE IS REAL AND IT IS WITH YOU.

A s you might have gathered by the quote at left, I am a fan of the *Star Wars* franchise of movies. I like the fact that they created a mythology of characters who embody basic metaphysical principles, all of which have to do with energy. When I embarked on my journey, I met many strange and wonderful psychics along the way, some who inspired me with their respect for the **FORCE** and some who repulsed me. I was able to reflect on what I *did* and did *not* want to be as a professional medium with each encounter.

THE ULTIMATE READ

To illustrate an example of a medium who did NOT use energy for the right reasons, I need to start with a story about Larry King. I don't know if you ever do this, but I like to pose hypothetical questions and situations to myself all the time. One such question arose from a conversation that I had with Larry King in 2003 when I was a guest on his show. He talked about the "ultimate interview" and the person he would love to sit down with if he could choose anyone. I thought that was an intriguing idea and it stuck with me. Shortly thereafter I was invited to Larry's seventieth birthday party and wondered, what gift do you get Larry King? Suspenders? Hey, you know you went there as well!

Instead, I asked his assistant to surreptitiously inquire who Larry's top five "ultimate interview" guests would be and was told that the short list included Jesus Christ, Winston Churchill, Abraham Lincoln, Adolf Hitler, and the pope, John Paul II. The only person living at the time was the pope, and since I didn't have Big Poppa on my speed dial, I knew I couldn't make that happen. My Guides, on the other hand, have a wicked sense of humor and I laughed out loud thinking that they were attempting to tell me that I could *connect* with four out of the five with their help. Suddenly, I got that feeling you get when a teacher calls on you in class and you are goofing around instead of paying attention. Then my Guides showed me a paintbrush.

"Am I supposed to paint this?" was my first reaction.

Clearly, my Guides have developed a sense of patience with me over the years, the way yours will with you, when it comes to understanding how easy it is for their messages to get "lost in translation." Anyway, it finally became obvious that I could make this happen by hiring an artist to sketch a picture of the "ultimate interview" that included all five of Larry's wished-for guests. Long story short, I surprised Larry with the framed original and I kept the approved sketch as another reminder of my Guides' clever handiwork.

I couldn't help but continue to think about whom I would choose as my "ultimate interview." A few years back, I remember being contacted by another medium who lives overseas; he asked me to have a meeting with him and "his people." I am not really into socializing when I am traveling for work. I don't usually sightsee and barely go out while on the road. I am immersed in the energy of working, and I stay in that mind-set as much as possible. Most people don't understand this mind-set. They can't imagine going to a foreign city or country and not taking in the scenery, and to a certain extent I agree. But I feel it is my *duty and responsibility* to make sure that I am rested, relaxed, and not overloaded with excess stimuli before any reading or speaking event. So it would be wrong of me to run all around and exhaust myself and then have no energy left for the real reason that I am there. In this book I will impart to you many examples of ideals like this. Obviously, I am unable to tell you what to do in your own work, but I hope I will inspire you when it comes to understanding the weight of the responsibility and sense of duty you must have if you want to do readings for others.

So although I hesitated, I did finally agree to this particular meeting of the mediums. One of the questions the other medium asked me was, *"Who is your MUST read?"*

I didn't exactly know what he meant and asked, *"Must read?"*

At first I was thinking about writers like Stephen King or maybe someone more metaphysically inclined, like Paulo Coelho, author of *The Alchemist*. But that isn't what he meant at all. He clarified that he was talking about doing readings for Hollywood celebrities. At this point I laughed so hard that the Diet Coke I was drinking almost went flying across the room. The medium did not even crack a smile, and when I realized how serious he was, I quickly pulled myself together. I could tell that his entourage was hoping to get me to work with him (which was never going to happen) and waiting with baited breath to hear what I was going to say.

"Honestly, I sometimes don't even want to read the people who have been on my waiting list for seven years. I am not looking to add famous ones!" I answered with a bit of exasperation.

Please don't misunderstand me: I love my work and I am extremely passionate about it, as you must have gathered by now, but I am also human. Just like you, I have things that I love to do but sometimes the thought of having to do them can be tiring in the moment.

"Who is YOURS?" I asked to take the pressure off the uncomfortable shift in energy.

Quickly, as if anticipating my question, he said dramatically, *"LA STREISAND."*

After I responded that I think she's an amazing performer, he wanted to know if I had ever read for her. I said no, and quite honestly, even if I had, I would have said I didn't, because I don't talk about my famous clients. I have a lot of them. I don't speak of them by name. That's tacky and would violate their confidentiality. It also implies that celebrities carry some sort of importance in validating my work . . . and they do not.

It kind of irks me when I see other psychics touting how they read certain celebrities or famous people in the hopes of raising their own profiles. Don't get me wrong: I have certainly done readings for celebrities who have agreed to be on camera at the time, but it was more about their choice to validate the work than about validating me. Here's the deal: if you are good at what you are doing and your Inner Monster is in check, you don't need to brag—it's that simple. At this point in a workshop, I always mention Arthur Miller's *Death of a Salesman*. During one scene in the play Willy chats with Bernard, the son of Willy's neighbor and friend, Charley. Bernard, a lawyer, casually mentions that he is going to Washington, D.C., to argue a case. Later, Charley tells Willy that Bernard has achieved a huge mile-stone—he will be arguing a case in front of the Supreme Court. Willy is surprised that Bernard hadn't boasted about his accomplishment. The simple response was that Bernard had confidence and grace, and telling everyone wasn't necessary. He knew what he had achieved and that was enough. Point made. I never forgot it.

> **Remember this message, please:** It is less important for you to tell others how gifted you are than it is for you to know how amazing it feels to use your ability to help someone through a difficult moment.

After my experience across the Atlantic and thinking about the hypothetical idea of my "ultimate reading," I came up with the per-fect person: Albert Einstein. I would love to have a sit-down with him to ponder the concepts of Life after Death and the ability of the soul to communicate from beyond the grave. After all, he *is* "Mr. Energy." He was clearly onto something with the concept that energy can't be created or destroyed. I wonder what his thoughts were regarding the Afterlife while he was here in the physical world, and it would be awesome to have his consciousness back it up from the Other Side in some way. He's on my list of people to look up on Facebook once

I am on the Other Side. Imagine, if you could, what that would be like. I am sure that there is some sort of network of communication, but maybe it's more like *Soulbook*. We are all connected by our energetic thoughts, both here and on the Other Side. The only difference is that while on Earth we are slowed down by the density of the physical world and its vibrational frequency. When we are just energy on the Other Side, we are not.

This chapter has been a tough one for me to write in terms of the development aspect. I am trying to find just the right way of expressing a couple of critical principles here, while also telling you that there is *so* much more. The task at hand gets complicated because I want to make sure that you understand the vastness of the concept of energy—like the ocean or space in its immensity. I think there is so much that humanity has already learned, but so much more that will be revealed over the next century. And in your personal development, I feel like I am giving you an overview of the important principles, while trying to really emphasize that this is just the beginning of a long journey. This begs the question—how far down the rabbit hole do you want to go?

One of the best documentaries that I think has been made in recent years is a film from 2004 called *What the BLEEP Do We Know?* I highly recommend that you watch it as soon as possible, if you haven't done so already. Immerse yourself in the concepts and let yourself see the world in a completely different way. Yes, this journey we are on is an interactive experience and all good teachers give homework, right?

The reason why I like this documentary so much is that it takes you on a journey of understanding energy by using quantum physics. I consider myself to be a student of quantum physics and could fill an entire book with a whole set of questions and answers regarding these concepts. But for our purposes, here is what I want to address: *currents of energy.*

TUNING IN TO POTENTIALITIES

You probably have used or heard the phrase "We are on the same wavelength" from time to time, which illustrates that you and someone else understand each other or are in harmony. Let's address this idea a bit further.

To return to the instrument analogy mentioned in Chapter 1, if you play an instrument you need to keep it in tune. The same concept is essential for all modes of transportation, such as automobiles and planes, and is also wise in regard to computers and other machines. Wherever energy is expended, a tune-up is vital from time to time to ensure operation at peak efficiency . . . and this definitely includes people, as well.

For our work is all about harnessing and fine-tuning the energy so that the frequencies we are working with are on a positive and productive level. Have you ever heard an out-of-tune piano or guitar being played? How far would you get in a car that is not tuned properly? Would you even want to step foot on a plane that hadn't had its regular maintenance work done? So why the hell would anyone want to see a psychic who is not tuned-in properly? Consulting an energetically depleted psychic or one not "in tune" could be extremely dangerous for the client.

> **At the risk of repeating myself because I can't stress it enough:** when you give a person any type of psychic information, your words have an enormous responsibility.

Every person you read for is vulnerable to some degree to your input and insights and is usually seeking direction. This direction is something that your clients have to figure out for themselves by using their own free will. You MUST NEVER tell them what to do, even if you believe that you *know* what the potential outcomes will be for them. People have to learn their own "lessons" and it is not your job to stop them or get in their way. There are not enough psychic development books to possibly prepare you for how difficult a task this really is to put into practice.

Here's an example of what it will feel like when you know something is going to potentially take place for your client. Imagine you are on the top of a hill looking down at someone who is wearing headphones, listening to music, and walking on a train track. As this person is walking along on the track, you can see a train coming quickly behind him, but he can't hear it because of the loud music blaring in his ears. You then notice that the conductor is looking down and not paying attention. You are seeing it all from a distance, hundreds of feet away. And no matter how loudly you yell, there is nothing you can do in that situation. You have no control. Even though you scream, throw rocks, and pray to God, you can't stop what will happen. There are several potential endings to this scenario, and you can see all of them clearly, flashing in front of your eyes. Welcome to the world of being psychic.

Obviously, this example is a dramatic one of life and death proportions. Thankfully, most situations will be a little more subtle in their tone, but life-changing nonetheless. **You must always remember your role in your clients' experience: to provide insights in a positive way to enhance their life and to assist in their decision-making process.**

So let's go back to the currents of energy in life: yours, mine, and the world's. Every time you have a thought or action, it sends out a bullet of energy attached to a line of probability. These lines of probabilities are potential realities for you that will cross and intersect with others in your life. If you are a fan of the TV show *Lost*, you can see now why I like it so much and have referenced it in this book. If you read my novel, *Final Beginnings*, you will understand why I wrote it with all the characters' lives intersecting and having a common point of connection. We are not dissimilar in that way. I am writing a book that at some point in your life you are now reading. It connects us by linking what I am doing to what you are learning. Every action does have a reaction . . . but metaphysically speaking, alternative potential outcomes do exist.

POTENTIAL REALITIES

These are what you will be tapping into when you are doing a reading for someone or, more importantly, examining your own life. You will see opportunities and situations that are glimpses, not absolutes— never absolutes. Learn that everything is interpretational, and keep the Inner Monster at bay from trying to adorn your ability with perceived accuracy.

Back when I was first dating my wife, Sandra, one night we went to see the movie *Wolf,* starring Jack Nicholson and the beautiful Michelle Pfeiffer. In the middle of the movie I saw a glimpse (vision) of a large jet. My next flash (thought) showed the inside of the plane filled with Asian passengers. The next flash was that same jet crashing on a runway, blowing up, and a large 0 (zero) coming at me. All this happened in a brief second of earthly time. But metaphysically, time is irrelevant. Often you will be hard-pressed to explain how you received your information because it is *just there,* which is why I call these flashes of insight *"downloads."*

I turned to Sandra and whispered to her what I just saw. She stared back at me with her popcorn-filled hand frozen in mid-air: "*THEY showed you this now? WHY?*" I had no clue. But I *knew* that this airliner was going to make an emergency landing and crash on impact. It was going to blow up and there would be no survivors. Later that night, I dropped Sandra off at her house in Queens Village and drove back home to Glen Cove, Long Island. We both turned on the rebroadcast of the local news, which showed the exact scene of what I "saw" earlier that night. And then the big reveal happened. The plane had made an emergency landing and all the passengers aboard were Asian. It did explode on the runway, but not until *after* all the passengers had been evacuated. The *zero* I saw in my vision meant no casualties: Thankfully, everyone survived. The important lesson for me that night was to be aware of how my logical mind got in the way of what I was actually seeing.

Even though I was on a date and enjoying a movie, my Guides saw this frightening event as an opportunity for a lesson. When you are engaging in this type of intuitive work and choosing to live a conscious life, you are actively enrolling in the "Universal School of Awareness."

"YOU'RE F••••D!"

Listen, most of us have dropped the "F bomb" on occasion. I just don't like the way it looks on paper. But I need to use it to explain how life-changing it can be to fully develop your psychic abilities. In the late '80s, I had the pleasure of meeting a psychic by the name of Virginia Pomilio and we bonded immediately. She was the Judge Judy of psychics, meaning she had a no-nonsense, "don't waste my time" kind of energy when she did readings. If you wanted someone to candy-coat information—well, she wasn't the person to call. She was accurate to a fault, but as Bugs Bunny might have said, a little finesse from time to time wouldn't hurt. But we shared some of the funny moments of my early career.

On our way to a psychic fair in Staten Island, New York, Virginia startled me with a shocking statement. I will never forget where I was in that moment. We were in my car in traffic, right in front of the North Shore Towers on the Grand Central Parkway, when she said, *"You know you're f****d, right?"*

"Huh?" I was flabbergasted at her language, considering she was my mother's age at the time.

"Yeah, it's a shame, poor kid." She looked at me in a maternal sort of way, and I had to fight the urge to yell at her. How could she say that to me, not to mention while I was driving!

"Honey, it's like this. You are so far more advanced than you even know yet. You are on the accelerated program of development for what they are using you for and you will not be able to get away with some of the mistakes that other people can. You will not be able to say you didn't know any better, because you really do, even if you consciously don't know it yet."

I never forgot that conversation. It tied directly into my first year of doing this psychic work when my Uncle Joey pulled me aside and said, *"You know that if you embark on this journey, your life will never be the same. Are you sure you want to take on that responsibility? You're only fifteen!"*

The ironic part is that several years later I made that same exact statement to my protégé and friend, Jonathan Louis, after he started doing readings. He trained in the philosophies of metaphysics for many years before he was instructed by both his and my Guides to develop his skills further. After studying with me for a few years, I tuned into my Team ("the boys") and they gave Jonathan permission to begin to do readings. His first reading was an impromptu one that happened over the phone when I was working in Phoenix. One of my staff members traveling with me had recently lost her mother. Jonathan just happened to call as we were leaving a movie theater, and he asked whom I was with at that moment. Teasing him, I said, *"Ask your Guides to tell you"* and they immediately did. His Guides then opened him up even more, and he made an amazing connection with this woman's mom. Since I already knew that he was clearly born to do a medium's work, it was a beautiful moment to witness. I felt like a proud father watching his son graduate.

Shortly after that, I knew that Jonathan needed more experience in the reading department to learn how to interpret his information and listen to his Guides more accurately. I began scheduling people for him to read over the phone. I wanted him to realize that he needn't be in the room with his client and to learn to trust only what he was seeing, hearing, feeling, and downloading.

His second phone reading was with a family from Florida that I knew only a few things about. He began to make a connection on the Other Side with the patriarch of the family before the reading even started. I reprimanded him to wait until the phone call, because I saw him getting nervous and anxious. I was watching him come undone and I was becoming annoyed. I told Jonathan to meditate and ask his Guides to intervene and quiet his nerves. The father had a lot to say and Jonathan started spouting this information. I could tell he was looking to me to validate him, and I didn't feel comfortable with this whole situation. From a skeptical point of view, it felt like he was looking for something to be right about before he got on the phone to speak with the family.

If you think that my passion for taming the Inner Monster is evident on the pages of this book, let me assure you that you have NO IDEA what I am like when dealing with a student who is about to do a reading. I berated Jonathan and told him that he sounded like he was fishing for information before the call and that I did not know anything about this family. I did, but certainly not what he was talking about. Actually, it all sounded completely wrong, but I was afraid that if I did say *"No, that's not accurate,"* it would shut him down and he wouldn't be able to do his job.

It was finally time for the call. I talked to the client first and told her the ground rules. I explained that she was to be the spokesperson for everyone listening and to reply only yes or no to anything Jonathan said. She was not to reveal more information or to help Jonathan in any way. She completely understood that he was a novice and that this was only his second real reading. I remember instructing her to be patient since his information wouldn't come through very quickly since he was so new to the work.

I put my phone on mute and had Jonathan pick up the other receiver. He began. *"Holy shit"* was all I kept saying to myself. What I witnessed shocked me. It was like a geyser of information pouring out of him. Details, names, and situations flowed for over an hour. It was like I was not even sitting there watching Jonathan as my student. Instead, I was watching someone who was destined to help people, a *medium* born to do this soul-touching work. I was looking at myself through Virginia's eyes. When the reading was over, he hung up the phone and the client said to me, *"I thought you said he was new at this."*

When Jonathan came back in the room to hear the assessment of the reading from the family as well as my feedback, all I could do was smile and say *"You're f****d."*

The Doorways of Potentials Exercise

I would like you to imagine that you are standing in front of a doorway. When you open the door there is a hallway that leads to three other doorways, and when you open those doors, you see more hallways and more doors. But some of those hallways will intersect and double back to many of the same doors. Maybe a better analogy would be riding along on a highway. Intersecting with the highway are expressways, parkways, interstates, country roads, residential streets, and unpaved paths. Many of these will take you to the same destination, just with different scenery and different people along the way, and that is where your choice or your client's choice will come into play.

* * * * * * * *

THE ENERGY IS THE WORK

Every time I make a statement about what it means to be a professional psychic, there will usually be someone who will feel the need to disagree with *my* experiences, either by sharing their opinion during a reading or, my personal favorite, interrupting in the middle of a live event to say how *their* abilities are different than mine and that "they can do" whatever it is that I am saying can't be done.

My favorite example has to be a woman who stood up in a room with at least five hundred people present and launched into a laundry list of her assessment of my abilities in comparison to her own. It was such a grotesque moment of the Inner Monster that I knew she had to be working with lower-level entities, not Guides, and I felt sorry for all the people who had crossed her path in this work. Honestly, I felt badly for her in this particular moment, because as *psychic* as she thought she was, she couldn't feel the distinct level of disdain directed at her from the audience members who were horrified at her display of self-promotion. I even had to make a joke about it to break the tension in the room and told her that the only thing she forgot to mention was her website address and phone number. She laughed but still didn't get it since she went on to share her contact information while quickly adding that her rates were far cheaper than mine and she can download names when I apparently can't. The irony is that names and initials always come through during my sessions, including that night, but obviously it was ALL about her.

Ego: When it is all about people only embracing their ego, the Inner Monster will never allow them to see, hear, feel, experience, or realize anything that doesn't feed, stroke, encourage, or worship their ego. It's actually quite similar to the behavior of a drug addict.

There was also the time that several people were distributing advertisements for their own psychic events at my speaking locations. They were planning shows in the same cities that I was visiting, trying to capture the people leaving my events who might be disappointed because they were not read by leaving these fliers in the restrooms and on cars in the parking lots. I wish I was kidding, but I'm not.

These Inner Monster energies come in all forms. Some people mask their negativity by asking a question to make it appear that they are curious about my answer, but really it's just to share with everyone how "special" they are. These "look-at-me-now" types just want to gloat because John Edward is going to validate them in front of thousands of people. The list is long and tiring, to be honest.

During an event in Austin, Texas, a young man who was clearly in love with fame (and himself) asked me, *"So how did you get so famous and what do I have to do to be famous, too?"* The question made me really nauseous and energetically shut me down. I remember thinking, is this *really* the message I am sending out? *"Not at all,"* my Guides answered my thoughts; it was his Inner Monster issue and his warped perception of my work. I had to remind myself that I can only be responsible for driving *my* car. I responded to his question by saying that I simply put my energy into my work and people noticed.

I am the first person to humble myself to the process and I am always talking about how *"it's not about me, it's about the work."* I find that intensity of Inner Monster celebration disgusting and consider it to be low-level energetic noise. **You need enough ego to allow you to do this work, but anything more gets in your way.**

* * * * * * * *

I APOLOGIZE TO YOU HERE AS I CONTINUE TO WEAVE concepts and stories, digressing from them and then returning. It really is intentional, meant to build on previous aspects of the foundation of my—and hopefully your—psychic development. I tend to teach by example and, I hope, will entertain you with my experiences. It is fun for me to share them with you, and the idea is that you learn some valuable lessons along the way.

TIMING IS EVERYTHING

In looking at the timing of things, both when they are happening in your life and in the future, it is important to understand the mechanics of what went into creating certain outcomes and what is needed to manifest change.

Why are you reading this book now? There is a reason. You need to explore that. For 98 percent of the people reading this, I promise you it is NOT to do readings. Your Team has put this book in your hands to get you to listen and see life differently. They want to give you an enhanced understanding of what lessons you are here to learn, experience, and teach. And if you are currently doing readings or desire to do so in the future, this book can provide you with a strong foundation for that work as well, maybe even correct some elements or bad habits you might have already fallen into.

Psychics and timing are like oil and vinegar: They can go together but really have to be worked on to become one item. They are two separate ingredients coming together for one purpose . . . a potential outcome.

In the psychic projections you make, your timing may be off simply because of free will. This is not a psychic cop-out that I use or am giving you to use—it's just the truth. In looking at the lines of probability for a person's choices, you may tune into one of them stronger than the others. Usually, it's because your client is also leaning and projecting their energy toward that line as well. This does not mean you are reading a person's mind. You are looking at where they are in their life today and seeing the bullets of energy that they are shooting out, their FEAR and LOVE bullets and the realities they will be manifesting as a result. And then you are speaking about it. Here is an example of what I mean.

Mary is engaged to Steve. Their wedding date is set for next year. Mary was previously engaged to Tom, but he left Mary to marry Diane, whom he accidentally got pregnant. Diane was aware that Tom wasn't in love with her, but she didn't want to raise a child on her own and believed that the least Tom could do was take responsibility by marrying her. She told herself at the time that the love would follow. Six years have passed and Tom is now leaving Diane. He has not seen, called, e-mailed, or reached out to Mary since they broke up, but she is still the love of his life and he feels like he made a mistake. Tom wants to reach out to her but because of the fear of rejection he is hesitant.

That's five lives with multiple probabilities at stake. It's five lives, not four. Why? Mary, Steve, Tom, Diane, and their child, Tommy Jr. Because of the emotionally charged bullets of desire that Tom is emitting, all their lives are affected in ways that are not understood in the physical world, but let's examine the situation from a universal, metaphysical standpoint.

Mary doesn't know that any of this is going on, but as she is planning her wedding to Steve all she can think about is Tom, and this is perplexing to her. This is causing her to question her feelings toward Steve; her confusion just erupted out of what feels like nowhere with no reason or cause.

Steve is now feeling something different from Mary, an energy he has never felt from her before: uncertainty. This doubt is now pushing buttons in him and is on the verge of shifting his energy in how he deals with Mary, their relationship, and their future. Maybe the hot, flirtatious co-worker whom he has not responded to previously will get a little bit more of his attention.

Tom is pining away for Mary and reconnecting with her energetically. He is replugging into old feelings and experiences . . . and if there was sex involved, that level of connection is a direct plug into a person's source energy. He basically is firing away the bullets all day long, and if he starts to fantasize about Mary sexually, they start to become cannonball shots of energy.

> *WARNING! WARNING!* I need to be LOUD and CLEAR here so you can understand just how karma works. It would be unethical, inappropriate, and even deemed "Black Magic" to intentionally send harmful energy toward an ex-lover or any other person, for that matter. The negative repercussions to you would be huge! I repeat: Do Not Go There. The psychic "bullet" you send out with malicious intent to hurt someone will return as a heat-seeking missile to your life. **Don't Do It.** Now you know better and so there is no excuse karmically—regardless of how victimized you may feel. Leave it up to the Universe to handle the karmic payback; it's not your job.

Diane is sure that Mary, whom she never has met, now is the one to blame for her relationship breaking up because she can't imagine that she herself did anything wrong. She will play the *"We have a child!"* card on Tom followed by a heavy dose of guilt: *"How can you leave us?"* And simultaneously Diane is firing all these bullets of negativity toward Mary.

Poor Mary is under an energetic attack and hasn't even heard from Tom in six years! And now her potential future has a new channel of negative content as a result—a new door and hallway, lines of probability being developed, all because of Tom.

WHAT'S THE LESSON?

There are many lessons to be learned here. Let's just look at a few of the obvious ones.

Hopefully, you now see the overwhelming need for practicing psychic self-defense. If Mary was properly protecting herself (see "Psychic Self-Defense Exercise" in Chapter 1), she might get one or two "hits" (thoughts) of Tom and they would be quickly followed by messages of self-empowerment, such as *"He doesn't know what he missed out on"* or *"That's the past . . . let it go"* as opposed to *"I hope Tom is okay"* or *"I wonder if I should contact him?"* and other open-ended maybes that would clearly mess with her thinking in regard to her future with Steve.

Tom is not dealing with the realities of his present situation because he is trying to plug into his past. So instead of learning lessons and moving on, he perpetuates staying in this energetic grade. Even if he doesn't remain with Diane, he will attract another relationship just like it and be back "in school" to deal with the same lesson all over again.

Diane does not own any responsibility in why she and Tom are done. She is just playing the *victim*. She is doing what many of us do when a romantic relationship breaks up. The very thing that is illogical and magical in the beginning, people always want to make logical and analyze at the end. Never try to understand all the intricacies of a relationship, because then you spend time trying to define and understand one half of something you don't have access to.

Instead, I recommend that you spend time honestly owning your part in the failure of the relationship, processing it, and then letting it go. And only then can true growth and healing take place. If you hang on, second-guessing everything, blaming, or reminiscing, you become vicious and venomous about "why this is happening to me." And now you know (especially if you watched *What the BLEEP Do*

We Know?) that if you come from a negative space, you start shooting out negative energies and attracting more negative situations.

Tommy Jr. has a whole other set of highways in front of him based on the decisions his parents are making, and his free will also play a role in his thought processes even at the young age of six.

The above example has many other lessons, but I just wanted to highlight a couple. This way of thinking should help you to understand how we are all connected by the power of our thoughts, and the crucial need for psychic self-defense as a practice against all negative attacks.

I also hope that I made it crystal clear that it is inappropriate for you to superimpose your free will or intent on another person. It is a *universal violation.*

VALUABLE ASSETS

When I first began my journey into the world of psychic energy, I had a life-altering reading done for me in 1985 by Lydia Clar. The results of that reading put me directly on my path to becoming a professional medium. Lydia was invited to my grandmother's home to give readings at a party hosted by my mother. My mom's side of the family was really into readings, but my father was not. Even though I was not close to my dad, I had adopted his police officer skepticism toward anything deemed psychic. Lydia agreed to come to the party only if she could meet me. Apparently she had felt my energy through my mother during a previous session. My mother gave me the strictest of orders to be polite and respectful, because she and Lydia shared mutual professional friends. I agreed. Lydia read many friends and family members that day, but when it came time for me to get a reading, I declined by saying that I wasn't giving this woman any money to tell me a story. My cousin Roseann challenged me to do it and said she would pay for the session. I laughed and told her she was wasting her money as Lydia would not be able to read me anyway. Well, not only was she able to read me, she was able to foresee what would ultimately be my chosen Destiny: my psychic work and teachings. Lydia predicted that I would change the way the world perceived psychics and the Afterlife. I laughed. All these years later, whenever I see her, I always joke and say, *"Look what you did!"* and her response is always the same: *"No, I just acknowledged what you had the potential to do. I'm glad to have been a part of it."*

The Universe then directed me to Sandy Anastasi. Sandy ran the Astrological Institute of Integrated Studies, which was on Long Island at the time. She is the only person who can ever claim to be my "teacher" in regard to my psychic development and the only person whom I allow to say so publicly. Keep in mind that if you think studying with her is going to make you just like me—please go back and reread what I wrote up until this point and highlight the Inner Monster moments. However, I do encourage anyone interested in studying metaphysics seriously to work with her or learn more about her teachings, which can be found online at www.InfiniteQuest.com.

Sandy helped me to shape my views on so much of my work and experiences and has always been a divine source of wisdom and sage insights and, more importantly, a good friend. She gave me some of the best cornerstones to build my foundation of development on.

She taught me one of the first lessons with a simple question. *"Would you ever go look in your next-door neighbor's bathroom window and watch her take a shower?"* I immediately blushed because I had a hot next-door neighbor who was only a couple of years older than me. I gave Sandy a slightly puzzled look because I wondered if she knew of my secret crush. I recovered and quickly said, *"Of course not!"*

Sandy replied, *"Then make sure you **never** do it psychically. Just because you have the ability to look into places in people's lives doesn't make it okay!"*

Point made. Direct hit. Another *universal violation* to steer clear of: **the Peeping Psychic.**

GREATEST GIFT OF ALL—BEING WRONG?

But I would have to say that the greatest gift in my early development that Sandy gave me was the permission to be wrong.

I was given the freedom to explore this world of energy devoid of the ego that gets created by having to "get it right." Too many people working in this field take on the weight of *being psychic* and think that if they don't come up with the right answer, or for that matter any answer, they have failed somehow.

Over time, these same psychics may lose sight of the fact that they can be wrong and begin to believe that their ability is untouchable. This Inner Monster invincibility becomes very dangerous because it can cause clients to make choices based on this false belief, as opposed to providing insights for them to make their own informed decisions.

I have been studying astrology for a few years, but I am not an astrologer. I would recommend a client to seek out a professional astrologer in the same way I would refer a client to a dentist if I psychically saw something wrong in the mouth. I wouldn't ask them to open up their mouth so I could give them my assessment of their teeth and gums or attempt to pull out a tooth in my office. For most of you, this book is meant to be a recipe book, not blueprints for a restaurant. I borrow this metaphor from a fellow medium, Suzane Northrop, whose book, *A Medium's Cookbook: Recipes for the Soul*, talks about psychic development as well.

A COLD, DARK PLACE

Some psychics who are not mediums feel the need to give information about loved ones who have crossed over. Unfortunately, because they can't really do that type of work and don't recognize their personal and professional limitations, they blame the lack of connection on the people on the Other Side, who can't communicate because they are stuck or unevolved.

Many years ago, a woman who lost her son came to me for a private reading accompanied by her son's best friend. As I was conducting the session, the mother seemed to have absolutely no reaction, while her son's friend nodded with enthusiasm at what his best friend was coming through with. It was clear that he had brought this woman to me in the hopes that he would be able to help her in her grieving. At the end of the session, after the son came through with some amazing validations for his family, I looked at his mom, who still was unresponsive, and said, *"Did any of this help you?"*

She nodded unconvincingly.

The best friend, knowing the session was coming to a close, looked at me desperately. He looked back at the mom and said, *"Tell him!"*

The woman began to go into detail about how some pseudo-psychic had informed her that her son was in a cold, dark place longing to be with his mother. Her eyes welled up as she revealed this story to me.

I am only half Italian, but I am 100 percent passionate. I think I know what it feels like to have a stroke, because it felt like I had one sitting there listening to this woman. I also know that if that psychic wanna-be who shared this "information" with this grieving mom had been in front of me, I would have become violent. I was that incensed and angry. I quickly tried to put my rage aside in the moment, as I knew that my window to make a difference here with this mother was closing rapidly.

"Ma'am, may I ask you what types of validation this psychic gave you to make you believe him?"

"What do you mean?" She looked directly at me for the first time during our time together.

"Well, did he say . . ." I went over all the key points that her son had told me during our time together. We spent another forty-five minutes talking about the significance of validation during a session

and how that assists the medium as well as the sitter to know if an accurate connection is being made.

She replied, *"No."* So the "psychic" had just dropped this bomb of information and moved on to something else. I believe it happened over the phone and through a friend of the family, as if he solicited the call in some way. I can't even express the levels of wrong he did to this woman.

"Well, your son DID say all those things to you today through me, didn't he?"

"Yes." She replied tentatively at first, and then she became more animated. *"He did!"*

"Then I need you to know that your son is not in a cold, dark place, and I assure you he is not longing to be with you, because he already is."

I saw the lights go on in this woman's eyes. The realization of that fact was priceless. Her eyes started to overflow with tears, but they were tears of relief, with a touch of elation. She turned to her son's friend and said, *"He is okay! He is okay!"*

This reading happened many years ago, and my eyes are still welling up as I relive it for you. At the end of the session, I asked them to give me the name of the person who had called her, but after seeing

LET ME BE YOUR SANDY ANASTASI!

Be who you are. Develop your abilities to be the best YOU and live the most empowered life possible. Don't do so to become a professional psychic, astrologer, or medium. Later on we will discuss tools in the psychic development process. Hopefully, you will pick one and that will be your key to assist you in unlocking your abilities even further.

my reaction, they decided not to share his name. I can only cringe at how many other lives this arrogant, unprofessional, Inner Monster–feeding bastard affected in an adverse way.

In keeping with the previous story, the following might not be what you want to read from me, but I have to say it. As much as you are enamored with spirit communication, it isn't likely that you were born a medium. I am sorry to say it so bluntly. Your personal losses may have brought you to understand the importance of the work, and you might have had some amazing experiences of your own, but that does not constitute an occupation or a need for a career change.

Don't try to convince yourself otherwise. You may do more damage in your life and the lives of others if you don't honor that fact. If you know that you are a medium, you don't question it. You have the ability. To quote my colleague, Suzane Northrop, once again, *"Mediums are born, they are not taught."*

A PSYCHIC STANDOFF

Suzane and I participated in the making of the HBO documentary *Life Afterlife* a number of years ago. A portion of the film featured a study conducted at the University of Arizona's Human Energy Systems Laboratory (now the Veritas Research Program) under the leadership of Dr. Gary Schwartz and his wife at the time, Linda Russek. If you want to read more about what happened there, check out the book *The Afterlife Experiments: Breakthrough Scientific Evidence of Life After Death.* The part of the experience that I want to share you won't find in the book or the documentary.

There were a number of phases of this study that I participated in, as in science you need to replicate and extend data in order to substantiate your claims and findings. For the most part, I love science and technology, and to have someone who was willing to explore my passion and work was a dream come true for me. I am happy to report that Dr. Schwartz has continued to push the envelope and explore various subjects under the category of Energy. I am excited that more and more accredited researchers and universities are embarking on exploring Energy in metaphysical modalities.

Back to Arizona: We were all sitting on couches in a living room at Canyon Ranch in Tucson, talking about Energy and the study of it, when the conversation came around to teaching. Someone posed the question, *"Can you teach mediumship?"*

"No!" Suzane replied emphatically while I simultaneously said, *"Yes!"*

We looked at each other with a mutual appreciation of each other professionally and personally, yet holding firm to our answers. All of a sudden, the two of us could have been transported back in time to another life during a Western standoff at twenty paces. I spoke first.

"Suzane! You teach workshops on psychic development! How can you say 'No'?"

"Mediums are born. They are not taught," she said in a nonnegotiable tone.

"But how can you teach then if you feel so strongly about that?"

"Mediums are born. You are born to do this work. You don't develop an interest and study it. You don't lose a loved one and become a medium. This deal was set before you got here!" she said with finality, eyes flashing.

It was apparent to me, as it was to everyone else, that the conversation was over. There was an uncomfortable energy in the room, like a fart that happened at a dinner party—we all heard it, but we are adults, so we just moved on. Okay, this is a bad example since I would definitely crack up if that happened!

It took a few years, but I completely agree with Ms. Suzane "Mad Dog" Northrop (my pet name for her because she reads so quickly it makes me look slow). I came to respect and understand her point only after I began doing the TV show *Crossing Over* in 2000. It seemed that everyone and his mother wanted to be a *medium*. It became trendy to talk to dead people. I actually have had clients who lost relatives and, after enlightening and empowering sessions with me and my colleagues, then decided that they too were going to be mediums and write a book about their experiences and work. To me, that is like waking up after successful heart bypass surgery and saying, *"You know, now that I survived that, I can be a heart surgeon. Lie down and let me take a look at your ticker."* It sounds ludicrous in that example, right? Apply the same concept to my line of work.

There were psychics and card readers who now were calling themselves "psychic mediums" because of the level of attention that *Crossing Over* brought to me and to the subject matter. People started adding the moniker "Medium" after their titles, and then there was the ridiculous practice of people advertising "Gallery Group" for their psychic events.

Paul Shavelson, the executive producer of *Crossing Over*, was the one who coined the term "Gallery" to refer to the viewers in the TV studio. He did not want to call the folks attending the show an audience. He listened to me talk for hours about how passionate I am about connecting with people and argue that we needed to make sure the show was about the process and not about "John Edward." I wanted to be clear that this was not about celebrating *me* on television, but that all the people watching it should be able to identify with and appreciate the experiences of the families getting read. I knew that this show would be life-changing for many people who previously would never even have thought that it was possible for their loved ones to be okay on the Other Side. I wanted to make a difference and touch their hearts.

One day we were standing on the set while it was being assembled and Paul looked out and said, *"Welcome to the Gallery."*

"Gallery? Is that some TV jargon for audience?" I asked.

"No. You said you will be painting portraits of energy, right? That is how you define your work. We will be hanging that artwork for everyone to see it here. You hang artwork in a gallery."

I was mesmerized by his level of "getting it" and we've been friends and have continued to work together ever since. And if you see anyone using that term in their advertising, be wary of attending the event—because I'm sure most psychics don't even know what that word means in the context of doing a reading.

To this day, I watch people who are doing this work and literally hear my words falling out of their mouths:

"That's their way of validating themselves to you."

"They are above you, or to your side, or below you."

"Psychic amnesia."

"A me-too syndrome."

"They are pulling back."

"That's their way of letting you know that they are here and okay."

Oh, the list goes on and on.

My wife recorded a medium she saw on television who literally sounded like she was just "being John Edward." Later I sat there watching the taped show with this weird feeling. Part of me was honored, and part of me was freaked out. Now, here's the deal: they say that "imitation is the sincerest form of flattery." Well, I don't know who *they* are, but to a degree I am cool with it. I am comfortable with it if I can inspire someone to honor the process and put ethics and responsibility first at all costs. But I am not okay with someone copying my style, verbal patterns, or even how I stand.

I was horrified at this copycat syndrome, which was happening more and more. It was like the genie was out of the lamp and it has been that way ever since. Michael Logan from *TV Guide* magazine asked me how I felt, since I helped to create a new genre of programming. I laughed. But it really is true. Unfortunately, I don't resonate with most of it. A lot of it is stereotypical bullshit that is totally FEAR-based. But that is because most of the people making the decisions in television and movies are producing to the lowest common denominator and their number one goal is to make a buck.

I talked about Jonathan Louis earlier. He really does sound and read like me. I trained him so it is bound to happen. Simply put, if you are mentored by someone, you will reflect that person's style. But in addition to my mentoring him, the last part of his training included "deprogramming John Edward" from his work.

My second television show that I produced and hosted was called *John Edward Cross Country.* In my last season of that series, in 2008, I produced an episode called "The Four Psychics," which included Robert Brown, Char Margolis, Jonathan Louis, and myself. When Jonathan was standing on the stage doing audience readings, I was in the control room watching him bring through a son who had crossed himself over. Jonathan delicately delivered this boy's loving messages to his mother. As this was happening, the executive in charge of production walked into the control room and began watching Jonathan while standing right next to me. After a few moments, he happened to glance in my direction, saw me standing next to him, and did a double-take between me and the screens in the control room, while pointing at Jonathan.

"I thought he was you!" was all he said and then looked back and said, *"Holy crap, he sounds just like you."*

There were moments I would watch Jonathan on television or listen to him on the radio and have to turn it off. Why? Because at one point it was like seeing or hearing myself. He has since worked on taking my teachings and being the best Jonathan Louis that he can be; otherwise he and anyone else would just be a knock-off. The message here for you is the same. **It is imperative to be the best YOU that you can be, not a copy of anyone else.**

SHIFTS IN REALITY

My hope is that with the coming shifts in planetary consciousness that are upon us we will see more people developing their intuitive voice and abilities. This development in society will help raise the positive vibrations of the planet. There are huge shifts already occurring, and yes, all that 2012 stuff is based on the Mayan calendar and certain metaphysical philosophies. But I don't believe that it will be an Armageddon-like, end-of-the-world kind of event. Instead, I think it will be a massive potential shift in consciousness in how people examine the world we live in—from organizational religions to technology, science, the environment, and more. It's about *change* and the hope that our newfound awareness will be used for spiritual gain and will lead to positive action in our vibrations evolving as a society.

The action for you is to recognize the world of energy that we live in and to utilize that force for positive manifestation in your personal life, sending out ripples that will touch others around you.

Not a Secret

In the last few years there was a great repackaging of the metaphysical idea of the Law of Attraction. It came in the form of a little book and DVD called *The Secret.* When I first watched the DVD, I was excited to see how well it was produced for a commercial marketplace. It blew up in popularity and made instantaneous household names of some of the people who were interviewed. Because it was featured on the *Oprah Winfrey Show* and in magazine articles and radio programs, many people were exposed to valuable information.

The danger with the Law of Attraction, or manifesting your own realities, is that people almost always seek to attract the most obvious things. (Again, please save your letters and e-mails.) I know this to be true from the enormous number of questions I was being asked about it. People were telling me that they were doing their visualizations and making their "wish boards," but they still had not obtained what they desired.

Most of the complaints were about not receiving money or material possessions. Next on the list was not manifesting the perfect relationship. Here is the problem with *The Secret:* nothing. There is no problem with it. The problem lies in the *perception of entitlement* that the people utilizing the principle embodied.

If EGO is the monster, then ENTITLEMENT is its bitch. Put those two together and you have a recipe for stagnation in your life. The message of *The Secret* is simple: create and manifest your best life possible without limitations. You are a great person who can achieve all that you desire. The Universe is your blank slate to write your future on. Nowhere in there was it stated that you are entitled to a new car, spouse, pair of shoes, engagement ring, house, et cetera. There is no promise of all those things.

The promise is the same as it is in this project: **Build the best YOU possible. The principle of the law of attraction is simply that you attract what you are putting out there.** If you are putting out negativity, you attract more of it. If you are putting out positive energy, you attract more of it.

Everything is happening for a reason. Figure it out for yourself and learn from it. If there are patterns you don't like, try to understand them. Recognize the bullets of energy you are firing in a machine gun-like fashion, creating similar lines of probability, and then own them and apply the law of attraction to them. Alleviate the fear and try to raise your personal vibration and emanate what you want to attract.

> Remember that what you are seeking to achieve from external aspects of the world is abundant in the source of who you truly are within. The potential is yours to create.

SCIENCE AND PSIENCE

So going on the principle that energy exists, and we are energy, and the entire Universe is made up of that energy that shifts and transitions, how is energy harnessed for psychic usage?

This chapter is the one that I struggled with the most. I knew that in writing this book, it could really have been turned into multiple books that put together would create a metaphysical series. I like the science of metaphysics a lot and truly believe that science will one day validate the existence of an Afterlife and survival of consciousness in a huge manner.

Meditation and *Prayer* are the two tasks that I put forth to you as methods of harnessing the energy of the Universe and turning it into fuel for your own usage. When you bring up the word *healing* in regard to energy, people immediately think of faith healing. True energy healing is working with the universal energy and allowing it to flow through the healer as a vessel and directing it toward the recipient. I believe that the healing happens in the heart of the recipient, just as chemotherapy heals cancer. It is a force that can affect a great change within the structure to which it is applied.

Meditation and *Prayer* have the same ability to help you harness that Universal Force. So take the time to do them every day, as often as you feel necessary. Structure is important, and doing your meditation and prayer at the same time and place when possible is one of the keys to your success. It helps you to build a strong foundation by raising your vibration and enabling you to be in the essence of your spirit. It allows you to quiet the physical body, work from your higher self, and open up to higher planes of energy and consciousness, including your Team.

We discussed the power of *white light* earlier and I believe it definitely has divine frequencies attached to it. Always remember that you should encircle yourself within that force for spiritual and energetic protection as often as you feel the need, repeating to yourself:

**I encircle myself in the white light of
God's love and divine protection.**

4

PREDICTION
or
PROJECTION

DESTINY & FATE: Does Free Will Have a Voice?

One of the things that I wrestled with early on in my development was how much control I had over my own life. Josephine, my maternal grandmother and a source of unconditional love for me, always said that things happened the way God wanted. When it came to death, she claimed that God lit a candle the day you were born, and when it went out, it was time to go to Heaven.

Really? That's it? This roll-over-and-surrender idea was not working for me. When I was a child I always asked questions that adults didn't want to answer, mostly because they were not equipped with the knowledge or the patience to do so. Some kinder relatives just said that I was "precocious" and others called my endless questioning "a pain in the ass." I often was given replies like *"Why don't you go play in traffic?" "Children should be seen and not heard"* and *"Why did we ever teach you how to speak?"*

All comments made in jest, of course, but said to me nonetheless because I pushed boundaries by asking *"But why?" "How come?"* and *"What if?"* The ironic part for me is that my son, Justin, is now doing the exact same thing. I love his open-mindedness to the *"What ifs"* of life. I am so happy for my children, partly because I feel that they are being raised with a huge edge in life since my wife and I are encouraging them to be freethinkers in every possible way. And this is the same *edge* that I want to impart to you.

HOW DID THEY KNOW JESUS SPOKE ENGLISH?

When the miniseries *Jesus of Nazareth* was on television in 1977, it was a huge must-see for my family. I remember sitting on the floor in front of my grandmother's nineteen-inch RCA TV, surrounded by a number of my family members, including my aunts, my cousins, and my mom, all watching this epic, moving depiction of Jesus's life.

All I could think was, *How did they know he could speak English?*

So when the movie got to the Sermon on the Mount part, I couldn't stand it any longer and I stood up, blocked the TV, and demanded to know, *"Shouldn't Jesus be speaking ancient Bethlehem-ese?"*

My entire family shushed me and told me to sit down. I just wanted to know how the moviemakers knew the story happened this way. Everyone was making me feel that I should just accept it as fact, but I was pretty clear I was watching a fictionalized movie and not a documentary or Mary and Joseph's home movies. Finally, when my mother realized that I would not shut up until someone answered me, she said, *"Wait until the commercial."* So I sat down and waited.

When it finally came time for the commercial, I remember looking at her impatiently for some answers. Her explanation was just what I needed to hear.

"Let's just say that there was this great and amazing man known as Jesus Christ. Some see him as the Son of God, some believe him to be God, and some view him as a prophet. Regardless, this inspiring man's life and message was documented in the Bible. Even though cameras were not actually there to capture what we are watching, it is based on the story of his life and his teachings. The actors and actresses are portraying an interpretation, but nonetheless, there is something important to be learned and appreciated. Understand? Just pay attention to the message!"

"Yes." I acquiesced.

"Now, shut the hell up before we all tie you up and stone you!" my aunt Roseanne, fondly known as "Big Ro," said, laughing. The whole family laughed, including me.

My point is that if as a young child I would questions the nuns, or the story of Jesus, of course I would continue to question everything else. Even my grandma and her proclamations were not spared from my query.

JOHN CALVIN VS. JOHN EDWARD

When Mr. Welch, my high school European history teacher, taught our class about Calvinism and the doctrine of predestination, I was just embarking on my psychic development. I would sit and engage him in these metaphysical "what if" questions and I think he believed I was just totally engrossed in the subject. I was not. I was just formulating my own thoughts and philosophies about life, based on what I was studying *outside* of school.

Not to go all historical on you, but the Calvinist movement is a series of theological beliefs first promoted by John Calvin (1509–64), one of the leaders of the Protestant Reformation. One of its most basic tenets discusses predestination and whether you were part of the "elect" that God has chosen to redeem. The belief is that all events throughout eternity have been preordained by divine decree, including each individual's ultimate destiny.

All I kept thinking was how sad it was for those who believed that their life was totally plotted out in its entirety. How do you learn from life? Why would you try to improve yourself or strive to do better? You wouldn't. You would accept that this is your lot in life, based on God's will.

I wasn't all right with this concept at the age of fifteen, and at forty I am definitely not okay with that theory. Let me tell you what my Guides have shared with me, and what I have seen in the last twenty-five years. There *are* aspects of our lives that are *predestined,* just in the same way a curriculum is planned for a college student enrolling to obtain a specific degree. You know that there will be certain prerequisites that you will have to take, and then you will build upon that foundation by studying. You need to earn credits toward your degree in order to graduate.

It has been shown to me that we decide what it is our souls need to learn and experience before we *incarnate,* or arrive on the Earth plane.

Life is the University, and your evolution is the degree, with an ultimate graduation back to the Other Side, where the learning still continues. What's the job? Be the best YOU, soul, energy that you can be, whether on this side or the other, and evolve in your ability to get as close to unconditional love, God, that Divine Source, as possible.

Then we pick the scenario that will best teach us those lessons and give us the greatest opportunity to learn them. That means you decide where in the world you will be born, the culture, the environment, and yes . . . you choose your parents. If you were to ask my children what I am known for saying to them (besides *"I love you"*), they would instantly reply, *"Thanks for picking me to be your Dad!"*

The reason I honor that choice is that I see the spiritual tasks beyond the normal responsibilities of parenthood: food, shelter, clothing, and love. I know that my children are here to learn just as you are. I also know that my life experiences, choices, and lessons plus the lines of probability that I have set forth—as well as their mom's—and our collective circle of family and friends help to create the current environment for them to evolve into and within.

EDDIE AND THE GAME OF LIFE

"What is the meaning of life?" "Why am I here?" These are two of the universal questions people ask themselves, discuss with each other, and even pray to God to get answers for. How many times have you looked up at the night sky and gazed at the moon and stars, wondering what your true purpose is? How often have you felt completely lost and frustrated because you felt this inertia in every direction? My friend, you're not alone. I felt the exact same way.

My cousin Eddie is only one year older than me. Over the years, we spent numerous holiday parties and family events together, including a fun trip to Jamaica and the occasional game of chess. I am happy to report that most games wound up in a stalemate. When he did win, it annoyed me, but what irritated me even more was that Ed, as he is now known, knew at an early age that he was going to be a child psychologist. He grew up and became a child psychologist. He had a clear vision of what he wanted to be and did it. In contrast, I felt clueless.

I asked Ms. Ewing, my high school guidance counselor, what was wrong with me because I didn't know what I was going to do for my career. She laughed. *"Honey, I still don't know what I am supposed to do. Just do what you like and make sure you like what you do. You will have more choices and opportunities unfold than you realize. Open your eyes and pay attention."* What great advice.

All of us can learn from Ms. Ewing in that respect. Open your eyes and pay attention, not just to people and situations, but to what the Universe itself is whispering in your ears. The Universe

LOOK FOR THE MAGIC IN THE MOMENT

Maggie Kerr, a well-known astrologer of whom I am quite fond, gave me a bit of sage advice when I was recently on tour in Australia: *"Look for the magic in the moment."* It directly applied to a Saturn transit that was occurring in my life, but I think it is a great message in general. I believe the Universe is just waiting to assist you by making energy happen for you.

doesn't send you a text message or e-mail that comes with instructions like you see in *Mission Impossible;* no, it is way more subtle than that.

In my adolescence, I was all over the board when it came to my future occupation. I clearly don't remember scoring high on the SAT in the "Talking to the Dead" section of the test. Actually, my actual score was kind of average. My first thought was that I wanted to own a deli, and then I imagined I would go into business of some sort, and finally I developed a sense that I was supposed to be in a healing profession. This career path led me to the health care field, both on the clinical and administrative side.

My strongest feeling has always been that I am meant to be a teacher. It never mattered what position I was holding, I always wound up training other people about that field. When people ask me, *"Why do you think you have had so much success in becoming known when there are so many psychics in the world?"* my answer is simple: *"I am a teacher."* I believe the Universe utilized the perfect storm in my approach, desire, ability, and perseverance in honoring the process. I always put the work first and try to raise the awareness of those around me regarding life and the world of energy.

Some of you may have had Eddie's experience and know your lessons and what you are supposed to be doing with your life, yet for some of us the classes or courses that we chart out in this lifetime become clear over time. Others make a decision not to turn the Universal lights on at all and live in a darker consciousness, choosing not to grow and evolve. Ultimately, you have the free will to apply as you wish.

FREE WILL

When you enroll in college (life), you work with a guidance counselor (Spirit Guides—your Team) to determine your career goals (life path), the degree necessary to reach them, and what classes (life experiences) you need to obtain that degree. Just because you show up at college doesn't mean you will graduate from it; sometimes people drop out early (suicide), are put on academic probation (illnesses), or take on additional classes to become a teacher (accelerated program). All of it still about learning and creating new lessons. Think of your life path as a GPS navigational system. It charts out where you are going and gives you turn-by-turn directions. Some of the more sophisticated devices show pictures and maps, and others pick up traffic patterns and alert you to alternate routes. You have the ability to heed the direction or plan a different course. If you make a decision to go against the recommended route, the GPS will adjust and start picking up the next path to the same destination.

Your free will comes into play in the largest way possible. The more energy and effort you put into this experience (lifetime), the more you will extrapolate from it. It goes back to the simplistic boomerang theory of energy—what you project out comes back.

I call the *Destiny* or *Fate* moments the ones that are supposed to happen and are charted out for you as part of your *Core Curriculum*. These *Life Check-in Points* are necessary to graduate with the degree of YOU for this lifetime. How you get from point A to B is all free will. You are in control over your life today, tomorrow, and every day. **Live passionately and be a force for the Universe to use.** You can accomplish a lot, or you can stagnate and slow down the process—ultimately, your destiny is in your hands. Isn't it so much easier to just blame it on "the man upstairs" and say it's entirely his fault that these things are happening in your life? You could blame your parents or your childhood experiences. As of today you know differently and you no longer can use anything or anyone as an excuse.

HOW DO I LEARN ABOUT MY CHART?

If I can take a moment to allow my Inner Monster to speak out here, I promise I will quickly beat it back into submission. You are fortunate to be reading this book now and to have these insights organized for you in the manner that I am laying them out. I did not have such an experienced earthly guide. I am so excited to utilize my journey to create this roadmap and place the billboards on the side of the road. I am happy to point out the rest stops and the speed limits. I am giving you some very important insights that absolutely apply to your empowered journey in Project YOU.

During the first few years of my psychic development, I studied everything that I could get my hands on that was deemed occult, paranormal, metaphysical, and mystical. I learned about many different courses of study that are available to all of us to provide us with deep insights as to who we are and why we are here.

I have talked about your journey and I brought up the analogy of your chart for this spiritual evolution. I am sure you are now asking where you may learn about your chart. Well, think of the chart as something that acts like that GPS device that you and your Guides utilize to get the most gain and result. We can use many lenses of metaphysics, such as numerology, tarot, I Ching, rune casting, et cetera, to discover facets of this so-called chart and the aspects of your journey, but perhaps none so clear as looking and exploring with the science of astrology.

NATAL CHART

The astrological system of knowledge and its language are completely fascinating to me. My entire life I had heard about the zodiac and knew that I was a Libra: the sign of the Scales, lover of beauty, fair-minded, creative, indecisive, romantic, diplomatic, and so much more. We all have read our sun sign horoscopes in magazines and newspapers, and they are ubiquitous on the Internet. As a child, I knew that Libra began on September 23 and lasted through October 22 because I had a plaque hanging in my room that said so, and that was all I needed to know. I couldn't have been more wrong.

I read everything I could find in the first few years of developing my abilities. Back in 1985 I felt like I had read a lot about astrology and yet understood very little about it. I instinctively knew that I needed to focus more and eventually was drawn to psychometry and card readings, and then the spirit communication started to happen on a more serious level. In my studies, I learned about all the various tools that would help me to develop and unlock my psychic powers and expand my senses.

Around the same time, I met and became lifelong friends with a psychic named Shelley Peck. Besides her uncanny ability to communicate with the Afterlife, she was an equally adept psychic and astrologer. When she looked at my natal chart, which is a snapshot of the heavens at the exact moment and place I was born, she told me that I had a natural ability to be a medium . . . something about Neptune being in the twelfth house. She urged me to take her astrology class. *"Okay, if you say so,"* was all I said to her. I didn't need astrology to tell me—seeing, hearing, and feeling the energy of those on the Other Side told me I was a medium more than any piece of paper with space hieroglyphics on it ever could. It looked more like a foreign language than anything else. Shelley laughed and told me I just didn't get it.

Shelley always said that I would make a great astrologer and begged me to let her teach me. I didn't really have a desire to study it, although I became fascinated by it. In the following years, my Guides would give me astrological information and, having no clue what it meant, I would call Shelley to ask her to interpret it. She would chuckle, but then get annoyed and tell me that I was cheating. She would remind me of when her next astrology class was starting, and I would politely decline.

In the mid-1980s I was in high school and had a part-time job managing a local mom-and-pop video store. One afternoon when the store was completely empty a woman walked in. It was her first time in the store and as I looked at her I saw superimposed over her face an astrological chart.

I blurted out uncontrollably, *"You are an astrologer!"*

This stopped the woman, who I found out was named Dee, in her tracks. She raised her eyebrows and replied dryly, *"And clearly **you** are a psychic—nice to meet you."*

What happened from that day on was life-changing for me. Dee would come into the store and we would have amazing conversations about metaphysics and astrology. I would go back and talk to Shelley about them and she told me that Dee wasn't getting all her information from astrology alone. Instead, she was using astrology as a tool to psychically receive the information. Astrology was the key to unlock that door.

Dee, the astrologer, would insist that she was not psychic, but was only interpreting my chart. She said she did "old astrology," not this "new stuff" that people were practicing now. Somehow I felt like I was brokering a relationship between Israel and Palestine, with each side unwilling to listen to the other's arguments. When I suggested that we three get together and discuss all this for fun, they both declined.

Dee offered to read my chart and I thought it would be an awesome experience. In all the years of knowing Shelley and Sandy Anastasi, I hadn't ever thought of asking them to interpret my chart. I will not go into the details of Dee's reading except for one. She predicted to the hour my mother's death. My view of astrology changed dramatically after that moment. To say that she got my attention would be an understatement. But since astrology isn't really about predicting those kinds of things, I knew that Shelley was right about Dee's psychic abilities.

Shelley never shifted her opinion of Dee's ability to interpret charts psychically, but she did acknowledge her accuracy.

STAR SCHOOL

When I was in college, my aunt Roseanne told me she wanted to attend Shelley's beginning astrology class. She was embarrassed to go alone and asked me if I would accompany her. By the third class, I was very clear on one thing: I would not continue studying astrology. When I explained to Shelley that I was already enrolled in twenty-one credits that semester as part of an accelerated program for my master's degree and that her class was like taking a physics class, she laughed. It was a science and mathematics class combined . . . too much work for me at the time.

There were no computer-generated charts then, which meant you had to learn the actual mechanics of casting. I felt like the great navigator Magellan painstakingly looking up longitudes and latitudes, consulting several books just to create one chart. I knew that learning astrology was not for me, at least not then. I told Shelley that I wanted to wait until it was possible to use a computer to create the charts, not to mention that I needed to finish college. *"Are you crazy?"* was all I kept saying to her when Shelley told me it would get easier with practice. Shelley was disappointed at my decision, but my aunt Roseanne studied with her for over a year and loved it. I think on a psychic level Shelley knew that when I returned to the subject matter, she would no longer be on the Earth plane to teach me.

BACK TO SCHOOL

Starting in 2003, my Guides told me that it was time for me to return to student mode and that astrology was to be the focal point. Why all of a sudden this sudden urge to look up at the celestial heavens and learn from the stars? I truly had no clue, but I knew that my Guides were serious about my revisiting the subject matter one day soon. And now I had no excuses with the proliferation of computer programs available for generating charts. Maybe it was just time.

When my Guides speak, I listen. Always.

They had instructed me much earlier in my development that my role as a teacher would be to create a school. Back then, I immediately thought it would be a real brick-and-mortar building. As this educational edict evolved, my Guides let me know that the school would be worldwide and theoretical. Now, that idea didn't make any logical sense to me. I would have people from all over the world coming to study at my psychic academy? It's like I was creating the psychic ideal for Hogwarts! They referred to it always as the "BIG U" in my head.

When the Internet started to gain momentum as a means for global communication and websites became essential for all businesses, I realized my school was clearly going to be an online virtual experience.

The answer to why I needed to study astrology became immensely clear when I was developing the concept of BIG U into a reality. "The boys" knew that one of the cornerstones of this website would be to encourage students to examine their lives and the world through the lens of astrology. Realistically, how could I embark on creating a school that would delve deeply into a subject without learning more about it first myself? For me the answer was obvious: I could not. Reflecting back, I realize that my rekindled desire to learn more about astrology was to prepare me to build my school, InfiniteQuest.com.

Looking Up

They say that when the student is ready, the teacher appears. Of course the teacher appears, since you manifested the opportunity. I called Sandy Anastasi to tell her that I needed to be a student again and that I wanted to introduce her to the psychic I was mentoring as well. I felt it was time for me to pass on my mentor to him. I asked Sandy what she felt psychically I should be studying. I was thinking maybe Kabbalah would be interesting, even though I knew my Guides had already told me astrology; I was half-heartedly trying to wiggle out of the hard work I knew it would entail . . . but she replied *"astrology."* She told me that although she would love for me to attend her classes, the fact that she was in Florida and I was in New York would make it impossible. Not to mention she didn't want other people in her classes freaking out that I was in their class and hoping that a loved one of theirs might come through when they were supposed to be studying the planets and signs. Sandy suggested private lessons whenever I could find the time to visit her in Florida, and I agreed that might be the best option but I would need to juggle my schedule to make it happen.

I started going down to the west coast of Florida to study with her again, bringing my student Jonathan with me. Sandy's teaching style and methodology make it so easy to understand these very difficult and complex insights from the Universe. After the first intensive weekend, my aunt Roseanne asked me how it went and what I learned. Sandy covered with me in one weekend what Shelley had covered with Aunt Ro in over a year. Once again I realized I was on the accelerated program. But what was the rush? I had no intention of doing astrological readings. What was this urgency that I felt? I thought maybe it was not about me, but that my Guides wanted me to bring Jonathan to Sandy and I was merely the intermediary, in the same way I was for my aunt with Shelley.

In our very first class, Sandy started talking about the cells in the body, protons, neutrons, nuclei, electrons, and orbits. I was staring at Jonathan and wanted to have a confident "isn't this great" kind of energy, but instead it was complete confusion. All I was able to think about was why we weren't talking about Libra, Leo, Mars, and Venus? When Sandy looked at me she saw my confusion and laughed. She explained that to really learn what's happening out there in the cosmos, we had to understand the smaller universe of what's happening in here, as she pointed to her physical body.

Remember when you were in high school and learning all about chemistry and energy? You thought to yourself, "I am never going to

AS ABOVE, SO BELOW

"That which is above is the same as that which is below." This principle is widely adhered to in astrology, and almost all systems of magic claim to function by this same formula. It is attributed to the Emerald Tablet of Hermes, a text that is the original source of Hermetic philosophy and alchemy, dating back to at least the tenth century. The significance of this phrase is that it is believed to hold the key to all mysteries. In astrology it is used to simply explain that the stars do not rule us nor do we rule them. It is a more symbiotic relationship than we might first imagine.

use this information." I was starting to feel that way about Sandy's class. I was listening and writing down what she was teaching, but was thinking and wondering *"Have my Guides lost their minds?"* As Sandy began to delve deeper and deeper into the subject matter —the elements (Fire, Earth, Air, Water), the Modalities (Cardinal, Fixed, Mutable), and then the planets and how they tied into the signs, I began to get a glimpse, and I mean a slight hint, of this amazing science.

After the glimpse came the reality of knowing that I was never going to be a professional astrologer. Even if I could download a chart now, I felt this was not part of my path. I studied for over a year with Sandy and then I became very busy, and getting our schedules to align became nearly impossible.

The idea of my virtual school was still in the back of my mind, but when I did what's called a wire frame for it and had program-mers give me estimates on the finances of launching what was deemed phase one, I had to abandon it. I just couldn't afford to do it the way it needed to be done. I knew that it had to be right and not just another website. I figured, as with astrology, I would one day revisit BIG U. One day soon after my decision, I signed on to check my e-mail and saw that two separate people had sent me the same electronic newsletter about astrology. It was written by an American astrologer named Alan Oken. I thought it odd that I had received this newsletter in light of my walking away from astrology for the second time. Within two days of receiving those e-mail newsletters, someone else asked me if I knew who Alan Oken was. Now, the name sounded familiar, but I was thinking of an actor for some reason and couldn't place him. A few days after that, I received a package in the mail from Sandy Anastasi with books by Alan Oken!

"Oh, come on, guys!" I exclaimed. My Guides are RELENTLESS to a fault. They were clearly leading me to Alan for a purpose. I went back online and started to look at his materials and teachings and

was blown away by the level of expertise and the many arenas he writes about. Now, what was really quite odd in a "nothing happens by accident" kind of way is that Alan was born in Queens, New York, just like me, but was now residing in Portugal. Portugal? The same country that my wife's entire family is from? The signs were too obvious to miss. I just sat at my computer and laughed.

So Alan Oken, an accomplished astrologer and metaphysical scholar residing in Portugal who only takes on a few students each year for private tutoring, accepted me as a student. I didn't reveal anything about me or my profession when I contacted him, but when he saw my name he asked if I was the same guy from the television shows. After we had a brief chat, the lessons began.

Even though I had learned so much from Sandy, I asked Alan to start from scratch. For me, I just knew that there was something very important that was going to come from this connection. We made it to the fourth class when he startled me by saying, *"Do you know that you are supposed to launch a metaphysical university on the Web?"*

I jumped up from my desk with my headset still on, stood with my arms extended, and said, laughing, *"Well, can you look at my chart and tell me who the hell is going to pay for all this?"* and Alan confidently, yet quietly uttered, *"You will."*

There was a quiet knowing that came over me. I can't explain it. It was like a feeling of "you need to use your voice and name to make this possible." InfiniteQuest.com was launched in 2009 with Alan Oken as my cofounder.

AN AHA MOMENT OF ACCEPTANCE

There will be moments in your life when you just *know* something. You will see the direction so clearly as I did over twenty years ago with the concept of Infinite Quest. For me, the timing and technology weren't right in the early days of knowing that I had to build the educational component. But even when it was ready and I could, there was a blockage or fear around doing so. Should I embark on such a huge undertaking? Could I afford it? All these normal and practical questions come up in our pursuit of learning and evolving on all levels.

Think of it like this: you might look at a puzzle for a long time and then all of a sudden it becomes perfectly clear that it is in a specific shape, or you realize while watching a movie exactly who the culprit is. You will also have these breakthrough moments psychically. You will seemingly just "know" what the answer or information is. The reality is in what you do with it.

When Alan was talking to me, he was looking at my natal chart and explaining where I came from, what shaped me to be me, and what my projected future would be. When he uttered the words *"You will"* in regard to the BIG U, I knew in that moment that I needed to hear that message. It only validated what I already really knew and didn't want to admit.

I now understand that the years of learning about astrology were preparation for Infinite Quest. They gave me the confidence to be able to speak of astrology with respect and appreciation and to allow me to develop it into an aspect of the website to help the members understand their charts on their journeys. So to you, the reader, fellow student of the YOUniverse, please know how significant a tool astrology can be in understanding who you are, your purpose, and your blueprint for your current lifetime.

For me, astrology shouldn't be used solely as a predictive tool. My recommendation is to look at it as insights and foreshadowing of what's to come energetically, like a weather forecast . . . and to prepare accordingly. Ultimately, I recommend that you utilize it to explain and explore who you truly are.

Going back to the destiny and fate theme we are discussing, astrology really can illuminate some of those lessons you are currently learning, as well as what's coming up, and how you can benefit from them to get the most out of life. Why work against the flow of the Universe when you can flow with it?

Know Your Chart

If you aren't already familiar with your astrological natal chart, here's your chance. Visit my website www.InfiniteQuest.com to run your own personalized chart. All you need is your birth date, time, and place of birth. Find out what makes you tick from a planetary point of view. You can use the offer in the back of this book to enroll for a free trial membership so you can access the astrological services plus all the other interactive features on the site.

5

Taking
Chances
& Making
Choices

DESTINY IS COMING. LIFE IS HAPPENING.
FREE WILL EXISTS. These realities are the building
blocks that help to create the stage for us to act out the
drama of our lives.

Almost my entire practice has involved seeing clients who were in an emotional place where the thought of the unknown or changes that were happening were creating an imbalance in their lives. Some were simply afraid. In Chapter 2, I mentioned how the FEAR principle can harness and inhibit a person's evolution; this issue is discussed in offices of every metaphysical counselor or therapist across the globe. People don't normally seek out a reading or session because their life is great; they do so in the hopes of improving their lives and to make themselves feel better.

My grandmother used to get so frustrated when she would hear me say to my clients that they didn't need to see me because they could learn to pay attention to the signs and symbols all around them, instead. I believe that life is like a soap opera in the sense that if you are watching closely enough, the writers give you a foreshadowing of what's coming up for the characters. **You and the Universe are the writers and you are the star in your own life's drama.** I often suggested to my clients that they study metaphysics, meditate, or just learn to listen to their own intuition. My grandmother would exclaim, *"Why are you saying that? You are not going to have any business!"* I just laughed, and I still do to this day when thinking about it.

WHAT'S LOVE GOT TO DO WITH IT?

William Shakespeare made the ancient metaphor *"we are all actors on the stage of life"* famous in his plays and the adage lives on to this day. Now that you are probably getting a good feel for my perspective on things, you can guess that I want to be the actor, writer, producer, director, ticket taker, set designer, and even the floor sweeper, for that matter.

Being in control and creating balance in your life is key for your personal growth. Developing into the best YOU possible and utilizing your intuition and astrology—or whatever metaphysical tools you connect with—can help you to understand the energetic flow of the Universe and how it impacts your life. It can assist you in understanding what you are supposed to learn from any given situation, as well as how *not* to handle things. Trying to change your thinking and how you are generating actions in your life through your thought processes is a huge element in your ability to evolve. If you disconnect from the harnessing and restrictive powers of the *Fear Principle* and shift your perspective of the same situations but come from the *Love Principle* instead, things will begin to immediately transform within and therefore evolve all around you.

Some events and circumstances might yield an immediate change, a universal instant gratification, while others take more time to develop. Just be careful that you don't start looking for your reward because you said a prayer, read a chapter, and started to think about things slightly differently. The transformation is more subtle and deeper than you can imagine at first.

I can't even begin to count how many people will complain to me that *"Nothing is happening!"* even though they say they are doing "the work." *"I'm doing what I'm supposed to so why aren't things changing for me?"* Ugh! I get annoyed just typing those sentences and thinking about all the folks who are programming their energy with such a self-defeatist mind-set. If you didn't know this concept before reading this book, now you should understand how this kind of questioning just perpetuates more of those very same thoughts they are trying so desperately to move away from.

I admit that the mental, emotional, and spiritual process that I am describing is daunting, yet it must become a way of life if you really want to see it work. It is difficult to use just one specific analogy, but I think it's easier to understand when compared to the world of physical fitness. If you are overweight and know that you need to make a change in your habits, watching an infomercial on the latest fitness equipment, buying nutritious food, or joining a gym is not going to do a thing. **You need to create and manifest that positive change.** You must take the actual steps to lose the weight. You have to go to the gym regularly and work out, eat healthier meals, and be more conscious of your relationship to food and what you really need to do to reach your weight-loss goals.

It takes an enormous amount of mental and physical energy on your part to make the necessary changes and it is not done overnight. There is no quick fix. A lifestyle shift has to happen and only then can real change take place.

For me, if I didn't pay attention to how I was living I would weigh three hundred pounds. When my personal trainer, Frank Sepe, told me that ice cream was not actually a food group, I was devastated. Okay, I already *knew* it wasn't, but here are a few of my favorite foods so you can see what I was up against: fast food of all types, especially burgers and fries; chocolate chip cookies, cakes, and soft drinks; and everything Italian, including pizza, pasta, meatballs, and fresh mozzarella cheese. And my favorite food of all, ice cream. I could really be a professional ice cream eater. Some people can eat one scoop and think it's enough; I am a double pint eater. That's right—you read that correctly.

If I was not coming from the *Love Principle* in my life, which includes loving myself and respecting my health, I would really be outrageously overweight. Now, I doubt I am ever going to grace the covers of fitness magazines as Frank has, but I will always maintain some sense of healthy balance when it comes to my eating and working out. When I was rapidly approaching my thirtieth birthday, I joked and said that I ordered six-pack abs and they apparently were on back order. Now that I am forty, I just want to be healthy, and if the appearance shifts as well, then that's the icing on the cake.

The *shift* is the key I want to discuss. The shift that I have had in the last twenty years regarding my physical fitness is almost entirely a mental approach. Sometimes I am extremely diligent about my eating habits and working out, and at other times I am very lazy, but I always know that I will keep some balance because I truly desire to be healthy.

I want to address the same shift in regard to the spiritual energy between you and the Universe. That subtle way of shifting your thoughts can create an amazing outcome. Spiritual fitness can be viewed in exactly the same way as physical fitness. It's impossible to run a marathon when you weigh five hundred pounds, but you can work toward the goal and slowly lose the weight so that you can make it happen. You shouldn't do a psychic reading without having a true understanding of your own spiritual evolution, a deep respect for the ethics and responsibilities needed for this work, and a comprehensive knowledge of the mechanics and tools of metaphysics. **You build a house upon a strong foundation or else it will collapse.**

When you move from a place of Fear to a place of Love, the shift creates a new concept for you to embrace, one that I refer to as the *Taking Chances–Making Choices Principle* (TCMC). The *Taking Chances–Making Choices Principle* can assist you to feel empowered about the life you currently are living and can give you the tools necessary to create the changes you want for your future.

In keeping with the spiritual fitness theme, TCMC would bring your healthy diet and fitness regime together to create the changes in your internal and external health in a huge way. When I need to make a physical change in my eating habits, I get behind the TCMC principle and use a thought such as *"I am eating for fuel, not for fun."* I visualize the purpose in my eating with every bite and morsel. I force myself to acknowledge that consuming two pints of ice cream in one sitting is equivalent to about two thousand calories, and thirty-five hundred calories will add one pound. I take responsibility for the fuel that I am putting into my body and understand the result. It really is that simple. And I believe it is equally simple with energy and spiritual fitness as well. The major difference is not being able to see the obvious results, such as the pounds melting away or your cholesterol going down, as a barometer. The spiritual results play out very differently for every one of us. It is important not to *look* for the instant gratification or the immediate reward. One step at a time. You see, feel, and experience life through a different lens and that is the true prize—knowing that the decisions and choices you are making today in the present will yield a more amazing tomorrow.

"TRUST THE WIND" AND "HELP IS ON THE WAY"

In my opinion, David Friedman is one of the most amazing and intuitive songwriters and composers living today. His music and lyrics have been skillfully executed by many singers, including Diana Ross and Nancy LaMott, and his many soundtracks for movies and musicals encompass spiritual themes in everyday life circumstances. "Trust the Wind" and "Help Is on the Way" are two of my favorite songs because they are about trusting the energy of the Universe. I believe that people utilize their psychic abilities in a variety of ways, and David Friedman clearly uses his to inspire people through his music, opening hearts and touching souls with his words. You might enjoy discovering his music and listening for yourself. His messages are universal in their appeal.

Another person who probably wouldn't define himself as being "psychic" is Dr. Wayne Dyer. Dr. Dyer is one of the world's most respected authors and motivational speakers on the power of the human experience. His heartfelt teachings have inspired people all around the world. One afternoon several years ago, he was on a television show called *CNN Talkback Live.* I was just out of the shower and getting ready to speak at a seminar on the road and the show caught my attention because of the subject matter: changing your life in a moment.

I don't recall which best-selling book Dr. Dyer was being inter-viewed about at the time, but I remember the host seemed a little cynical in tone while speaking to him. Never once have I seen Dr. Dyer lose his cool or get ruffled when addressing someone who might be challenging his knowledge or doubting his message. The question put to him was right to the point: *"Dr. Dyer, do you truly believe that you can change your life in a moment?"*

I expected him to launch into a lengthy example from his new book, delving into some meaty ideas and philosophies. Instead, his reply was a simple and emphatic *"Yes!"*

That one-word delivery was profoundly impactful to anyone watching it, myself included. Your life *can* change in one moment— one bullet of positive thought to manifest the change you need to make. Just be mindful that sometimes the way you think things should be is not how they will turn out. Remember what happens when you fire those bullets of thought and energy, so keep your inten-tions positive, no matter what.

> Take the time to make things happen for you instead of letting them happen to you.

I told you that I believed that fear and love are the two major motivations that we have in life. I know that there other motiva-tors, like ambition, anger, greed, and ego, but I view them as derivatives of the big two. Let's explore the *Taking Chances–Making Choices* mind-set and look at some of the blockages that might get in our way.

PAYING PSYCHIC ATTENTION

There are moments that take place for all of us when we are forced to examine what our potential outcomes might be depending on the choices we make. We assess what is happening and how we are feeling and often we can see only the downside of a situation. Our perspective is intrinsically shaped by our past and helps us to define our present and affects our view of the future. It is normal and healthy to weigh all the options and explore every opportunity or potential, both negative and positive. Unfortunately, most people can't get past the negative—perhaps even dwell on it purposefully—and choose not to set themselves up for disappointment by thinking about the positive potential.

What is at play here when this happens? Who is speaking to you in that moment? Certainly not your Spirit Guides. Your Team would not be doing anything except giving you the wisdom to understand your present situation and the tools to improve it; remember that is their job. So the real question is: *why are YOU getting in YOUR own way?* You guessed it—back to the *Fear Principle* once again.

My friend and colleague, Char Margolis, will often define fear like this:

False **E**vidence **A**ppearing **R**eal

Every time we are doing a speaking engagement together and I hear her use that acronym, I smile. Although its origin is unknown, it has been made famous by author Neal Donald Walsch and is used by many motivational speakers. Char is the one who passed it on to me, and now I am sharing it with you. I know that after all the years she has dedicated to doing the work of a psychic, she has learned many of the same lessons that I have. We never had to sit and discuss the *Fear Principle,* because we see it all the time in our practices. Fortunately, we also know that we will continue to learn from the events taking place in our lives and that we can choose to shift the energies of our own free will.

I want you to be able to see exactly where the *Fear Principle* harnesses you and also visualize where the growth lies in your own future.

You can picture what it is that you fear and also where the growth can come from and hopefully make unbiased decisions to keep yourself in balance. Live in the reality of the life you are creating. But what are you afraid of? Success? Hard work? Failure? Love? Rejection? Happiness? The list can be long and changes often.

Now, I know that many of you are just not accepting the idea that you have the ability to transform your life and yourself. You are ready to put this book down so you can e-mail me to defend your fears and explain again why you are different and have a special set of circumstances. Later on, I will address how you're not that special when it comes to certain things, and this happens to be one of them. Fire doesn't burn selectively for some people and not for others; it's just fire. The same holds true for thoughts.

Remember, you are reading this book for the insights that I am revealing. I believe that these insights do just that . . . they keep things in your sight. They are not promises to change your life—I can't do that! But YOU can! I will continue to repeat and emphasize specific aspects to drive home how certain things can hamper your intuitive growth. If your eyes are closed, you won't be able to see what is right in front of you. All of this is meant to open your metaphysical eyes to get a clearer vision of the Universe around you.

SINK OR SWIM IN
THE OCEAN OF FEAR

I want to address this concept not from the psychological standpoint of the fight-or-flight theory, but from how in certain moments of fear we erect barriers to receiving and interpreting psychic information. This in turn creates blockages and unplugs us from our Guides and Higher Self. Realize that your Guides are a source of divine wisdom and they are ready, willing, and able to download information to you in all aspects and situations. Keep in mind they are not there to do things for you, but to assist you in creating and manifesting. So please don't walk around surrendering your free will while desperately looking everywhere for signs and symbols from your Team. This is about YOU and your choices, not them. If you pay attention, your Team will make their message clear enough for you to understand.

FEAR AND THE AFTERLIFE

As you might imagine, a recurring theme in my practice involves people whose fears manifest through their grief. **When we lose a loved one, their physical body ceases but their soul and essence of who they truly are lives on.** We are still able to connect with that consciousness of love, and we don't need a medium's help to do it.

Our loved ones and friends on the Other Side still want to maintain healthy relationships with us and will go out of their way to let us know that they are around. Because we have spent our lives dealing with them only in the physical capacity, we condition ourselves that without the vehicle of the body, we can no longer connect. The fear of that thought creates a natural barrier that over time becomes a blockage in communication.

One of my favorite questions to ask an audience is this: if death wasn't physical death in the way that you know it, but instead meant only that you lost the ability to speak the language that is your own and now had to be able to speak ancient Aramaic, what would you do? The answer is simple: you would learn ancient Aramaic. This is a clear-cut example of why it is important to develop and evolve your energetic self and project YOU. This book will help you to raise your awareness to the place where you can open yourself up to recognize the subtle energy language Spirits now speak to you in.

So because your thoughts manifest your realities it is imperative to "think positively." You need to honor your feelings of grief and physical loss, while simultaneously understanding that the ability to connect with your loved ones is still possible. Your emotional fear of not seeing them, hearing them, and feeling them in the physical world can block you from experiencing them from the Spirit World.

You need to look at the moment when the information from your Higher Self and your Team becomes blocked and seek out where and why your intuition has been silenced. This feeling, left unattended, can make you feel as if you are stranded out in the ocean with no sight of land in any direction. Here is what I encourage you to do:

This is such an important concept to understand. I am not saying to deny the feeling of fear and pretend it is not present; instead I am sug-

> Honor what you are feeling in any given moment, not just what you are fearing.

gesting that you embrace it. See it, hear it, feel it, be it, own it, and then let the fear go and move forward. Make the decision to swim . . . otherwise, fear will single-handedly sink you.

MS. KRAUT AND CHINA

Discussing psychic development forces me to reflect on my own, and since a great deal of it occurred when I was still in high school, I will frequently use examples that are etched in my mind from that time. Often the hardest teachers are the ones you remember the most. While I was still in eighth grade, I attended my high school orientation and one of the teachers we met briefly was Ann Kraut. She was an ageless and energetic force—a short, militant powerhouse of a teacher who expected you to be fully present in her class, whether you were interested in the subject or not.

While most of the teachers were painting an exciting portrait of our upcoming freshman year, she took her introduction to a whole other level.

"You should pray you don't get me on your schedule next year. I don't teach from a text, I teach with lectures. I don't repeat myself and I don't

tolerate any insubordination. Don't be late, study hard, take good notes, and we won't have a problem."

Right in that moment, I knew down to the core of my being that I was going to be sentenced to Ms. Kraut's boot camp next year. The last bit of advice she gave to her terrified audience was, *"If you want to ace my class, teach yourself shorthand over the summer."*

A week later my fears were confirmed: next year my seventh period would be Ms. Kraut's Afro-Asian History class. As soon as I got home after school that day, I called my mother while she was still at work and told her of my plight. At the time she was employed as an office manager in New York City.

"Just because I'm a secretary doesn't mean I know shorthand," Mom replied.

"You have to find someone who will teach me or I will fail Ms. Kraut's class. She told us!"

"I am sure that no one else is flipping out about wanting to learn shorthand. You will do fine without it."

I couldn't stop thinking about it. This teacher meant business, and I felt that if she went out of her way to inform you during an orientation that if you were unlucky enough to get her as a teacher you should learn shorthand in order to pass her class . . . well, I had to pay attention. I tried to tell myself that it was just an act on her part to scare unsuspecting freshmen, but I failed miserably in convincing myself.

My mom, as she often did, came through for me. Apparently, after we hung up the phone, within five minutes two books landed on her desk. They both covered something called Alpha Hand. It wasn't exactly shorthand, but that summer I taught myself how to do this type of speedwriting and I will say, with great confidence, that I was very good at it. I was armed and ready to go head to head with my seventh-period nemesis.

The first day of Ms. Kraut's class came and I immediately sat down in my seat, ready to capture word for word what she was going to say. And I did. In all seriousness, I could have handed her my notebook at the end of the semester and she would have had her own textbook.

But beyond school and Ms. Kraut, that year a bigger issue had me seriously afraid. It was my health. I had been told a couple of years earlier that I might need to have a urological surgical procedure done at some point in the future. I was alone in the doctor's examination room when that little bomb was dropped on me. When my mom came in afterward, the doctor told her the same thing, but said he would leave it up to me to tell him if it was necessary. If it became painful, or if I started to have difficulty urinating, then we would know that it had to be corrected. An aside to anyone in the medical community reading this: don't ever inform a twelve-year-old boy that you might want to cut his "equipment" in any way. I didn't care if I had to urinate through my fingertips; that surgery was not an option. Because of my intense fear of the procedure, I didn't tell anyone that I was actually having some problems and they were growing painfully worse.

One afternoon, in the middle of my writing word for word Ms. Kraut's recitation about the Ming Dynasty, she paused for what seemed like a long time. I glanced up to see why. She was gazing right at me in a way that made me feel like I just got caught doing something wrong. That was impossible because all I was doing was diligently taking notes. Ms. Kraut said the following:

"When your body is making you sense pain, it is telling you that something is wrong and needs to be corrected."

She stared directly at me when she delivered that statement. I looked to my left and right to see if anyone else noticed that this had just taken place. All the other students were still looking straight ahead or taking notes in an attempt to keep up with Captain Kraut. She then took her ruler and whacked it down on her desk loudly and said, "Are you all with me?"

I was frozen in shock. I raised my hand and asked if it was okay for me to use the bathroom pass. She allowed me. I walked out to the pay phone in the middle of the school and called my mother at her office. I told her what had just happened. By six-thirty that night I was sitting in a urological surgeon's office and the next morning at six-thirty I was having surgery performed on me.

After my recovery and upon my return to school, I went to see Ms. Kraut to thank her. I told her how her words made me honor my feelings and release my fear, and I was able to stop permanent kidney damage in the process. The ironic part of this experience is that she did not recall speaking that sentence, and no other students in my class remembered her saying anything like that.

So what actually happened? I honestly believe that because of my highly focused note-taking, the experience was a form of meditation. While I was in this semi-altered state, I was very receptive to the information being sent from my Guides. They knew that I was in physical trouble and utilized Ms. Kraut, someone I respected and closely listened to every day, to get me to pay attention.

Your Team is just like mine. They want to get your attention so they can help you swim, not sink, in the ocean of your life. You just need to open your eyes, ears, mind, and heart to allow them to truly be your Guides.

My point in sharing this story is simple. I was allowing fear to be a motivator for me. And although there are situations when fear can actually be a positive force, especially in times of physical danger or when it pushes you to work harder—for instance, I learned shorthand due to the fear of Ms. Kraut's wrath—ultimately it is a showstopper in more instances than not.

Fear tends to keep you from accomplishing your goals or even attempting things at all. In this case my fear of what was going to happen to me if I told the truth about my health could have had seriously negative consequences.

TINGLING AND RUSH

No, this is not a new band being played on the radio or a new dance craze sweeping the clubs. These are the moments when energy is coming through you like a force flowing in a very direct and abundant way. Something is about to happen and there is this feeling or crackling of energy all around you that you can almost see, but you absolutely can *feel*.

If you have ever won anything in a casino, you know exactly what I mean. It is the moment when you have this amazing sense of clarity, but it is backed by a force of energy . . . like a flash flood of information.

This *Rush of Energy* can be harnessed and controlled to a certain extent. The more you open yourself up to your Guides and your Higher Self through meditation, prayer, and the white light, the more you will be able to experience this free flow of energy. During a TINGLING OR RUSH you are being bombarded with energy and intuitive information. A very basic example that demonstrates this is when you are standing next to a roulette table. Somehow you *know* that nineteen is going to be the winning number, you have a physical reaction of excitement, and you put twenty-five dollars down on it. Nineteen rolls around and you win!

Another easy example can be seen when searching for an item that you have been wanting for a while. One day you literally feel *drawn* to a specific store, garage sale, or eBay listing . . . and there *it* is, waiting for you to find it all along. Your Team is giving you the answers to questions you haven't even asked them yet. They are trying to download the information to you, so pay close attention to the *feelings* you receive in any given moment.

You had this inexplicable RUSH of energy that was telling you what to do. The trick is learning to recognize it and make positive use of it before it's gone.

FALSE FUTURE

Part of our intuitive development is to be able to imagine the future. We already discussed earlier in this book what creates the future—bullets of energy that we emit draw lines of probabilities that help to shape various potentialities. When these potentialities meet up with the courses that we have enrolled our soul selves in, we create our teachers and lessons for our immediate future. So with that philosophy close to our heart and soul, we will be armed for manifesting the best potential futures for ourselves.

The glitch in the system occurs when fear gets in the way and creates a block, or *stagnation*. When we stop our energy from flowing we become stagnant, just like putting a car in park. Some of us sit idle, waiting perhaps for something to happen, and eventually run out of gas. Now we are going nowhere at all.

The obstacle of stagnation, being caught up in self-doubts or endless questioning, is a huge game that people play with themselves. They think that they are just looking at their options one more time, weighing them out, and trying to decide on a course of action. Instead, they are allowing fear to keep them idle and stagnant, void of a direction. *Just move.* Move in a direction and stick with it. How do you feel about where you are at the moment?

Remember to trust the wind and always listen to your heart.

If I had a dollar for every person who ever said to me, *"What do you think I should do?"* my great-grandchildren would not have to work a day in their lives. All right, maybe that is a slight exaggeration; just my grandchildren would have it easy. The great-grandchildren will have to get jobs.

You get the point that I am trying to make here: **Fear allows us to create a False Future.** The potential of what the fear is broadcasting is not one based on your free will, intuition, and logic.

Think about a personal crisis that you experienced in your life or perhaps one that you helped a close friend to navigate at some point. It's almost always easier to see the lesson in someone else's life than in your own. How did you handle the situation at the time? Take a moment to reexamine your actions and consider how you might do things differently now if you had the chance.

When I teach this valuable lesson to my kids, I want them to be able to look at life through this same filter of understanding with the stimuli of other adults, kids, and media all factoring in and helping them to formulate their directions. I want to give them permission, and to you my students as well, to be empowered and to move into their future in a positive manner. No "False Futures" allowed, my friends. Don't let yourself or your Inner Monster (or its bitch, entitlement) create a blockage that stops you from moving forward.

Screenwriter's Exercise

You might want to create a journal to do this or use the one online at www.InfiniteQuest.com. Pick any television show that you enjoy watching (you can substitute a favorite movie or book if you prefer). I think a drama is more interesting for this particular exercise but a comedy would work just as well. In any case it should be one in which you already are familiar with the history of the characters, understand their personalities, and know something about their underlying motives.

Take one episode and examine how your favorite characters could have done things differently and then consider why they didn't. Try to understand what the motivating elements are in their most singular form and how they complexly weave together to create emotional blocks or false futures that your characters might be envisioning. Most likely the show's writers are not giving you this information in the dialogue and you will have to explore this subtext on your own. If you know other people who enjoy the same show, see if you can get them to play along and listen to your thoughts and findings.

The reason why I suggest this exercise is to help you start to look at life through a pair of metaphysical glasses. It is important to understand that everything happens for a reason and that the mysteries of the universe are simple yet complex. Once you get yourself to notice these motivating trends of blockages and energies, you will more readily be able to spot them in your own life and those of the people around you, including your clients if you choose to do readings.

What you will soon discover is that you have always *known* these things, but might not have been aware of just how significant a role these hidden motives play in the choices people make and the impact these motives have on a person's future.

6

PROGRAMMING

WHEN YOU THINK about the word *programming*, two areas probably come to mind: television and computers. But have you ever thought about yourself as being programmed? Since I am a student of the Universe, my Guides are always introducing me to new perspectives on life, and these concepts take me to deeper levels of understanding about this world of energy we live in.

W hen my television show *Crossing Over* ended in 2004, many people asked me what I was going to do *now*. I actually found this to be an odd question because I was going to do what I had always been doing—my work. My plan was to continue reading for clients in private and group sessions, continue lecturing around the world, and perhaps get back to writing another book. I had made a conscious choice not to build my personal and professional life around this television show, even though all the executives involved tried really hard to get me to make it my sole priority. It was not. In fact, it was only a fraction of the whole of my life.

My Guides made it crystal clear to me that if I defined myself by this one show, then when it ran its course, I would be lost when it was over. When the end came, as it comes for most things, I was relieved in a way. I remember feeling literally like I could finally exhale after four years. Now don't get me wrong: I will always consider it as one of the most amazing experiences of my life.

After two years of retirement from television, I started to get bombarded by e-mails from clients and fans of my work *demanding* that I go back on air. I used to laugh at the way many of these e-mails were written. They were more like edicts of passionate need rather than simple statements such as *"I miss your show."* Yet I really couldn't picture myself walking into the local network affiliate and announcing that I was back and ready to talk to the dead again, so put me on and move over, Oprah!

These e-mails always came at unique moments, usually when I had thought that I was totally finished with mainstream media and doing my work in such a public fashion. I knew they were my Guides' way of communicating with me the importance of my teaching through the medium of television.

Finally, these heartfelt messages led me to return to the air to host a show called *John Edward Cross Country,* which was picked up for international syndication.

In the world of television there are high-powered executives programming the networks, selecting what shows are produced and aired. They must project in advance the viewing habits of their target audiences, and then they shape and mold their lineups based upon those projections. That is why you will often see a surge in certain types of programming all at once. That is not a coincidence at all; it's called *following the herd.* If a particular show, genre, or subject matter pulls in a large audience, not only will executives produce more episodes of that show or topic, but other shows will copy it and do the same thing.

I know that if you turn on television during the day, you can see a whole array of shows covering the *Who's Your Daddy?* DNA paternity testing theme and the popular *Makeover Madness* segments, in which some poor person walking through a mall is accosted by a team of professionals telling her how frumpy she looks and that when they are done updating her hair, makeup, and wardrobe she will be new and improved. Of course her entire life will be better too, right? But that magical transformation is what many people will stick around to watch, making the advertisers for hair products, cosmetics, and clothes very happy.

Now, I am sure you are once again wondering why, in a spiritual development book, I am off on another tangent, digressing about television. It is a simple correlation I am making here: *you are your own station.* My goal is to make you think about the management team you have in place choosing what's to be played and projected. Are you in charge of your station's programming? Are you allowing other people to tell you what shows to produce and when to air them? Do you really want to see other shows play out on your station but someone else is stopping them from getting on air? It is all about recognizing that you are like those same executives with their assumptions and beliefs about what others want to see. You are deciding what makes it to "air" in your life depending on the motivating factors of fear and love. For me, the ultimate goal is to have you be your own #1 station in the Universe, writing and producing the best content for your viewers and developing "Must See TV" for your future as well.

All this programming that you are producing has to start with one simple thing, a thought. Remember that your thoughts are those bullets of energy fired from your brain, creating the lines of probability to pull in the situations that will help you to experience your life lessons. In applying our broadcast model to spiritual development, we now have to take that concept a little bit further.

First things first: we need to look at what the current lineup is on *your station,* so think of this as your very own programming guide. Why? Simply put, as the broadcaster you need to cater to your current viewers and keep business running as usual. But the good news is that you are going to transition your role into being a conscious viewer of your station as well. The goal here is for you to know that you are the viewer already, and by being more proactive you can control what the broadcaster is supplying you with to watch. Remember, if a television show is not rated favorably by its audience, the network will pull it off the air. Are you with me? If there are things in your life that are playing out in a negative way or not generating much interest, you can alter your show or cancel it altogether and start with something new and more exciting to watch.

Ultimately, you manifest your future by raising your awareness of how you can positively program your life to bring out the best You Network possible.

What's Your Channel? Exercise

Take a moment to describe your personal network. What are the "shows" that play on a regular basis for you, and which ones would you like to cancel, update, or start as a brand-new series? Does your network have a balance of different types of shows or is it just playing one genre most of the time? What would your network be called? Would it be a channel you want to watch as a viewer? If not, what would you do to make it more interesting to you? You are the programmer and the number one viewer, so think of ways to produce shows you will enjoy for the future.

* * * * * * *

MOVIE IN MY MIND

I don't know about you, but I love my TiVo. I remember when VCRs first came out and they were the coolest things on the planet. The videocassette recorder revolutionized home entertainment and kicked off the video store industry. To this day I can still remember that my first one cost $662. Technology has come so far since then and today we have the über-VCR: the digital video recorder (DVR). I love the fact that you can pause or rewind during real-time shows, fast-forward through commercials, and record programs in such an effortless way.

The DVR concept made me think about how we all have a built-in ability to be our own personal recording device in life. In case you are not familiar with all that it does, TiVo allows you to create your own viewing list and choose a "season pass" for your favorite shows, actors, or genres so that you do not miss anything you might wish to watch in the future. It will even track your viewing patterns and make recommendations for other shows that you might want to see.

I came to realize that people do this type of mental programming unconsciously all the time. If we can fine-tune technology in such a manner, then we can certainly learn to do it with our own personal energetic wiring. You can create the playlists of your station to attract positive things into your life.

GENETIC CODE

Deoxyribonucleic acid, or DNA, happens to be one of my most remembered words from high school biology. Even though science was always a fascinating subject to me, I seemed to instinctively comprehend the concept of the double helix that is our genetic makeup. I was intrigued by how the arrangement of our chromosomes and the genetic programming of our ancestors worked to help create who we are—not only physiologically and anatomically, but in a behavioral way, too.

When I was a child, I remember my grandmother having a conversation with my aunt about a family member's negative behavior, and hearing them say, *"It is in his JEANS."* I couldn't help but wonder why he was allowed to even wear those jeans in the first place and why they didn't just empty out whatever was in his pockets that was making him act in such a way. I now laugh at the silliness of that thought. But when I took high school biology and learned about genetics, that phrase had a whole new meaning to me. Science teaches us that our genes help to create our physiological being and composition. This biological history, an amalgam of mother, father, and their family ancestry, passes down to us gifts of life and programming that we as the next generation play out and, if we have children of our own, pass on to the next generation.

BALI HI FROM ALAN

While writing this chapter, I had an interesting conversation with Alan Oken, master astrologer and cofounder of InfiniteQuest.com, about doing a speaking event for him in Bali, Indonesia. When he asked me what I was currently working on, I told him about this project and he got excited. He talked about how I am honoring the potential of my natal chart by moving into more of a teaching capacity. He said that he was happy that people weren't just going to think about me as *"the guy who talks to dead people!"* and I couldn't help but laugh.

Since I was fortunate enough to have access to such erudite wisdom, I had to ask him his opinion on my philosophy about spiritual evolution and what his thoughts were from an astrological standpoint, and here is Alan's response:

As we develop our consciousness, we begin to see ourselves and the world around us as interconnecting energy patterns. When you are born, such an energy pattern is born with you and this is revealed in your horoscope (natal chart). In effect, this celestial portrait is your terrestrial blueprint and reveals what is natural for you to express and be during the course of your life. It is therefore an incorrect assumption, albeit a common one, that the positions of the planets at your birth "cause" you to be a certain way. Both you and your planetary picture are reflections of a Greater Cause, a *Force of Life* that transcends both planets and people. This Cause has many names, the most common of which is God.

There are many factors which are synthesized into making up who you are; the natal horoscope is but one of these. Many people can be born at the same moment in time and they will all have the same planetary imprint. Yet the complications of being human are such that the astrological energetic pattern has to merge with these other factors. There is first the matter of our DNA, something I like to call our "biological karma." This characterizes us by race, family patterns, and inherited psychological and physiological structures. Then there is the matter of our sociological environment and how that influences us in so many ways. Ten people are born at the same moment in time, one to a high-caste Hindu family in India, another to a family of farmers in China, another to a wealthy Italian industrial dynasty, etc. Each of these individuals will play out the same astrological "energetic drama" but on very different "stage" settings.

The question of who and what we are should therefore not be one of conditioned behavior based purely on family and environment, as many psychologists would have us believe, or solely of the DNA make-up, as biologists might argue. Nor should this be founded upon a fated karmic life as designated in the horoscope, as many astrologers often proclaim. Who and what we are is a fusion of these three elements and something else, something that goes beyond both astrologers and psychologists. This is the *Great Mystery* of the Universe.

YOU'RE NOT THAT SPECIAL

At my speaking events, when I discuss our energetic programming being passed down to us, I often see many people actually frown and become annoyed. This perplexes me because I am there to bring through their loved ones to connect with them. I surmise that these annoyed attendees don't want to surrender their individuality, or equate behavioral issues with family members, or even look to their lineage, because that makes them feel less unique. Most times I think people want me to be like the type of customer at McDonald's who places the order and there's no idle chit-chat or information given— just give me my family super-pack and let me be on my way. It just doesn't work like that with me at the Big E Restaurant of Spirit Communication.

My initial reaction is **"Well, you're not that special."** Believe it or not, this is a line that I use quite often and it is usually met with surprise. I know, there I go being *harsh* again, because it sounds like a mean thing to say, but I like to break down barriers with words and energy . . . actually, I intentionally do it all the time. I know that when I have a group of people sitting in front of me, I can't allow one person's issues to cloud the experience for everyone else. I have heard other mediums say that they don't believe that one individual in a group setting can affect the programming experience, but I assure you in my twenty-five years of work, I have seen it happen firsthand.

Most of the time, when I get in someone's face it is done to make that person just listen to what I am saying. By assuming an energetically aggressive posture, I am usually able to persuade people to drop their guard and recognize that I am not the enemy and not responsible for the passing of their loved ones. My goal is to raise their awareness so they can heal and grieve, and I am only able to do this by validating the information that is coming through. Other times, it becomes a matter of pride because the individual does not want to acknowledge the information in front of an audience, sometimes even after he or she knows exactly what I am speaking about. All of these are manageable situations because communication is taking place, and people can learn what they need to know whether it's in the moment or later on in their own process.

> **Death is the great equalizer of life, coming in all shapes, sizes, and manners. Some deaths are expected, and others shock us to the core of our being and force us to redefine life as we know it.**

Many times people will have unresolved issues with their loved ones who have crossed over, and when I begin making the connection with those Spirits and start passing on their messages of validation, an immense healing and closure occurs. On other occasions, I will get a shut-down wall of energy deflecting the very same connection people supposedly hoped to have when they came to the event. There are various reasons that people close down in such a manner: fear of dealing with the death, fear of not hearing from their loved ones, fear of disappointment, fear of not being read, or fear of what they might be told. Other times, people get what I call "psychic amnesia," where they forget who they are, who they are related to, and all pertinent family details that can support the fact that their relative is present. Many times I feel a sense of anger and entitlement projected toward me, which makes me rage internally. I don't care who the person is or what my connection is to them in that moment—I get mad.

This recently happened to me when I was in South Africa doing a few small group readings with my friend, Char Margolis. Char is a spiritual force to be reckoned with and I have the utmost respect for her psychic ability and her passion for teaching. We had an amazing time with our audiences, and almost everyone was respectful of those who received readings. The feedback we were given in return was appreciative, and when a few people were not read, they acknowledged their disappointment, but seemed to sincerely understand the process. The fact that people were so gracious makes this a part of the world I wish to return to again and again.

The audiences were able to witness over four hours of intense connecting between myself, Char, and the Other Side, and I think many folks were very touched by the experience. As a medium I know that I start off my job at a huge disadvantage and have to remind myself that no matter how hard I work, it is NEVER enough, nor could it be. People don't really want to have to sit with me to talk to someone who has passed over; instead, they would much rather be with their loved ones and have them still physically present in their lives.

Unfortunately, even though I know all this, it is still disheartening to see some people allow their ego and own personal sense of entitlement block what they feel was "supposed" to happen. During one of the small group events, I had to deal with an unhappy woman in the audience who for whatever reason was not read. Instead of learning from the experiences of others, she concluded that she was not read because I was prejudiced. In addition to my apparent racism that I demonstrated against this woman's family, she believed that I also infringed on her time because I brought Char out on stage instead of continuing with my readings.

Listen, anyone who attends a private session with a medium can't be guaranteed a reading or a connection from the specific person they may have wanted to hear from. In a larger group setting, the reality is that those who are supposed to get the reading will receive one. But everyone attending the event is experiencing the connections as well, and I believe that the collective feeling of joy is even more significant than the personal message for the individual being read, even if it doesn't feel that way at that moment. The realization that the bond of love never dies and that we are connected even after death has a subtle but lingering effect on one's heart.

I was disappointed at this woman's arrogance and lack of appreciation since, after having the opportunity to participate in well over four hours of spirit communication in an intimate environment, all she walked away with was "*What about me?*" I detest self-importance, and I disliked the way this woman thought she could define another person's motivations when she had absolutely no clue. So I "fired" her!

I know she will not be reading this book since I fired her. Yes, you read that correctly: I fired her as a client. I made sure the event organizer sent her money back and told her that she is now officially on the "No Fly Zone" list in my office and for any future events in South Africa. If her name or family name comes up on our radar, it is an immediate decline.

Debra, the organizer of my events in South Africa, called me to say that she felt the e-mail I had written was (you guessed it) "harsh," and in this case I own it. Debra was concerned that this woman could tarnish my image if she was further offended and went to the media with her grievance. *"Bring it on,"* was my immediate response. Now I will admit to feeling a lingering "hostility hangover" after this experience, which is what I had to accept as a consequence of sending out not merely a bullet but a cannon of negative energy toward someone—I had to own and work on that. But in this case, I felt it was a necessary course of action. I did have to engage her in some way . . . normally, I do not feed into this type of negative energy, but when a certain energetic line is crossed in regard to the work I do, I need to respond in order to create structure and boundaries and to clearly demonstrate the parameters for my work moving forward.

In this chapter about programming, I want to show the inter-relatedness of everything we discuss here. If I were to temper in any way what I wrote in that e-mail, I would no longer be honoring my feelings and coming from the love of myself and the work which I have dedicated my life to. I would instead be motivated by the Fear Principle—the fear of someone having influence over my reputation in the media.

I only wish I had the opportunity to explain this to her face, so I could let her know that she is not that special and that a person's grief does not justify a sense of gross entitlement. This is something that people forget. For me, the reality is simple. Appreciate how much energy it takes for your family to come through from the Other Side and stop your whining because you didn't hear what you wanted or have the kind of connection you expected, whether during a reading or in a direct visit from them in your own life.

So what is it in this woman's programming that made her think that she was more important than every other person who was going home without a personal message from their family? Why was her loss greater than the loss felt by the people sitting next to her? And instead of doing a character assassination of me, why didn't she try to understand the communication process better? Now, I need to be clear, I really do not know this woman and I want to be sensitive to whatever pain and grief she may be processing, but because I have dealt with others who have had similar reactions as hers over the years it sounds to me like the Inner Monster could be at work here. She was clearly coming not from a position of love in her handling of the situation, but from one of fear and anger, and that will only perpet-uate a negative circle of energy and behavior. Ultimately, I sincerely hope that whatever programming brought this woman to a place of darkness in her own life will shift and change, because it will be to her own detriment if she keeps firing such harmful bullets to those around her.

Consider how you react when things do not go "your way." Are you quick to judge the situation from a negative or blaming viewpoint, or do you stop and think about the experience as a whole and what valuable lesson might be there for you to learn? How you program your experiences makes all the difference in the world.

WHAT BREED ARE YOU?

People love when the furry four-pawed family members from the Other Side make a cameo appearance during my group events. They smile and laugh when Fluffy shows up with Grandpa, but don't want to equate their life to that of a canine because that might be seen as downright insulting. Well, Fido, here's what I teach:

When folks talk about their pet's or animal's habits in general, they often use a scientific tone. If a dog is aggressive or bossy, people will say *"It's in her breed to do that."* Could you imagine if we acknowledged people like this? You would be considered prejudiced or stereotypical in your thinking if you described people in such a way. But if you take a moment and are truly honest, you can think of some of those "stereotypes" that fit your own family more than you might want to admit. Pick your breed, my friend, because the pack, flock, or herd you travel with is based on your own family's genetic ancestry. There really isn't a way to get around it, no matter how much political correctness you want to assume.

Now you might be thinking that you used to like me when you watched my show and even respected what I had to say, but now I just told you that you're not that special and equated you with a four-legged animal, and you're not so sure anymore. But stop for a second, put your ego aside, and try to understand that I am only saying these things to help you think in a certain way. We all belong to the planet in different biological categorical definitions. For our purposes, I want you to see that we are born into a certain type of programming, or "breed," and if you are more aware and accepting of the fact, you will have an easier time of making real changes when necessary.

ANIMAL INSTINCT

Think about the tsunami that devastated Southeast Asia at Christmas time back in 2004. The casualties from that crisis were largely reported to be people, not animals. Why? The animals trusted their instincts and moved to higher ground or more inland. You didn't see animals down on the beach when the waves were coming, capturing the moment with cameras, going for a swim, or surfing. They didn't stop to analyze what was taking place and wait for someone to tell them to run: they just *reacted*. This is often the case where animals are concerned in regard to floods, earthquakes, and other natural disasters.

The reason why I use this as an example is I believe that we, as a human species, have the same survival instincts that other animals have, but perhaps we were more in touch with that part of ourselves in earlier times when we lived more in balance with nature than we do today. The major difference is that we have distanced ourselves from our instinctive behavior by becoming more "civilized" with education, rationalization, and technology. We like to believe we are the most advanced species on Earth, and yet perhaps we have lost some of our best natural skills and use of our senses in the process of our evolution.

We can once again address the network analogy for you personally. You are your own local network station, and it is connected to other affiliate stations such as your extended family. What they do, you will do to an extent. Your genetic predisposition for certain types of behavior is part of your family breed, and you really need to understand that concept without too much resistance so you can work to create your own personal energetic network for improved future programming and growth.

For example, if you are short-tempered and quick to fly off the handle just like your mother was, you need to be aware of that trait when making decisions or reacting to certain situations. If some of your family members had problems with alcohol or drug abuse, you should certainly examine your own dependency issues as a preventive measure as you go through life. The list of personality traits goes on, negative and positive. And although I think it is valuable for everyone to understand how these traits can affect the way we go about our lives, most people can really see this message hit home when it applies to the family history of physical illnesses.

If all the men in a particular family have heart disease and some of the elders pass on before the age of sixty, it is clear to the relatives and their doctors that this is a serious issue to treat proactively. If several women in the family have breast cancer, it is something that the rest of the women will need to pay close attention to by doing regular self-exams and mammograms. They are forced to do so because their lives may be in jeopardy. But our genes, or genetic programming, can also be less obvious, and we can only learn about it by reflecting on our family dynamics and our own individual patterns of behavior.

Genetic Code Exercise

Take a few minutes and jot down in your journal some specific characteristics that were "passed down" from your family and heritage. Clear your mind of any notion of what is right or wrong; no one else has to read this but you. Try to be as objective as possible in the process. For example, is everyone in your family loud and boisterous, or super competitive about everything? Perhaps there is a stubborn streak, a fear of heights, a talent for cooking, or a love of animals carried down from each generation. Look at both physical and personality traits from both sides of the family and see which ones you might have inherited, both genetically and conditionally.

DAD

I have previously discussed the lack of connection I had with my father in my book *After Life: Answers from the Other Side* and more recently in an interview with William Shatner on the television show *Shatner's Raw Nerve*.

My mom and dad separated and later divorced when I was in junior high school, and even though he was connected to my mom afterward, for years my relationship with my father consisted of virtually *"Hi...put your mom on the phone."* I am happy to report that since my father's passing, I now feel a much stronger connection to him. I am positive that when he crossed over, he did his life review and has since evolved beyond the role he played here as "Captain Jack," freeing himself to be the loving energy of "father" that he couldn't be here on the earthly plane. I wanted to share my personal story for everyone reading this who didn't get a chance to have a relationship with someone who has already crossed over, especially if there were problems that you couldn't fix with a person. It is my knowledge and experience that you still have the ability to mend relationships once the person is gone. Please don't use this as an excuse not to repair a relationship of importance to you while people are still alive. I instruct my clients to try and communicate the things they are feeling while the person is here on the earthly plane because it always sounds better coming from *you* rather than from a medium after the person has passed on. But there is hope if you truly want to create a better connection in the Afterlife, and it's possible to do even without a medium's help.

The uncanny aspect for me was watching family videos and *seeing* myself in my father. I don't think I really look like my father, but I will definitely say I see him in my mannerisms and personality . . . as they say, *"it's in the genes."* I might not have had my father's daily influence on who I am, but his genetic ancestry is undoubtedly a major factor.

Think about those stories of twins who are separated at birth and later reunited only to find out just how similar their lives are. I think much of that can be attributed to our genetic programming and how it shapes one aspect of who we are, but I also think there is another programming at work here as well: the *Energetic Code.*

THE ENERGETIC WEATHER

I touched upon the understanding of energy patterns earlier in the book when I discussed your astrological chart and how it is a blueprint of who you are. This blueprint, or course of study that your soul chooses, is used to create situations, opportunities, and lessons that enable you to discover and evolve in your soul's progression. The ultimate goal is for you to manifest the best potential YOU, while learning about unconditional love and evolving as highly toward the Divine as possible.

When our genetic makeup combines with our spiritual makeup, it creates our very own unique *energetic code.* This helix works in conjunction with our biological self and spirals together with our spiritual self and creates somewhat of the perfect energetic storm in our lives.

I want to make sure you understand this concept so let me recap for a quick second. I am telling you that I believe that our scientific composition, our DNA, conjoined with our soul's energetic purpose, or spiritual lessons we're incarnated to learn, will set forth currents of energy to manifest certain situations in our lives. Still with me?

Many clients have sat in front of me in sincere dismay about how and why they were repeating the same relationship lessons over and over again. Many played the victim and didn't understand why this was happening to them; I had to answer with *"you're not that special."* Others felt that they had taken the initiative to do what would be right for them, yet they were still repeating similar mistakes, and my reply was to *"check the energetic weather patterns around you."*

The use of the weather as a metaphor for the energetic climate is important and along with your "station" can help you to shape your future even more. If you are living under a certain negative energetic weather pattern, you have to make a conscious move to not experience it. I am sure you have heard people say they feel like there is a *"gray cloud"* or *"black cloud"* hanging over them. They need to figure out what is causing it. This weather pattern that you are ultimately responsible for generating will also pull into it the people and situations that you are traveling with, and they contribute to creating the programs that are running on your network.

Weather Patterns Exercise

Consider the "clouds" you live under in your daily life. Do you walk around with a sunny disposition, looking for the best in everyone and in every situation? Perhaps, instead, you find yourself wondering why nothing seems to go right for you, or maybe you are somewhere in between the two extremes. Try to describe your changing attitudes in weather terms and see what you arrive at. Are you "partly sunny" or always "stormy"? Now expand that thinking to consider how your "weather patterns" change in different environments—work, home, in your car, out in the community—or around different people—family, friends, coworkers, strangers. Finally, add in the weather patterns of the people that you are around on a regular basis—spouse, partner, boss, office mates, friends, and family. Notice how your weather shifts when you're in the company of certain people. When looking at your energy in a different light, you might see some interesting patterns that you may want to happen more often and those you wish to change.

I know that this is a lot of information to digest. You're a breed, you're a station, you're a viewer, and you're a weather pattern . . . I bet you want me to make up my mind. I just want you to be the best

YOU possible and that starts with understanding the foundation we are building upon, so I am going to use every metaphor possible to help you learn these lessons.

One last thing and I will move on from this chapter. There is another aspect to your programming that needs to be mentioned as well and that is what is learned from your environment.

I left this last because it is more the backdrop and stage upon which your experiences are occurring. It is a contributing factor or amplification of what we have been discussing and is sometimes the reason why people feel an innate need to move. Whether you move to Hollywood to become famous or to a warmer climate for health reasons, your environment factors in as the canvas for your programming to be painted on.

I think the genetic and energetic codes of programming are the forces that shape who we are and our potentials of what we can achieve, combined with our free will. What we learn in our environment, either consciously or unconsciously, also will season our outcome. Be aware and know that it too can, for better or for worse, impact your today and definitely your tomorrow.

7

The Application: UNDERSTANDING YOUR PSYCHIC POTENTIAL

AS YOU DEVELOP your garden of spiritual understanding, the root system will grow, and over time this seed can develop into a forest of energy.

The objective of this chapter is to help you understand your own intuitive energy and psychic potential. Think about how many times you can recall knowing that the phone was going to ring and who it was on the other end, and it had nothing to do with caller ID. The last time I was on *Larry King Live,* Larry asked me how I felt about having "my gift." I really don't like referring to the work I do as a gift, because in many ways it makes it and me more special than necessary. I like to refer to it more as an ability, something we all have in varying degrees and can all enhance. The same issue came up when a client told me that she thought that God had bestowed upon me a beautiful gift. This was a woman who had no remaining family; all her loved ones have crossed over. They all came through during her session and validated their presence so she knew that they were happy and fine on the Other Side. When she paid me this compliment, I thanked her. I then told her that I didn't feel that God gave this ability just to me but to all of us. Some have developed it naturally more than others and not every person will develop at the same rate. Just think of it like this: we don't all have the same

SOAPBOX MEDIUM ALERT

You won't become the world's greatest psychic just by reading this book; it doesn't even begin to include all the training you'd need to be a professional psychic. To do this work professionally takes years of study and above all practice and dedication . . . at least it should. In the last twenty-five years there's been an overwhelming mainstream interest in the various aspects of psychic phenomena. People are recognizing that they're more than just their physical body; they are learning that there is a universal power that they possess and can work with to help them be more empowered. But how do you harness it? Not everyone who develops their intuitive abilities will ever be able to do an actual "reading," but that's okay. This is about something more personal and bigger than just doing readings. It's about Project YOU. Your desire to develop psychically shouldn't be about predicting the future or connecting with someone's Aunt Tilly. The real goal should be to live a more fulfilling and spiritual life.

aptitude for music, sports, or art. That doesn't mean that we can't enjoy those activities. We just don't all have to be Barbra Streisand, Babe Ruth, or Picasso.

Everyone has psychic abilities. Everyone has the ability to be intuitive and has the free will to embark on a journey toward human enlightenment and their own spiritual quest. Even though I believe that "mediums are born," all people have the ability to tune into the frequencies of love and energy from their own families and friends on the Other Side. It doesn't become an issue for me until a person feels the need to start doing it for others. You don't throw a young kid with a great pitching arm into the middle of a Yankees game thinking he should be allowed to play. It doesn't mean he can't enjoy the energy of "the game" in his own backyard.

INSTINCT AND INTUITION

Imagine removing everything from society that we all worked so hard for and often take for granted—our educations, jobs, houses, cars, and all modern technology; just strip it down to the most basic form of civilization—what would we have left to rely on? Our basic instincts and intuition. Modern technology and even advanced education have an unintentional way of deadening our intuition. We are taught to rely on scientific evidence, the latest inventions, and rational concepts that only equations can prove. When was the last time you got out of your chair to change the channel on a television instead of using the remote control? Do you even remember half the phone numbers that you used to know by heart but are now stored in your cell phone? These are just the simplest of examples to make you stop and consider how much we increasingly depend on technology instead of ourselves. My goal is to teach you to listen to the voice of your intuition, use your psychic logic, and allow your Team to assist you in your everyday pursuits.

When we were children, we were so much more open to this spiritual energy. The filter that we develop with training and conditioning as we mature is not yet actively in place when we are young. We innocently interact with the world of energy we live in until we are told again and again to stop it. I have heard hundreds of stories of children who have walked over to a family photo and started to acknowledge a deceased grandfather that they never knew. Children haven't learned to question this ability or their sensing of energy; they just react to it. How many of us had "imaginary friends" as children that we were made to feel foolish about until we left them behind? Perhaps they were just figments of our imaginations, or perhaps they were our Guides, but rarely were we encouraged to explore the possibilities; in fact, just the opposite, we were discouraged. Animals demonstrate their instincts and intuition in countless ways all the time. Biologist and author Rupert Sheldrake writes extensively about the phenomenal psychic abilities of animals in his book *Dogs That Know When Their Owners Are Coming Home* (1999). He documents many different species demonstrating their intuitive powers and concludes that humans "lost" these powers somewhere along the way in our evolution. ESP is a natural ability and it is possible to strengthen and train it, if you are willing to put in the effort. Remember, each person will develop differently, just as in singing: some people are born gifted with an amazing voice and others must work at just carrying a tune. But why not make the most of what you have?

PRACTICE, PRACTICE, PRACTICE

To develop a skill or talent, whether it's piano playing or downhill skiing, it is necessary to devote a certain amount of time to the process. It requires commitment and dedication. Because you are studying this material, you are already raising your awareness of the subject. The more you think about it, the more energy you'll put into your psychic development, the more you will actively welcome understanding the learning process. The more you practice, the more success you can expect.

When people are serious about developing their psychic abilities, I always warn them about the by-product of raising their intuitive awareness. I don't mean to make you think that your life is going to take a turn for the worse, but if you actually are working at it, your life as you know it will change out of necessity. You will be transforming the frequencies of energy around you and allowing yourself to be more receptive to the energies of the people in your life and more sensitive to their issues. You may even find that you feel more emotional. This receptivity can certainly make you more vulnerable, which means it is an extremely important prerequisite for you to study and work with some principles of psychic self-defense (see Chapter 10). You should also let the people closest to you know that you're working on opening up and raising your awareness. This way they can be aware of the changes that they may see in you and at least have an idea of what is going on for you, instead of possibly being confused by your behavior. If you are sincerely committed to doing this kind of personal growth, the individuals who stand in your way of developing for one reason or another will probably just fade to the background for a while, if not permanently. That is a natural part of the process.

You may find yourself having premonitions about global or local community events or even about your own family or close friends. What do you do about these when they occur? That all depends on what type of information you're receiving. If you are seeing something fun and festive, share it immediately; if you are sensing something on the negative side, be very careful in how you deliver that message. Remember, in the old days they shot the messenger for a reason. You don't want that to happen to you, even figuratively speaking. Negative events are most likely what you will think that you are sensing in the beginning of your development. What if you are wrong or misunderstood what you received? In addition to the messenger frequently being blamed for the message, you do not want to upset anyone needlessly. Tread very carefully when conveying your impressions and err on the side of caution, as your accuracy will be diminished by your lack of ability at this stage. Make certain that you explain that you are new to this work and you are only sharing what you saw, not necessarily your "interpretation" of it. For example, if you get a premonition of a car accident involving a friend, the message should be a gentle warning to drive carefully, wear a seatbelt, stop texting while driving—not "I saw you in a terrible car accident!" This is where the ethical responsibility of this type of work plays such an essential role in how you handle the information. You must always apply the Love Principle, not the Fear Principle, when sharing your psychic messages. Your goal is not to scare people, but to leave them better off as a result of your assistance. Encouraging someone to see their doctor for a routine checkup is vastly different from telling them that they have a disease.

I believe that you will also sense the positive messages simultaneously. However, bad news sells, so that will be what you will most likely pay the most attention to at first. In the beginning you won't be able to sufficiently trust or discern what you're receiving to follow up on it. That confidence and knowledge only come with time and practice. Not sharing what you learn can be tough, especially when the premonition or information regards someone you know. Think about your psychic ability like it's a new puppy. Is a new puppy house-trained? Of course not—you must consistently work on training it; otherwise the puppy will have accidents all over the place and you will constantly be cleaning up after it. Initially, that is to be expected, and you will need to be patient and gentle but firm with the puppy. In the same way, bursts of psychic energy will come through to you like an uncontrollable "accident" at first. But after a while you should be able to get the "puppy" to take care of its needs outside, although an occasional accident is to be expected while it is still growing and learning.

After a while you will be able to use your skills at the times you want to focus in and to work with your own energy. You must be able to train your senses just like you would the new puppy. You want to be able to turn it on and off at will.

PERMISSION, RECOGNITION, ACCEPTANCE

To begin developing your intuition, you must simply give yourself permission to experience this type of energy and information. After actively allowing yourself to perceive and receive energy, you must recognize it. The last step in the process is to consciously accept it. I am referring to the acceptance of what you experienced and the importance of not trying to rationalize or editorialize it. These three steps are simple, subtle, and to be done in your own way, and in doing so you allow something huge to shift in your life.

The basic keys to unlocking the door to your unconscious and your abilities are knowledge and meditation. Nothing negative will harm you as you work on developing your skills. You will *always*, and I stress the word *always*, be practicing some form of psychic self-defense or prayer work, so this shouldn't be a problem. The next step to furthering your growth is meditation. Meditation helps to calm the body and open the mind. This takes commitment and patience because it is a lifelong practice. It will require a daily routine of serious intent to learn how to quiet the mind and to really relax the body. Then my next recommendation is that you find a psychic tool (tarot, astrology, numerology, psychometry, rune casting, etc.) that you're drawn to using and that feels the most natural to you. Take the time to learn the intricacies of whatever divination system you choose; this process also requires dedication and practice. You don't pick up the symbols of tarot or astrology overnight. This tool becomes another key to unlock the door to your intuition, whether you do it just for yourself or attempt to read or sense someone else's energy. When using any of these tools for your own purposes, objectivity is essential. In fact, it is vastly preferred to see them only as sources for self-awareness, inspiration, and wisdom. Once you start using them in a predictive manner for yourself, the objectivity often gets lost in the process.

I know that I am sending out mixed messages here about your spiritual evolution. I am downplaying the idea of you giving readings but will also be teaching you how to do them at the same time. Now just because I discussed earlier in the book about not wanting you to do psychic readings, don't assume that I am stupid. I already know that many of you are going to attempt to do them anyway. It is not my first choice for your personal development—my preference is that you would just become a student of the Universe, studying and learning with an open mind and heart. Allow your ability to grow slowly and recognize the changes in your life. If you throw yourself into doing a reading for someone, you're more actively engaging with the energy than trying to understand how it works.

Once you have found the divination system that resonates with you the most, you must also recognize in what ways you are receiving the information. There are five psychic senses that can be used, whether you are obtaining information from your Guides or if the energy is being felt through your *auric field* and you are reacting to it.

PSYCHIC FAMILY REUNION

Science has taught us that all living creatures have an energy field around them. Mystics and psychics refer to this as the "auric field," an energetic amplification of the soul's energy. Consider it the result of the piano key being pressed. When you hit the key, the note is struck, and energy is created . . . this vibration or frequency is measurable and in musical terms assigned a note, chord, et cetera. In human terms, this energy shield, an invisible force field of energetic plasma, is like an energy membrane that shifts and changes as our emotional, spiritual, mental, and physical self transforms. Psychic self-defense helps us to strengthen our field to avoid its being depleted and to keep it pure.

There are five psychic abilities that your Guides will express themselves through. As I mentioned earlier in the book (see Chapter 1, page 15), I like to refer to them as the *"five sisters"* or, as they are more widely known, the "five Clairs."

Clairvoyance: *clear seeing,* the ability to receive impressions in a visual manner, whether in pictures, symbols, or daydreams.

Clairaudience: *clear hearing,* the ability to receive impressions through sound or in an auditory manner, usually in your mind's voice and not through your ears.

Clairsentience: *clear sensing,* the ability to sense and feel information. Gut instincts, tinglings and rushes, fear, and sympathetic and empathetic pain are experienced through feelings.

Clairalience: *clear smelling,* the ability to receive impressions through the sense of smell. This is a favorite for the Other Side when dealing with mediumship, as it is often the easiest way to drum up a past memory.

Clairambience: *clear tasting,* the ability to receive impressions through a taste in your mouth. Sometimes a favorite food or one that has significance for the person will be easily sensed.

The Clairs are the abilities that carry and amplify the energy of the unseen world. They represent our psychic eyes, ears, hands, nose, and tongue. We access the information through them and then process it with our conscious mind so that we can begin to try to understand what is being shared. In order to fully recognize the messages, you must first be clear on how you personally receive your insights.

Most likely, one sense will be stronger for some people than others. If you are more of a visual person, you will be better equipped to see psychic impressions vividly. If you find that you are more of a verbal person, you will be more inclined to hear "voices" in your mind. Most people are able to receive psychic information by feeling it as well, and this often works in conjunction with one of the other Clairs. Clairalience and clairambience are not as common, especially when first developing your abilities, but you may find that you have a natural affinity for one of them once you are further along in your practice.

The Five Sisters Exercise

To understand how psychic information can be received using the five Clairs, try these simple exercises and see what works most naturally for you.

Clairvoyance: Imagine your favorite cartoon character in as much detail as possible. The picture that you are painting in your mind is quite similar to the clairvoyant impressions you would receive, appearing like a daydream.

Clairaudience: Count in your mind from one to ten. Wait, now recite the alphabet. Okay, stop. Now do both at the same time, without thinking, A1, B2, C3. For those of you who have an easy time doing this quickly, you will find that receiving verbal messages will work the best for you.

Clairsentience: Think about the feeling that you get in the pit of your stomach when you're excited or frightened. That is the same way that a psychic message will make you react. Do you find yourself prone to taking on the feelings of those around you or are you deeply affected by watching the news? If so, this will be an easy way for you to pick up psychic impressions.

Clairalience: Experiment with your sense of smelling by asking yourself what memories are brought to mind when you smell particular scents. Is it easy for you to associate certain events or people with specific scents or aromas? Can you imagine a person or time just by smelling a perfume or cologne? Are you keenly aware of smells that others don't notice?

Clairambience: Next time you eat, explore if the taste of certain foods reminds you of a person or time. Are you a person who cooks by taste, not a recipe, or thinks of yourself as having refined taste buds? When you are thinking about a particular food, do you taste it instead of visualizing it?

GARDEN OF SPIRITUAL DEVELOPMENT

When I was a young child and took my first swimming lessons at the local YMCA, the group that I was placed in was called the "Minnows." I hated that name, and I really wanted to be a "Shark." I watched the "Shark" group of kids jumping off the diving board and immediately told myself that I could do that too, so I did. I almost drowned. In the same way, you are starting off as a minnow ... or a seed, in your own personal garden of development. This garden, if nurtured and empowered to grow, will sprout various aspects of your programming, as we previously discussed.

First you need to recognize which stage of your development you are currently at. If you are just exploring these ideas for the first time, you might just be that seed, needing water and encouragement to take root. Or you may have been on this journey for a while, and you are a young plant who requires more practice and knowledge to grow taller. Perhaps you already have the ability to flower and are now seeking ways to produce even more. And finally, there are also those of you who realize that your personal potential is strong and you're rooted in your abilities; you become a tree for others to be shaded by or climb onto, and you are still looking for ways to grow and branch out to be the most beautiful tree possible.

The key to understanding your garden is that if it is left unattended even for the shortest amount of time—not properly weeded or watered—it will grow chaotically or wither. With loving care and attention, it can flourish into a beautifully landscaped garden that is multicolored and multipurposed. Whether your garden is for others to appreciate, for growing fruits and vegetables for many to eat, or just for your own fulfillment, YOU are the one who is the gardener tending to it.

ROOTS AND RESPONSIBILITY

As you develop this garden of spiritual understanding, the root system will grow and, over time, what started as a seed can develop into a forest of energy. The most important thing for me to stress to you is the responsibility that comes with the use of your garden. Whether it be for yourself or for someone that you want to help, the responsibilities attached to this energy and work are enormous. I know I keep repeating myself but I honestly can't stress this point enough. Using your psychic abilities and passing on information to another person will have an impact on all parties involved. The bullets of thought and energy not only create lines of probability for others, but ricochet right back at you like a karmic boomerang.

HEED THIS MESSAGE:
What you put out there will come back to you.

When I was the "Minnow" jumping off the diving board into the deep section of the swimming pool, I saw other kids doing what

I wanted to do and then immediately experienced the reason why I shouldn't have made that futile attempt. I was not ready for that level of swimming. This world of energy is very much like that pool. You might not be a minnow; maybe you are a tadpole or goldfish, or perhaps you even believe that you are already a shark in this pool. Nonetheless, it will only help your growth in the long run to understand and utilize what I am putting into the pages of this book.

So many people approach me and say things like *"I can do what you do."* That statement never makes me want to pull up a chair and have coffee with them. Instead, I usually become annoyed and agitated. That is just their egos talking. I have worked for a very long time being a student of the Universe, practicing this work, and owning my own ability and power. As soon as people go to the Inner Monster zone and compare themselves to another person, or even worse try to put themselves above another to make them feel like they are better, they fail. It is like being a minnow and diving into the pool thinking you are a shark.

Don't drown (or get eaten!) because your Inner Monster is telling you something different. Stop and understand what I truly mean when I speak of the responsibility you have to yourself and others when interpreting the energy you are picking up or receiving from your Team. Over a period of time and with dedicated practice, your garden will grow into a beautiful landscape: of this I am sure. But let it take the allotted time, nurturing, and diligence it needs for you to be the best YOU possible. **NEVER stop striving to be better at who you are and what you do.** When your root system takes and your garden flourishes, you will understand that the scarecrow that is on display is really for scaring away those aspects of ego that hinder spiritual growth and evolution.

8

WHERE DOES GOD FIT IN?

LANGUAGE IS THE WAY that people communicate
with each other and religion is the way that people attempt
to communicate with God.

One of the things that I like to pride myself on is being neutral in the religion department when it comes to my work. I never discuss my religious upbringing with my clients because I don't want them to think they have to be Catholic, or practice any type of religion for that matter, in order to connect with their loved ones on the Other Side. This sensitive issue was something that I had to confront when I wrote my last book, *Practical Praying: Using the Rosary to Enhance Your Life.* That book was important to me as I was able to explain my personal process of utilizing the energy of prayer using the language that I was taught as a child.

I wrote that book because of a clear directive from my Guides back in 2003. I was in Sydney, Australia, at the time and I was preparing for an event that evening, and my ritual of personal meditation always includes the praying of the rosary. As I was sitting on the balcony, watching the ships in the harbor and the people bustling around the quay, I heard my Guides say, *"You need to write a book on the rosary!"* My immediate reaction was confusion. I do my utmost to remain nondenominational in my teachings so as to make the work I do an energetic process for people to understand, rather than a religious one. I felt that the moment that I wrote a book on prayer or the rosary, the line would be crossed, and I would never be able to return to that space of neutrality again.

My publisher had accompanied me on my Australian speaking tour, and soon after I finished meditating he told me that he had an interesting idea for my next project. I immediately thought he was going to ask me to write a book on what the Afterlife is like, but he surprised me with a completely different proposal instead. He suggested that I should write a book about how I pray the rosary before and after my speaking events. This earthly request, coming within such a short time of the celestial request from my Spirit Guides, was enough of a "coincidence" for me to really take notice. It seemed the message was clear and my next book was decided for me.

I mentioned in the book that I expected to be harshly criticized by everyone once it was published. Happily, I was wrong, because over the years I have received a great deal of appreciation for its unique message. My readers really seemed to benefit from understanding how I blend my religious and spiritual beliefs and why there doesn't have to be a conflict of interest in doing so. Other people told me that they gained a new method of praying with intention and were grateful that I had given them a tool for prayer that they could use on a regular basis and that fit so easily with their beliefs. In fact, some folks were just happy to get a clearer sense of the proper way to say the rosary. All in all, the feedback was surprisingly heartwarming and positive.

A few years ago when I was conducting a seminar in Fresno, California, someone asked me a question about God and religion in relationship to my belief system as a Catholic and my work as a professional medium. Someone else spoke up, quoted scripture, and claimed to be anti-psychic as a result of what she read in the Bible. This situation reminded me of another woman who stood up to talk during the first season of my TV show, *Crossing Over*. She told me she was not there to ask questions, but to make a statement, and she wanted to "save" me. This was not the first time a stranger had attempted to engage me in finding salvation, and it wouldn't be the last.

"I am here to tell you that you are doing the work of Satan."

When she began to speak, I could tell that the other audience members wanted to verbally pounce on her in my defense. I had to remind them that she had the floor and I asked everyone to be patient and respectful. When I asked why she felt the way she did, she told me that the Old Testament said calling up the dead is an abomination to the Lord. I asked her how the Bible was written.

"It was written by God," she quickly answered.

"God put actual pen to parchment?"

"No." She hesitated before starting again. *"The Bible was inspired by God in the hearts of men and written down for all to read."*

"INSPIRED . . . " I paused for a moment to let the word sink in. *"Yes. Do you know what that word actually means?"*

She cringed like a child who had just repeated something that someone else said and maybe didn't fully understand what it meant or where I was going with it.

"Let me help you with your argument," I said. *"The word 'inspire' comes from the root meaning 'to breathe' or 'of spirit.' And I happen to agree with you that the Bible was inspired, which means it was technically channeled material. So in my opinion, the Bible is actually the greatest PSYCHIC book ever written."*

Then I took the time to explain to the audience how human interpretation and frame of reference are major factors in helping people understand how the Bible was written. The woman didn't have anything left to say and my talk ended soon after that. It was a topic that I knew would come up again and again. In my heart I know that my work is about love and bringing peace, hope, and a message of empowerment to people. How could that ever be deemed wrong or evil?

During the Fresno event, another woman just cut right to the chase and said, *"You have this ability to connect with those on the Other Side and you are discussing your belief in God, so could you just tell us what the best religion is?"*

I paused and was about to launch into my normal explanation that I see my work as much more spiritual than religious and that I feel like I am painting a *portrait of energy* when I am doing a reading. How people choose to frame that portrait is completely up to them and their personal faith. Instead, something completely different came out of my mouth . . . a question that I had never asked before.

"What is the best language?"

I have to be honest that I was just as eager to hear what my answer was going to be as the audience was. My Guides were clearly having me approach this topic from a different angle and I was curious to know what *They* were going to say. My Guides answered through me by explaining, *"Language is the way that humans communicate with each other and religion is the way that people attempt to communicate with God."* So asking which religion is the best one is like saying that English is better than French. Of course that's not true; they are just different. When the event was over, I quickly wrote the message down so I wouldn't ever forget it.

I believe in God, the Source of all things, a Divine Power, who for me feels like the Principal of our School of the Universe—the Headmaster or Dean. I think it is imperative to have some foundational belief in this Higher Power, in whatever shape or form you so choose, in order to proceed in your spiritual development. I am not suggesting you have to go to a place of worship every week, but if that works for you as a way to get in touch with your God . . . well, then that is great. What I am saying is that you need to acknowledge and reflect that there is a Divine Force and you should want to tap into it. I know that by standing in that Column of Light, you are one with it. The Light can permeate your soul and infuse it with a higher energetic frequency, similar to being plugged into a "spiritual outlet."

If you are struggling with this concept of a Higher Power, I respect that. Many of you are reading this book because you feel like you are empty or missing something in your life or a part of yourself and I understand that. Humor me, your earthly guide, on this one. Give yourself permission to surrender to this potential source of energy and empowerment. Don't let the name of it, the dogma, or your previous religious experiences get in your way. Have faith

REVIEW YOUR PROGRAMMING

Maybe this is a good time to take a look at your own personal network and explore how to fit "God" into your future programming so that you can experience a deeper connection with the Divine.

and ask your Team for help on this journey if you need it. Find your inner plug and know that the outlet is always there for you. Let today be the day when you reclaim that Source for your future.

Experience the Divine Exercise

First, relax and take a couple of deep breaths. Now, close your eyes and visualize a beautiful blue sky. See a couple of white clouds in this endless blue sky. Feel the sun behind you, warming your entire being. Imagine how you feel when the warmth of the sun is all around you, filling you with its light and keeping you safe. Now, just add one symbol . . . a large hand filled with light descending from the rays of the sun. Know that this is the hand of the Divine Light and Source. Take a deep breath and inhale slowly for a count of six . . . hold it for two seconds . . . and exhale for a count of six seconds as well. Repeat as often as you like. If the image of the hand is too "fatherly," you could substitute any image of the Divine you feel comfortable with as this representation.

This introduction is as simple as it can be for you. Notice there was no mention of scriptures, rules, names, or organizations at all— just a pure and simple acknowledgement that there is this Divine Source. I hope you choose to work with this Higher Power every day as you move forward on your spiritual journey.

The interesting thing for me is that when I conducted workshops and classes on spirituality, I found that many people became uncomfortable when I began talking about God. The topic activated their current programming and past experiences. Sometimes it appeared to anchor them to their past and inhibited them to a degree. Yet when I asked them to plug into the concept of having a Team of Spirits on the Other Side that are willing to work with them, that was easier to handle.

TECHNOLOGY AND GOD

I am often invited as a guest on television and radio shows to talk about being a medium and to give quick readings, but when someone from CBS called last year and asked me to speak on religion and spirituality I couldn't help but be surprised. *CBS News Sunday Morning* was featuring a segment on why so many people were leaving organized religions and declaring that they were spiritual rather than religious in their beliefs. The producers were interested in my perspective on the topic.

I could absolutely understand what the statistics were indicating and thought I had a pretty good idea as to why the numbers were declining. I believe technology is one of the main catalysts. It used to be that people would obtain valuable spiritual inspiration at their weekly church or temple meetings. They would be able to participate in a like-minded community where they could find a social and spiritual connection with the other members of the congregation. But with the proliferation of the Internet, information and connection are accessible by a just few clicks, whether on Google or one of the many social networking websites.

Society as a whole is moving faster. This is not a judgment, but a fact. I often say that we live in a fast-food society and that when people seek me out for a reading, if they could order off a menu as if they were at McDonald's they would be happy. *"I will have the #3 special—Mom, Dad, and Grandma, please"* and then I am supposed to ask if they would like to *"supersize that with a side of Grandpa."* You might laugh when I say that, but I often feel that type of energy from the people sitting in front of me. They want the information to be downloaded instantaneously and I don't always sense that they are willing to understand the process. They want their connection and they want it NOW! It used to be that people would not shop online because they couldn't see, touch, or try on the items. Now, online shopping revenue continues to increase because people love the convenience of shopping from their computers or phones. You can shop any time of day or night, in your pj's, or while you wait at the dentist's office. It's almost too easy and most likely lends itself to a whole other level of impulse buying.

God is such a personal energetic experience, and I feel that you need to allow space and time to connect with the infinite wisdom—a source of spiritual fuel that assists us in all aspects of the life we are here on this earth to learn about. I am sure that almost every parish and house of worship is being forced to modernize its outreach by utilizing websites and social networking pages to be more available for its congregation members. Unfortunately, this cyber approach can unintentionally lead to a disconnected or fragmented group instead of a cohesive one. Raise your hand if you are following the Vatican's Twitter account or have the pope2you Facebook application to keep up with "Big Poppa" (as I like to refer to him). It's only in the last couple of years that the Vatican was even willing to validate the presence of the Internet. Finally, in just the past year the pope has decided to join the social networking scene and appears to have had a vast change of heart when it comes to the value of being online. It's a bit like a dinosaur trying to fit into the modern world; I can't help but wonder if it's even possible. I just shake my head and think that if the Catholic Church, and organized religion in general, don't get up to speed with the changing times in so many different ways, they will collapse. How can they not? There are things that are happening in our society that are not going away, and the Internet is just one obvious example.

As a result, people are seeking out in other places what they can't find in their religious institutions anymore, and that is simply a feeling of self-empowerment. Technology is making the search for meaning and a sense of spiritual community not only possible, but overwhelmingly convenient. People can connect with others of the same faith at any time from their own desk, laptop, or even their phone.

SUPER MARIO AND GOD

About a year ago, my seven-year-old son Justin asked me to Google some cheat codes for his Nintendo game handheld device. It was not like he asked to borrow the car keys for a date, but I still had a weird reaction. He looked at me as if I was confused and pointed at my Blackberry that was hanging on my jeans pocket.

I knew exactly what he was asking of me, but I had an epiphany in that moment. I saw so clearly how different a world he is growing up in than the one I knew as a child. I laughed out loud and he wanted to know why. I felt like one of those "When I was your age, son, . . ." kind of moments was happening and I told him that there was no such thing as the Internet when I was a kid. He winced as if I had just said there were no televisions, cars, or air for that matter. I then explained to him that being able to access the Internet from this little square device called a Blackberry to obtain codes for him to get to the next level on his little square device, his Nintendo DS, just made me laugh. Again he asked me why. I told him that when I was his age, I had to put a quarter into a big arcade machine to play the exact same game that he was playing on a postage stamp–sized cartridge that held thirty other games as well. He still didn't understand. *"What's the big deal?"* he said, unable to fathom how much has changed in my lifetime.

The big deal is that in a very short period of time our technological advances have been great, if not almost overwhelming, and arcade games and Blackberrys are just minor examples in the technological revolution. Even though we are always evolving on some level and technology is always improving, it just became very clear to me in that exchange with my son. In the times of my parents and grandparents, technology seems to have been more about advancements in convenience invented to change the way we lived: laundry machines, cars, appliances, televisions even. But for my generation, it seems to be more about progress not just in the way we live, but also the ways we think and communicate.

The following statement makes me feel old, but I have to say that I don't like some of the ways the younger generations will more than likely be affected by these technological growths. Don't get me wrong, I love technology, but I also think that it desensitizes us and possibly camouflages our ability to feel, think, react, and connect with each other. A recent report says that half of all American teenagers send fifty or more text messages a day, and one in three send more than a hundred text messages a day, or three thousand a month!

"A machine will just do it for me." Sound familiar? No ... I am not addressing you and your newfound dependency on a GPS device that gives you step-by-step driving directions to your destinations so you never have to look at an actual map of a city again. I am speaking about me and my impatience with astrology many years ago. Remember I said that I would get back to it when computers did all the complex computations? Imagine if everyone was as lazy as I was with astrology! The art of casting a chart would have become nearly obsolete. My guess is that almost all astrologers do use computers now to create their charts, and who can blame them—it is much faster and more accurate than doing the calculations by hand. The same could be said about so many inventions in this modern age that we live in ... but it does change us and the way we use, or don't use, our brains.

I apologize if I sound a bit preachy (pardon the obvious pun) because I have to also admit to being one of the first to go online to get the latest electronic devices and all the applications and software that go with them. And don't forget that I launched an interactive website called InfiniteQuest.com that features real-time events. But when it comes to communication and expression, the latest and greatest technology gadgets have literally redefined our entire society as well as the individuals relying on them.

Thanks to the inception of e-mail, with instant messaging and texting following in its footsteps, people don't communicate with as much of a personal energetic tone. Yes, you can add acronyms to express your mood or meaning, like LOL or LMAO, and emoticons like a happy or sad face, but there is something to be said about listening to people's voices when they are speaking, to hear their tone, feel their energy, and interact with them in a direct exchange. I just received an e-mail today from a cousin whom I have not spoken with in a few years and I felt like she was speaking in code as opposed to English, which left me unsatisfied with the lack of connection. It has even become acceptable to spell words incorrectly for ease of expression. In fact, there is a growing concern in schools that students are using their texting shorthand in their schoolwork, leaving teachers wondering if English as we once knew it will eventually become obsolete. And although Twittering is a fast, fun way to connect with large groups of people, the downside is that we are learning to express ourselves in only 140 characters or less.

I think it's important to appreciate all the different types of technological progress, but only as much as we continue to realize what they are actually developed to enhance—the human energetic experience.

You *can* simultaneously participate in all advances in technology and still feel the energy of the world we live in, but you need to make more of an effort to do so. So many people no longer pick up the phone to call; they text or Twitter instead. Even e-mail seems Jurassic when I hear how people utilize all the social networking sites that exist. Stop and think... when was the last time you wrote a letter and mailed it with a real stamp? The trick is to find a balance between connecting conveniently but still from the heart.

> **The energy exchange between people** face to face can never be duplicated no matter how great your Web camera works. There is no technological replacement for a hug or smile given in person.

FEEL THE ENERGY

How many times have you found yourself getting bent out of shape because the person you were texting with wrote something to you that annoyed you, but when you confronted him he replied that what you thought he said wasn't what he meant at all? It might not have been, but your interpretation was very different since all you had to go on was the abbreviated communication that was used.

Before you jump to conclusions and you want to de-friend the person who just texted you a cryptic message that you perceived as hurtful, take a deep breath and stop long enough to feel the energy that person is sending it from. Maybe he is boarding a plane and is rushing to shut his phone off, or he can't talk because his kids are vying for his attention. You read the brief message and feel blown off. But if you are *feeling the energy* of intent while reading it, now there is an energetic subtext for you to follow. Remember the exercise of watching the TV show and seeing all the potential outcomes? Feel the energy of the e-mail, text, tweet, or whatever form of electronic communication you are receiving, and think of the various scenarios it might be sent from. You can't take it all so personally without knowing what is happening on the other end. Take time to energetically read the energy within the message.

iGOD

I was trying to think of the best way of marrying technology and the Divine Force and made myself laugh as my Guides showed me the **iGOD.** Imagine if Apple came out with the **iGOD** in the next few years? Everyone would be walking around with one. There would be different colors and memory versions. Then I realized that I wasn't just being sarcastic, I was being psychic in that moment. My Guides wanted me to use that example because you all now completely get the message they are recommending. I say recommending because you can allow yourself to see God in the same way, as an *energetic force* that you can carry with you everywhere you go and power up on your terms. You might have many different playlists and various languages on your **iGod,** but all to support the concept of a Higher Power and your own infinite quest.

I *always* want to leave people better than I found them. I know that if you are working with meditation, practicing psychic self-defense, learning about your programming, and allowing the Divine Source to accompany you on your journey, your sincere efforts and pure intentions will be unlimited fuel for your spiritual tank.

9

DEVELOPMENTALITIS

REMAIN IN BALANCE and be

a warrior for light and love.

OOOOOOOOOOH AAHHHHHHH MOMENTS

As we are moving closer to delving deeper into the applications of your psychic development and spiritual empowerment, I want to address some of the issues that I have seen and experienced along this fascinating and sometimes surprising road. By sharing my insights, I hope to give you the best tools possible for traversing what may at times be rocky terrain on your intuitive adventure and to inspire you on your journey to become the very best YOU.

The moments of recognizing your intuitive accuracy and seeing what you *knew* to be true come to fruition are so significant and special. You will start to notice your psychic muscles growing in size and strength—it is similar to seeing your body's muscles develop and your waistline shrinking, noticing more definition in your abdominals and legs, and physically feeling and looking good. Your psychic "toning" will occur in various ways and at different times, and you need to understand just how it happens for you personally.

Keeping a journal and updating it regularly is extremely important throughout this learning process to monitor and track your thoughts, emotions, impressions, projections, and dreams.

As you are writing in your journal, you want to be very specific in how you receive the

JOURNALING

If you commit everything to a written record, you cannot bargain or rationalize with yourself how right or wrong you were or lose touch with how you're feeling along the way. You can learn from both your correct and your incorrect impressions and begin to understand what certain symbols or images actually mean. You are more able to keep yourself in check while discovering everything you can about how you receive psychic information.

impression of energy. Which of the five Clairs did it come through? Was it clairaudiently or clairvoyantly? Did you dream it? Was it just like a downloaded transmission from your Team, a flash of an image, or a "voice" in your head? How did it make you feel at the time it happened? Your journal will become a valuable tool for your development in many ways, including that you will be able to go back and recognize your strengths. This newfound self-awareness is not about trying to build up the other abilities faster—because you might not be able to; instead, the journaling should help you to learn how to weigh and interpret the importance of what you are receiving.

For Your Eyes Only Exercise

I am assuming you have already started a journal when working on some of the earlier exercises in the book, but if not, now is the time to start. You can either keep a written journal or create it online, such as the one available at InfiniteQuest.com. I want you to get comfortable writing in it every day while you are doing your developmental work. Your entries do not have to be long or overly detailed, but do make sure to jot down any impressions that you receive as well as how you are feeling about your progress. What messages are your Guides giving you during meditation or when your mind is quiet? When and how are the messages coming to you? Don't forget to pay close attention to your dreams, and keep your journal by your bed so that you can record anything you remember upon waking. After journaling for a couple of weeks, you will begin to notice some interesting trends that will help you to understand how your Guides talk to you. You might want to personalize the journal by adding inspirational messages and pictures and then fill it with your insights to make it a one-of-a-kind book just for you.

When I first began doing my work professionally, I met a woman named Grace, whom I identified as having the ability to actually do psychic readings. This situation—where I personally encouraged and professionally mentored an individual in developing her psychic skills—has happened exactly three times in my life. I've already mentioned Jonathan Louis earlier in this book; he is now working as a medium on an international level. Then there was a woman named Donna, whom I wrote about in my book *Crossing Over;* she is still affiliated with the world of self-help and empowerment. And then there's Grace, the first person I taught...well, let's just say that two out of three ain't bad! Grace's initial intuitive abilities were outstanding, but that's about where things ended.

I'm sure that there are other people who are walking around claiming that I taught them or that I started them doing this work, but now you have read it directly from the source: it's not true. There have only been three students whom I have taken under my wing. I am not saying these other folks are not doing good work or that they shouldn't be practicing—not at all. All I am stating is if they are out there broadcasting my name to elevate their own professional status, that should tell you plenty about their lack of confidence in their own skills. One shouldn't need to brag about a teacher, or school, or anything, for that matter. The work should speak for itself.

EGO: A FALL FROM GRACE

Are you tired of me bringing up the Inner Monster called Ego yet? It is the downfall of many metaphysical practitioners, professional psychics, and people with these intuitive abilities. I know I have said it already several times before, but I have seen it over and over again: individuals who believe that they are the *music* when they are simply the *instrument.* I believe it was the downfall of my first student, Grace, as well.

She was able to clearly receive the energy and information from her Team, but that's pretty much where the energy stopped working for her. She would end up making emphatic statements that came across abrasively in tone without any regard to the ethical responsibility behind the messages that she was conveying.

I remember her once doing a personal reading for me, and she simply told me I was going to get into a car accident—really, it was just like that! This was just another instance when I recognized how much I appreciate my Guides and their lessons over the years, as I instinctively knew not to take what she said at face value. I asked Grace to tell me exactly what she saw. She explained to me that she saw my car. That was it. She "saw" my car in her head. Somehow, in some crazy way, this image translated immediately to her as a car accident. I instantly thought of many other things that image could actually mean. A whole list of *"what ifs"* quickly came to mind. What if it wasn't an accident at all but that I was going to take a road trip soon? What if I simply needed to get my brakes checked? Or what if I was going to buy a new car? What if her vision had nothing to do with my car except that I had lost my wallet between the seats of my car?! Countless scenarios could play out here, which is why I stress that **you always have to be extremely careful in how you interpret your psychic impressions before blurting out inaccurate or fearful statements that could do way more harm than good.**

Grace's simple response to me was that she was *right*, no "what ifs" about it. I knew instantly that her growth as a psychic was quite limited because her arrogance would prohibit her from progressing much further. I immediately stopped teaching Grace because I wasn't comfortable encouraging her ego and did not believe that she would be ethically responsible in her work. As I've mentioned earlier in the book, Sandy Anastasi was my only teacher in my psychic development, and one of the best lessons she taught me was simple but immeasurably precious. She gave me the gift of knowing that it was all right to be "wrong." This lesson gave me the freedom to dig deeper and stretch my abilities to receive. If you don't have to be right every

time, you will feel safe enough to try harder and reach for the stars. I
believe this holds true for most things in life, not just psychic work.

> **If you are attempting to do a reading** for someone for the first
> time—or more importantly, if you are already doing this work
> professionally and don't realize that you are simply a pawn on a
> chessboard or an instrument of the Universe when using your
> intuition . . . **STOP!** You have to be humble before the process,
> in awe of its magnificence, grateful that you have been able to
> be a tiny part of it. Always take it seriously, respect it, revere it
> . . . all the while knowing that the "magic" has nothing to do
> with you.

REALITY CHECK

Fortunately, Grace appeared to get the message that she was not cut
out for this particular work and she suddenly lost interest as her abilities seemed to fade. I personally believe that the special Guides who
were in place to teach her recognized that she was not evolving and
developing from their teachings, so they moved on to work with the
next instrument they were assigned to assist. But what about the psychics who continue to have a growing Inner Monster problem? When
they becomes so narcissistic that all they want is attention, fame,
money, and all the trappings that go with it, without the essential
ingredients of responsibility, ethics, and humility? I can promise you
that those with larger-than-life egos leave themselves wide open for
psychic attack.

Lower spirit energies on the Other Side feed the Inner Monster
by actually giving it some accurate insights, manipulating the psychics into falsely believing in their own greatness, ready to share their
amazing gift with the world. Before they know it, they have lost touch

with the concept of being a simple vessel and therefore lost all contact with the higher entities. This disconnect allows a vampire-like relationship to form between the physical world and the spiritual realm— albeit a lower-leveled one—which can ultimately be dangerous to all those who seek out these psychics for guidance. Those clients have no way of knowing that the psychic is working with lower-level energies and not the higher ones a person would prefer to hear from.

When discussing some negativity that was lingering around me a few years ago, Sandy Anastasi reminded me that the currency of the Other Side is energy and that it functions in much the same way as money is used on earth. In the physical world we work really hard to accumulate money in order to exist comfortably. It is the same in the Afterlife, but with energy. The lower-leveled spirits who don't want to see the energy on our planet shift to the Love side of the equation create situations that generate Fear. That Fear becomes a spark that ignites more of the same, producing a level of energy that is like crack cocaine for the lower-evolved entities; they will do anything to get it and yet can never get enough. It's like an addiction to Fear, and unfortunately you can see it play out in energetic patterns all the time on this plane of existence.

Now I know that it sounds like I just stopped being rational and am heading off on some weird *Twilight Zone* theme. But people are people. Dead or alive. I am sure you have known some bullies in your life, either past or present—an intimidating kid on the playground, an overly demanding boss, a win-at-all-costs coach, a hypercritical parent, or even a passive-aggressive spouse. There are also bullies at large out in the community—the gang member pulling a gun on a gas station attendant for a few bucks, an entitled politician sexually harassing his staff members, or a financial lender threatening foreclosure in a menacing manner. All of the examples are fear-based energy motivators. The Other Side is no different. It is made up of many levels of evolvement and let me assure you that not all Spirits are good ones. The basic principles of karma are at work whether you are a person here on Earth or a Spirit on the Other Side. A negative entity has the opportunity to break its habit of feeding off the dark energy, but similar to being a drug addict, it is not an easy change to make. Conversely, Love is the energy currency that fuels positive, higher-leveled evolution on the Other Side.

So when the Bible talks about "false prophets" or I talk about the psychics who are working from their Inner Monster point, it is all the same thing—ego running amok.

> More than anything else it is imperative that you always remain pure of heart, mind, and soul when doing this type of work.

TRUST IN THE PROCESS

One of the more difficult things to accomplish in handling this developmental work sounds deceptively simple: **trust.**

It is not an easy task to surrender to the thoughts and emotions imparted to you from this invisible realm, especially after I just told you about the "bad guys" who want to prey on your vulnerability, ego, and fear. This is why this book is written and laid out in the manner it is. I wanted you to have the information about the subject matter first, before the application. Remember I said that I had my reasons? One of them is because of my past successful experience in mentoring my student, Jonathan Louis. My greatest accomplishment in being a teacher in this field so far was assisting Jonathan on his spiritual path to becoming a professional medium.

His backstory from my perspective is simple. When Jonathan and I first became friends, he had absolutely no interest in what I did professionally. Actually, he was one of the only people I knew who really didn't care about who "John Edward the medium" was; instead, he wanted to know *me*. I used to tease him all the time by jokingly asking him, *"When are you going to read one of my books?"* Jonathan's answer was priceless: *"Why read the book when the author can just share his story personally over lunch?"* Point made. Well, his Guides and mine clearly had an important mission in mind. They had me tell him all about my work and my experiences as a medium. What I thought were just simple casual conversations were actually training classes for him, preparing him for his own journey of development. When the time was right and our Guides told us that Jonathan was to be officially trained, it was like throwing a big electrical switch: all the lights came flooding on in that instant. He had years of theory under his belt before the instructional side even started. All of those "philosophy lessons" followed by intensive training have made him quite an accurate and successful professional medium in his own right.

I have written this book very much in the same style of my mentoring of Jonathan: I have given much of the theory and philosophy up front, before embarking on the application. Again, this is not so you can follow in his footsteps, but instead so you can create your own. You must listen to your Team of Guides and allow them to assist you in learning the lessons you are here on this Earth to learn, which does not necessarily mean that you will be a professional psychic . . . in all likelihood you won't. However, if you are supposed to do this work, you will know when the timing is right. The Universe will make it clear what instrument you are to play in its energetic orchestra. Whatever role you choose, just don't feed the monster lurking within. If you do, all the ability in the world won't be able to save you from yourself.

LOST AND FOUND

Death is an obvious way that we lose people in our lives; choices are another. Please be prepared to see people fall to the wayside in your life as you embark on this life-altering journey. When you begin to speak about your development and what you are learning, you will start to see shifts in the energies of those who are closest to you. Notice how your friends and family members react when you speak about numerology, astrology, or other tools in the psychic toolbox that you are learning how to use for your development. Watch their body language as you tell them about the latest prophetic dream you had that came true or a concern that you are having for someone that you love. You will soon be able to see which people will encourage and support your growth and which people will begin to energetically disconnect from you.

Whenever you attempt to make a difference in yourself from a self-empowerment perspective, those around you will immediately be looking at their own reflection in your eyes in a deficit way. It's normal human behavior to compare oneself to others, and you must be prepared to experience it as you change and grow.

This is not an overnight process, because at first your friends will say that what you are doing sounds interesting; they might even admit that they too once had or currently have an interest. The more you delve deeper into the field and, more importantly, yourself, the more you will create a shift in your energy that will be noticeable to everyone around you. That is when you will notice people start to either pull away or attack you for being different. Whatever happens, don't deny the change in you, because you are energetically different. You will not see it, but others will. Seeing the difference in you will force them to reflect and contemplate what they are not doing in their own life. Friends and family members will either embrace the positive shift in your life or become angry at losing the person you once were; they might even go on the offensive.

You can assuage much of the negativity or jealousy by remaining humble in your path and supportive of others in theirs, but some of your connections will literally just end. You will essentially outgrow those relationships, and it is a natural pruning process that happens so your garden can flourish. You can't expect to grow to be an amazing flower if weeds are choking you from all around. Release those who cannot support your growth, and soon you will be able to find others who are not threatened by your newfound strength, but inspired by it instead.

For those of you who decide that this psychic development work will be a conscious lifestyle choice, as it has to be for a practitioner, I am sorry to say that you will absolutely lose some of your close friends and family along the way. The Universe will ultimately remove the people who are blocking your spiritual path and attempting to stymie your growth. It is that simple. All the psychics I know could tell you their own personal story of the people who were literally removed from their lives. Most of the time, it will be those same people spinning themselves in circles due to the insecurities and fear in their own lives. Again, that is why utilizing psychic self-defense techniques and practicing a daily ritual of prayer and meditation, as well as honoring your Team and your place in the Universal Orchestra, are so significant.

I also want you to know that even though some people will be removed from your life, the amazing benefit is that there will now be more room for those who share your appreciation for life's magic, and your path will be cleared so that you can walk unencumbered with your new spiritual perspective and have more space in which to grow your garden. But I must warn you how essential it is that you have already worked through the steps of assessing and changing your personal programming, as discussed earlier in this book. If you did not make the necessary changes to your network before pruning the negative people from your path, you will just pull similar unhealthy energies into your field in the future, only to deal with the same lessons all over again. Before you go any further in this book, reexamine your programming to make sure it is playing on the highest potential frequency so that you draw in the kind of healthy people and empowering situations that you need in your life as a spiritual warrior.

THE GREATEST GIFT OF ALL

There is definitely something magical and universal about the lyrics to the song "The Greatest Love of All." Well, my lifelong love of music and keen attention to lyrics led me to thinking about music's energy and its vibrational power. After the terribly tragic earthquake in Haiti in January 2010, a group of incredible musicians and iconic musical personalities got together to raise money for the people of the devastated country by participating in a remake of the inspirational song "We Are the World." When you watch their music video or listen to the song, there's no way you can't be moved by all these talented "instruments" uniting their voices and spirits with such heartfelt purpose for such a humanitarian cause.

Please know that even though you are only one singular voice on the planet, when you dedicate yourself to being a member of the Universal Chorus of Love, you cause an amazing reverberation on our planet. This collective intent joins us in ways that can't be tangibly seen, but which raise the vibrational frequencies toward white light and positive change. Strive to be in tune and stay in focus at all times. Remain in balance and be a warrior for light and love. **Are YOU ready?**

ARE YOU READY?

I want you to understand that the Universe will not force any of these changes on you. The transformation is all based on your own free will and choice. I also know that at some point there will be a question put to you in some way by your life's experiences: "Are you ready?" You are the only one who can consciously and willingly accept the invitation for spiritual evolution.

10

PSYCHIC
SELF-DEFENSE

This is probably one of the most important chapters you
will read on your journey with me. Psychic Self-Defense is
a useful practice for your everyday living and an absolute
must if you are doing any type of energy work.

E arlier in the book I have touched on the value of psychic self-defense and some of the reasons why you need to practice it. Now I am going take this concept further to help you understand just why it is so important. In this chapter, I will explain some things that I believe you instinctively already know.

Let's start by looking at the physical world that we live in and commonplace protection methods that almost all of us follow. Do you lock your doors at night? Do you wear a seatbelt when driving? Do you have car, health, house, or life insurance policies? Do you have an alarm system for your car or house? Do you take extra precautions when you travel to a new location or an unfamiliar neighborhood? We protect ourselves from the weather by using coats, boots, hats, umbrellas, and gloves. We shelter ourselves from the external forces by constructing homes with sturdy roofs and walls. We place our valuables in banks, safes, and secret hiding places. We use passwords to access our computers and our financial accounts. Nations spend billions of dollars to protect their citizens from possible enemies and potential attacks. Maintaining our security is paramount and the list of our methods of protection in this day and age is overwhelmingly complex.

WHY DO WE PROTECT OURSELVES?

The answer to why we go to such lengths to protect ourselves is quite simply to avoid problems as much as we possibly can and ultimately to feel safe and secure. We see the value in creating security. Whether we choose to lock our doors or install an alarm system is still up to us, right? It's our choice to use protection, and our risk if we don't. Let's consider a group of assailants that are usually invisible to the naked eye, but which we still go out of our way to protect ourselves from: bacteria, viruses, cancers, and other causes of disease.

We are constantly informed by government agencies, the medical community, scientists, and the news media about countless ways to protect our health. For instance, we are told to eat vegetables high in beta carotene to prevent cancer, not to overcook meats or they may be carcinogenic, to wash our hands often when handling food because of salmonella poisoning, and to limit our intake of sodium, fat, and sugar. We know that if we are not very careful about how and who we have sex with, we can catch some sexually transmitted disease, which could possibly be fatal. Today, condoms are available at local drug stores and health clinics and even passed out in some schools. Why? To protect us. The "us" being protected is the physical part of us. But you already know or you are now realizing that there is much more to you than your physical body.

How many times have you tried to protect yourself from catching the common cold by taking extra vitamin C or the herb echinacea? You can get inoculated for the latest flu virus, maintain good hygiene, and practice preventive measures like doing lots of exercise, getting enough rest, and following a proper diet. Why? Certainly we strive to be at our healthy best, but we are also doing our best to avoid possible negative consequences. Preventive education is available all around us. It is easy to comprehend why we would pay attention to it for our physical well-being, but we need to apply this carefulness to our energetic health as well. This is where things get more complicated. Do you have to interact with lots of people at your job? Do you find that you are constantly helping colleagues do their work? Are friends and family only too happy to share their personal and professional dramas? Does your work involve physical touch, like a massage therapist or a health professional? Have you ever dabbled with metaphysical items like tarot cards, numerology, or any other psychic tool? Have you ever felt someone invading your space without their even taking a step toward you? Have you ever been attacked by one of those ambitious perfume pushers in the mall with the latest scent after you have taken your second step into their store? Are you physically tired or emotionally drained often, even after sleeping well? Basically, are you alive?

Well, I'm sure that you probably answered yes to a couple of these questions, and at least the last one for sure. So you better pay attention and keep reading.

CROSSFIRE

Our thoughts are like bullets that help to manifest our futures. Hopefully, we are aiming our intentions with purpose and are able to hit our target and create the future we desire. Sometimes we are careless in our aim and yet the "bullets" have to hit something once they are fired, which can have a negative result. But what about other people's thought bullets? Can they also affect us, intentionally or unintentionally? YES! Energy is not biased. Other people's charged thoughts and energetic fields can ultimately have a profound effect on us. Practicing psychic self-defense protects us from these energies. I don't want you to become paranoid now or "energy-phobic," but instead to be aware and to prepare. Worrying won't help; in fact, fear wears down your protective guard. This is why understanding the FEAR and LOVE principles discussed earlier in the book is so important. Strive to approach life and others from the Love perspective at all times for the best results.

There are many different defensive methods that can be employed when protecting yourself from negative energy. If you already have an effective practice for psychic protection in place, there may be no need to change it; just make sure to use it! Hopefully you find the information here helpful as well. This chapter can give you some options to add to your arsenal of defensive weapons. But if this is all new material to you, please take seriously what I am trying to convey ...you need protection and you need it now. I've been working as a psychic medium for over twenty-five years and it is imperative that I always use some form of protection. If you were thinking that what you just read sounds like I'm referring to sex, ironically enough, with regard to energy, the concepts of protection are very similar. When

I am conducting a reading I have to open my energy field to receive the impressions and communications from my Spirit Guides. In addition, any entities on the Other Side who are connected to the person being read will utilize my energy field to pass on their messages. Not to mention that I also have to tune into the energy field of the person I am reading to even allow this process to take place.

The intensity level of this type of experience is compounded by the attitude, energy, and type of issues the person I am reading is bringing to the session. Ultimately, my office is both an energy playground and a dumping field.

For the sake of getting across the message about the absolute need for protection, I am going to share an experience with you that I'm not eager to admit. I have occasionally forgotten to practice psychic self-defense to protect myself. I am not proud of this fact. Actually, it's plain stupid. I know the ramifications of not doing it. But like you, I am human, and there were times when I lost track of time before an appointment. Once or twice, I barely had enough time to do my meditation and prayers before the session. So what's the big deal? Well, keep reading and you will see for yourself.

One afternoon, I had a meeting with my publisher in New York City and I missed my homebound train from Manhattan to Long Island. I knew I could catch the next one, but I began to get anxious because I had private appointments scheduled later that evening. I was able to get on the next train, but unfortunately I arrived at my office at the same time as my clients. I briefly meditated and began my sessions without any time for my normal preparation.

My last appointment was with a family whose child had crossed over because of a malignant tumor in the brain. When he was alive, he was plagued with terrible migraines for days on end. Tragically, there was no medication that alleviated his pain. The session began and the boy came through to me immediately. He shared his name, how long he had been gone, and other validating details of his life.

Through what is known as *"sympathetic pain,"* he imprinted on my energy field the physical issue that he dealt with in his life—his tumor pain.

I was then able to feel the location of where the tumor was in his head by describing my own pain. This fact on its own helped his parents know that he was with them that evening. I was then able to convey to them that he was freed from his physical pain and no longer suffered on the Other Side. After the session ended, I drove home. That night, the same headache returned and lingered. Now, the child was not actively communicating with me any longer, but the imprint on my energy field remained. It eventually subsided after a few hours. Now, if I had taken the opportunity to protect myself properly, I know I would not have been adversely affected the same way.

My next example occurred in my personal life and is likely to happen to all of us from time to time. It is something that I refer to as *"energy dumping."* I had a long conversation with a friend who was having some difficulty in her marriage. She felt that her husband was allowing his family to control their relationship. I listened as a good friend should and offered my thoughts and support. Less than an hour later I found myself having a spat with my wife out of the blue, over some of the same issues that my friend spoke of in her marriage. My wife looked at me as if I were a complete stranger. I quickly realized that the argument had nothing to do with me and my wife. I was just sharing the negative energy of my friend's relationship, which I had picked up during our earlier conversation. I recognized that I was only reacting to the energy dump that I had experienced and I immediately apologized.

As I thought back over the day, I realized that I had been so busy that I hadn't taken my usual time to meditate and pray. By the time I spoke with my friend about her marital problems, I was somewhat depleted energetically and left myself vulnerable to picking up her issues. It is important to understand that it is those we love and feel the most connected to whose energy is the most likely to affect us. Our guard is already down because we care so much and perhaps do not feel like we need to be "defensive," since these are people that we feel safe around. Yet it is that same vulnerability that opens us wide open to receiving their energy, positive or negative. By all means I am not saying you should close down and not listen to those you love; in fact, I think being more intuitive enables you to be a more sensitive and loving person. The lesson here is to protect yourself so that you don't take on anyone's negative energy, no matter if it is a stranger, co-worker, spouse, or best friend. Practicing psychic self-defense is vital every day no matter who you are around or what circumstances you encounter. Better safe than sorry.

SMELLY ENERGY

Sympathetic pain and *energy dumping* don't just happen to me because I am a professional psychic. These same things happen to you all the time and you just are not aware of it . . . until now!

Think about how many times you are forced to interact with people that you don't know, whether it's on the subway, a large social event, or a meeting for work. We have all been faced with those uncomfortable moments in our personal or professional lives. In fact, maybe it was so awkward or unpleasant that you didn't want to be there any longer. There may not even be a tangible reason why you feel this way. They smile at you. They may dress nicely and appear to be very nice. But your energy is reacting to their energy and all you want to do is bolt. And you know what I say they're suffering from? *"Smelly energy."* But many times these interactions are necessary and you cannot react to the feeling by running away; actually, you have no other choice but to deal with these people. They might also be people you know such as your boss, co-worker, or an in-law . . . or it could even be your spouse on a really bad day.

That is why practicing psychic self-defense is absolutely necessary for everyone. Psychic self-defense isn't just about protecting you from strangers. It protects you from all types of negative energy.

Every living organism has an energy field known as the *aura.* This field of energy changes shape and color as your feelings and moods change. It is multilayered and has a mental, emotional, spiritual, and physical aspect. When you fortify your aura, you are protecting yourself psychically. But it can ultimately protect the whole you. **So your goal is to protect your aura.**

The external influences (bullets) that are around you can imprint your aura, but by practicing psychic self-defense, you are able to program your aura from the inside and resist those influences, like a firewall on your computer. By doing this, you are safeguarding yourself from any type of attack.

Practicing daily meditation and understanding the vital role it plays in your spiritual development is a great way to strengthen your auric field. Additionally, you must learn about *chakras,* also known as the energy centers in your body. An awareness of how energy affects each chakra and how to release it will greatly increase the spiritual power that you possess. I will go into more detail about working with your chakras later in the book.

Psychic Vampires

The reason that I recommend using psychic protection is that it helps to maintain the energy in your own aura field as well as keeping others from affecting it negatively or draining it. Most of us are familiar with the image of vampires, whether it's the old-school stereotype of Béla Lugosi from black-and-white movies or the young brooding *Twilight* vampires of recent popularity who come flashing to your mind. Guess what? There is a much bigger danger of losing your energy rather than your blood to a "vampire," and it happens more often than you might think. You have most likely encountered several *psychic energy vampires* in your lifetime and even been guilty of being one sometimes, as well. Now, please don't think that I mean sinking your teeth into the nearest person to charge up your batteries—it's not a "physical" act at all. **The attack of psychic energy happens on an invisible playing field.** Most of the time you don't even realize when you're doing it to anyone or that it's being done to you.

Here's an example to clarify what a psychic vampire attack can entail. Jane and Sue are good friends, and Sue is going through a difficult time emotionally. Jane is always a source of comfort for Sue because she truly cares about her well-being. As a result, Jane opens herself up to Sue's energy and her personal issues. Sue's marriage is draining her energetically and she feels depleted; her energy battery starts to run on low. Her first reaction is to call someone who she intuitively knows will make her feel better and lift her spirits. That is what her energy field is craving, an emotional jump start. She calls Jane because Jane is always willing to listen and support her. They talk for an hour or so while Sue shares her frustrations and Jane commiserates. By the end of the call Sue is laughing and feeling somewhat rejuvenated and more optimistic about her situation, but Jane is tired and irritable and heads straight for bed. In this particular case, Sue is the vampire, Jane the victim.

This is an example of a common energy exchange that happens all the time. Sue doesn't mean to intentionally drain Jane's energy, nor does Jane mean to play the victim. You can protect yourself by using psychic self-defense. It's also okay to not "invite the vampire in" by stating your limits when necessary, especially at times when you are tired or feeling energetically low. Jane doesn't have to "always" be willing to listen; she also needs to take care of herself. She is entitled to tell Sue that she is busy and would like to talk tomorrow instead. In fact, it is even a good idea not to pick up the phone every time it rings. Make sure you are giving yourself enough time for meditation and prayer so that you are well protected when you do connect with others. I am sure you can remember similar interactions like this one occurring in your own life. How many energy vampires are around you? And be very honest—are you guilty of being one with others as well? Now that you know what it means, do your best not to be one. Stop and consider what you are *dumping* on other people and what you might be *draining* from them.

People who study shark behavior respect the animal's powerful force and the potential danger that it might offer to humans. Marine biologists may wear shark repellant suits and some stay protected in cages, but danger can still be very much a part of the experience. We need to wear a psychic self-defense suit when dealing with the psychic vampires in our lives. These are just normal people who are lacking energy and vitality in their own lives and without any conscious thought can drain healthy or more vital people of their energies. When you act as a vampire or if you are a very sensitive person, you may unintentionally take on the energy of other people. But what if their energy is in worse shape than yours? What if they're sick, depressed, or angry? You then are making yourself susceptible to their issues and could find yourself feeling things you don't even understand. So be aware of the energy leeches, and watch your own tendency to be one. They come in all shapes and sizes—some might be cute little kids in a classroom, while others are the elderly in a nursing home. They're not aware that they are draining others or affecting you in an adverse way. Their neediness is just taking over anyone who comes close to them. You must always think about where you are spending and mixing your energy. Additionally, keep in mind that the energy in groups can take on a purpose of its own. Once again, **be aware and prepare.** If you are "wearing protection," the effect will be a lot less damaging.

THE PRACTICE OF PSYCHIC SELF-DEFENSE

In my lifetime of studying psychic phenomena, I've come across some of the most intense and slightly unusual practices that deal with metaphysics—especially in regard to psychic self-defense. I found some of them funny while others seemed extremely ritualistic. Searching for obscure ingredients that are required for some potion is already too energy-draining for my taste. If I need to stop what I'm doing in my busy life to go in search of a root or herb that I can't purchase locally—well, that's too much work. Later in this chapter, I will share some of the psychic defense exercises that I use. Trust me: they will be simple and not require a long list of hard-to-find items. I do not have the patience or the personality to do anything hokey. My sense of humor doesn't allow for such extreme measures: I would laugh too hard . . . which leads me to a funny story.

BEGONE, CAT

A number of years ago, Shelley Peck, a close friend and colleague of mine, was trying to sell her house. It was a gorgeous home that was decorated beautifully and above all was priced to sell. But for some reason, it just wasn't selling.

When Shelley mentioned to another psychic (whom we'll refer to as Ruth) that she was having trouble selling her house, Ruth told Shelley that she felt that the house had a dark energy residing in it that was preventing the sale from happening. Ruth said that she would have to perform a housecleaning immediately. Now, let me be clear and explain that she wasn't coming over with a mop and a bucket. Ruth meant a *psychic energy housecleaning.* Think of this as a spiritual spring cleaning, something that I believe should be done on your home and any other place where you spend a lot of your time.

This psychic housecleaning experience proved to be more than

I was expecting. In my opinion it was about as corny and ritualistic as something you would see in a bad horror film. Shelley called me and said that Ruth wanted four people to work with her in exorcising this energy. I asked Shelley if she even believed that there was such an entity present. At this point, since the house had been on the market for so long, if Ruth said that there was a Hawaiian native spirit in the house preventing the sale and Shelley needed to do a hula dance on the roof, I think she would have done it just in case.

So I agreed to participate in what was to be my first house exorcism or whatever you want to call it. The four of us consisted of Shelley, Ruth, Marvin (Shelley's very practical-minded husband), and me. It's important to note that Marvin was about as into the psychic world as a rock. He understood it. He knew that he was married to one of the country's top psychics, and he had developed a respect for my success in the field. But you would never find him in the corner meditating or reading tarot cards.

Marvin was a tall, quiet gentleman with a very deep and commanding voice, all of which contributed to his somewhat intimidating demeanor. Having him involved in this escapade was now setting the stage for my inappropriate giggling that was starting to surface. Ruth had us all meditate and do our own protection visualizations before we embarked on the "Big Cleanse" (Marvin's name for it). We were to start in the basement. Ruth had planned this task with great detail and determination. Shelley was to carry the burning smudge stick, which is a tight bundle of sage leaves. (Smudging is a smoke ritual of cleansing an environment by burning various herbs, with sage being the most commonly used.) Marvin had been instructed to smash an amethyst stone before we started and then carry its purple dust for sprinkling around the house. I got lucky—I was in charge of the big bell and was told to ring it only on Ruth's command. As we walked through the house, I felt like our "mystery van" should have been parked in the driveway, and spooky music should be playing all around us. I bet you're wondering what Ruth did; well, she led this pack of "energy busters" down the steps to the basement.

We entered a room and almost immediately Ruth acknowledged that she felt a "cold spot." Shelley was directly behind her, so I wasn't able to see her face. But Marvin was right next to me. He mumbled under his breath, *"Of course, she feels a cold spot. We're in the basement. There's no heat down here."*

At this point, I had developed a serious case of the giggles. I tried not to laugh, because that would be unprofessional and I would be mocking my own line of work. But I couldn't help it; I did laugh. I laughed as quietly and nondisruptively as I could manage.

Not ten seconds after Ruth announced the cold spot, she started screaming at the top of her lungs, *"GET IT OFF ME! HELP! GET THE CAT OFF ME!"*

Ruth was up against the wall in this room, and she told us in between screams that she was pinned up against the wall by a large cat that only she could see. She was shrieking and yelling dramatically that she couldn't move and begging us to get it away from her. For a moment the three of us stood there in a state of shock. Shelley and I were in this mode of complete and utter disbelief in what was happening. To my surprise, Marvin was the hero of the day, jumping in to rescue Ruth. He took the amethyst dust that he had so diligently created and threw it all around Ruth's feet while commanding in his deep voice, *"I COMMAND THEE ... BEGONE, CAT!"* At that point, Ruth became unpinned from the wall and began to regain her composure. I guess the big cat had met its match in Marvin. Apparently as a result of Marvin's magic, the phantom feline decided to permanently give up its residence in the basement. Ruth refocused her attention and continued uneventfully to clear the rest of the house, with all of us following behind her.

Here's the ironic part—the house sold in a week after the cleansing. Now, I'm sure you're wondering if Ruth actually *saw* this cat or if she had just forgotten to take her medication that day. To be honest, I have no idea what she experienced. Do I think there was some "dark energy" lurking about in the basement? No, I really don't. What I believe happened is that the exercise of cleansing the house allowed both Marvin and Shelley to release the lives they were living in that home so that it could finally be sold.

Just like doing a physical cleaning of your house, it is equally essential to psychically cleanse not only the space that you live in, but also your office, your car, and any place where you spend a lot of time. If you are moving into a new office or home, it is very important to clean and protect the area on an energetic level.

Energy matrixes, or "cobwebs," are formed over time, and it is important to dispel them because the energy in an area may build up and become stagnant. There are energy cobwebs around us and a psychic self-defense cleansing ritual can help to lighten up the energy of your space (see "House Cleansing Exercise" on pages 176–83). Believe me, you will feel a difference after it's done.

Whether you are actively practicing psychic work or just now developing your abilities, it is a must that you establish solid techniques for psychic self-defense. Just as people in certain occupational fields—such as firefighters, police officers, and members of the military—can't avoid occasional danger and conflict and must wear protective vests and uniforms, you need to constantly be aware of how to guard your energetic field. Now that you know that you can protect yourself from negative energy, I would like you to take a moment to consider if you can identify past situations where psychic self-defense could have helped. Think about what you could have done to defend yourself and learn from it. Always be conscious of the energy world you live in, release your fears, and fortify your belief system.

The power of prayer (any kind that works for you) is incredible and helps to strengthen your aura. There are seven major energy centers in the body known as the chakras, and it is through these centers that your energy flows (see Chapter 12). As you work on opening up your chakras, you need to practice some form of psychic self-defense. Just the thought of opening yourself up energetically and emotionally makes you more vulnerable to psychic attack. For instance, if you are holding the minority opinion in a group discussion and you have the majority of people directing their energy at you, telling you that you're wrong, you may still maintain your belief and convictions. But you'll be wiped out by the end of that experience from the energetic battle. It is important to be able to be aware and prepare for all different kinds of situations. I know from personal experience that I just can't handle spending time in crowds because I am so open and sensitive to the energies around me. It's not a claustrophobia issue; it's an energy thing. I know that I can't do it, even though the protection I use does help immeasurably. But it doesn't completely protect me from the aftermath of the experience, leaving me feeling energetically exhausted or drained. So I tend to avoid large crowds at all costs. So even with protection, there just may be certain situations that you want to steer clear of as you grow more open to the energy around you.

> Remember, when it comes to energy, prepare to be aware.

I just wanted to give you an overview on the practice of psychic self-defense. As you might guess, I could write a book solely on this topic, but I want to move on to the exercises that I promised you earlier. It is crucial that you develop a good, solid foundation and, in this case, a healthy strong aura as well.

STRENGTH TRAINING FOR YOUR AURA

At first, you probably thought that the whole idea of defending yourself against energy sounded weird, if not absurd. I'm hoping that you now realize why you should be aware of the energy around you at all times and why practicing some form of energetic protection is so important. If there was a psychic self-defense pill that I could purchase over the counter, I would take it every day for the rest of my life. However, there is nothing of that sort available. So you must utilize the exercises that work for you. Here are some basics to get you started. The first technique, and the foundation of all psychic self-defense, is the power of thought. You need to strengthen and fortify your aura field from the inside out. By doing this, you are allowing your energy immunity to develop. Think about this technique as similar to charging the battery on a cell phone. By reinforcing your aura with thoughts of protection, you are recharging it.

I have already mentioned several times the "white light" and how to surround yourself with it. This white light is universal energy that is available to all of us. The exercises below are basic and practical in nature. I will not be giving you a shopping list of things to buy like eye of newt and the bark of the giant naga tree . . . quite the contrary. These are mostly visual techniques, and they will fit into your everyday life and routine.

Affirmative Thought Exercise

Begin each day saying aloud: *"I encircle myself in the white light of God's love and divine protection."* Keep it simple at first, and remember that if you so choose, you can exchange whatever Higher Power you believe in for "God." In fact, when I taught workshops I used *"I encircle myself with the white light of Universal Love and Divine Protection"* so everyone in the class, no matter what their religion, would feel comfortable saying it. After you've been doing this affirmation for a while, you may want to tailor it to fit your changing needs. Please feel free to personalize it as much as you need. For example, maybe you're having a difficult time dealing with the energy of a person at work or in your family. You may know that you're going to be put into a situation where you'll be forced to deal with this individual. A suggestion would be to include the following affirmative thought: "I will allow nothing but positive thoughts and energy to affect me. I am not influenced by the negativity of those I encounter."

So in total, you would say: *"I encircle myself in the white light of God's love and divine protection. And I allow nothing but positive thoughts and energy to affect me. I will not be influenced by the negativity of those I encounter."*

Notice, I did not include a reference to the specific individual that you're concerned about. If you mention one name or situation, you would limit your protection. When you use sunscreen before going out to the beach, you distribute it evenly over your entire body. Targeting just one leg would be foolish. The same thing goes with affirmations. I also recommend that you include a prayer at the end of your morning exercise. The power and healing energy of prayer is something I believe in quite strongly. Throughout the day when immediate protection is needed, this is the exercise I will begin doing automatically. You can't say it enough, so don't hesitate to use it whenever you feel the need.

The Shower Exercise

This psychic self-defense technique is a basic energy cleanse. This can be done in the morning before you start your day, at night before you sleep, or even twice a day if you so choose. Frequently, people tell me they feel the most intuitive when they are in the bathroom, taking a bath or shower. I think the basic reason for this is privacy. Usually, it is the room in the house where the rest of your family gives you a little space. And even for those who live alone, it still provides an escape from doing housework, reading e-mail, or paying bills. (In the course of writing this book, it was called to my attention that some experts think that an additional reason people are more intuitive and get flashes of insight and invention in the shower is that most people are in the alpha brain-wave state, similar to the brain state in meditation—alert but relaxed.) This protective exercise actually can be done as you take your normal shower. Make sure that you focus your mind on the task of cleaning your energy field.

First, imagine that you just spent a few hours in a coal mine and visualize your skin being covered with a soot-like substance. The soot symbolizes the negative energies that we attract in our everyday lives. This exercise will wash all of the negativity away. Stand under the showerhead under warm, but not hot, water. Become very aware of the water. Feel it all around you. Use your soap to create lather. Know that the soap that you are using will cleanse not only your physical body, but also your aura.

As you are lathering up your body, watch the soap breaking up the soot energy that is on your skin. Now rinse. As you rinse, consciously watch the dirty water, the suds, all get pulled down the drain. Repeat the process. Lather, rinse, and watch the water go down the drain. And as you do this, know that you're working on a conscious level to clear your physical body's receptors. If you have trouble visualizing the "soot," just use the soapsuds as your focus.

The next step is to fortify and seal your energy field. Stand with your feet less than a foot apart, and allow your arms to hang down by your side. Tilt your head back slightly so that the water doesn't distract you by running down the front of your face. Close your eyes and become aware of the water falling all around you. As you listen to the water falling around you, take a couple of deep breaths and exhale. Make the water temperature slightly warmer for this next part. Imagine the water turning a bright white color. See it as if it was a beautiful ray of the sun. Allow the warmth of the water to relax your body and know that as the water washes over your body, it is cleansing your energy. You're strengthening your aura with this bright warm light splashing all around you. In your mind, imagine an indicator like the gas gauge in a car moving from empty toward full. When you see the lever hit full, open your eyes and know that you are finished. Notice how refreshed and clean you feel, inside and out.

The shower exercise is great to do after a hectic day. I don't know if you have ever noticed but if you take a shower after you have an argument with someone or get upset about something, you normally feel better. A shower will usually help to cleanse your energy and your aura, as well as your body. Once you have cleansed yourself and your energy field, it is very important to clean the energy that is left in the shower, and as you do you can imagine the rest of the negative energy going down the drain. A quick spray and wipe-down with a strong cleaning detergent will usually do the trick.

* * * * * * * *

EARLIER, I SHARED A STORY about the psychic cleaning of a friend's house. Remember the crazy part about the phantom feline pinning Ruth up against the wall? I still have to shake my head and chuckle when I think about how ridiculous I felt that afternoon. But, despite how silly it seemed at the time, Shelley's house sold shortly after that clearing ritual. Not because Marvin became a spiritual lion tamer, but because the cleansing of the energy in the house was successful. We broke up the energy cobwebs and cleaned them out, allowing Shelley and Marvin to "release" their attachment to the house. Because they cleared the house of their connection, potential buyers were able to feel a more open and inviting home when they walked through it. Don't you usually clean your house before having guests over for a visit? So why not do an energy cleanup to go along with the physical tidying up? You won't be the only one to notice not just how nice the place looks, but also how good it feels.

SMUDGING

Smudging is about purifying the energy around people, places, and things by performing a "smoke ritual." Smudging has been used since ancient times by many cultures as a ceremony of purification and protection. Spiritual groups such as pre-Christian pagans, Catholic and Eastern Orthodox churches, Hindus, Buddhists, and Cherokee and Lakota Indians have practiced different types of smudging rituals. Various herbs such as sweet grass, cedar, tobacco, calamus, red willow bark, dogwood, and sage can be used for smudging. White sage is the one most commonly utilized. This is not the traditional culinary sage, so don't raid your spice rack, but you should be able to find white sage at your local metaphysical bookstore or new age store, herbalist shop, and many places online.

The smudging process involves burning the sage and wafting the smoke in various areas. The smoke attaches itself to negative energy. As the smoke clears, it takes the negative energy with it, releasing it to regenerate into something more positive. It has been said that the smoke of burning sage literally changes the ionization polarity of the air. It is advisable to start at the lowest level of your home, or office space, and move to the top. Open a window or door during this smudging ritual so that you can visualize the negative and stagnant energy leaving the area. Sage is often used as a precursor to psychic events, including séances and readings, to ward off negative energy and to protect those stepping inside that experience.

House Cleansing Exercise

The first thing to do is to pick up a few items before you get started. You will want to buy sea salt, a spray bottle, large trash bags, cleaning supplies, and white sage. If at all possible purchase a sage smudge stick as it is easier to handle, but sage leaves work just as well for your purposes. First, you will take care of the outside of your home. In the first part of the following exercise, you will need only the sea salt.

You will now proceed to outline the perimeter of your home with the sea salt. Pour the salt along the edges of your house as you walk completely around it. Make sure to pay extra attention around the doors and windows, as they represent entrances and exits for energy as well.

As you sprinkle the salt, ask for your home to be protected and safeguarded from negative energy and events. You can use a tailored version of the affirmative exercise on pages 172–73 as a guide. Done. It is as easy as that. If you live in an apartment, condo, or townhouse, I don't recommend doing the entire outside of your building, just the walls where your space is located.

I suggest doing this first cleansing exercise in the early morning or late evening when you won't be disturbed by a nosy neighbor or any other interruptions. Focus on the words and ask for protection of your house or apartment (you can "house-cleanse" your office, too). Be serious in your intent and leave an energy imprint that keeps out any negative influences. Now, let's do the inside.

Once you are armed with your tools of defense, you should schedule a day to launch this plan of attack. Here are a couple of hints for success. Pick a day on which you know that you can begin early enough to complete the task by the end of the day. Try to be sure that you will not be disturbed during this process so you will keep the momentum going and will be able to finish in the time allotted. You might need to turn off the phone and step away from the computer so that you can really apply all your energy to this exercise. I also recommend that you do this project yourself, unless you absolutely need someone to help you. You must mentally oversee every aspect of this project so that it has your personal energetic stamp and not anyone else's.

You see, this process must be all about you. Nobody knows your belongings like the owner. The only exception to this rule is if your family members or roommates want to get involved. Preferably, all the people who live in the residence will want to do their part in the cleansing on the same day with you. This way they can be responsible for their own individual rooms. This will also cut down on the amount of work for you to do and will ensure that they don't feel that their space has been invaded or violated. Your children can sort through their games, toys, and clothes so they can keep what they actually use, and donate to a charity what they don't. This is a valuable lesson for children of all ages. Many families who are less fortunate might really value the things that your children never even touch any longer. Now I know that this is a time-consuming process, depending on how much clutter you have accumulated, but everyone will notice a positive difference once it's completed.

First, I want you to really *clean* your space. Yes, this psychic guy is telling you to clean and tidy up your house. Trust me—there is a good reason. I want you to clean each room as well as you can. Focus on areas that you might normally overlook when busy, which means that I want you to clean out the drawers and closets and move the furniture to get the dust bunnies underneath it as well. If it is reasonably easy to accomplish, I would recommend having you move everything out of the room you are going to start in, and then clean the walls, ceilings, and floors before you put the furniture back in place. The furniture and other items should also be cleaned before going back into the room if you choose to go that route. However, I am not telling you that you have to remove everything, but please move things around enough so you can be thoroughly efficient. I promise the end result will be worth the extra effort.

Whichever room you start with, do the closets first. Have some large garbage bags or boxes within reach because you'll need them for discarding and throwing away some of your stuff. **Yes, now I'm going to ask you to throw out the things that you don't use.** This is not a command. But consider it a strong suggestion. What does this have to do with psychic self-defense? Well, when there is too much clutter and no semblance of order, there is an automatic block in the flow of energy. And ultimately the house's energy becomes stagnant. Whenever I hear a person say that their mess is "organized," I can't help but think that's a lazy excuse. The simple truth of the matter is people learn to cope and manage within their mess, but it's not the healthiest use of their space. We can live more productive lives and feel happier in our environments once we have a better flow of energy. This is a very effective exercise in trimming the energy fat in your battle of the *negativity bulge,* and it can help you shed unnecessary pounds in your physical space, whether it is the kitchen, bedroom, garage, or office. Think about this exercise as an energy diet for your residence. Like dieting and exercise, if you don't follow your trainer's advice, you'll achieve only a small amount of success, if any at all. So stop your complaining and hit those closets. Once you are done, you will feel like your space is so much lighter to live in. Remember that this technique can also be used in your office at work.

Once your space is cleared out of all the unused and unnecessary clutter, you will find that you are able to be more efficient, which can potentially increase your productivity. The most difficult task is throwing away parts of you in your stuff. For one reason or another, you kept it, whatever it may be. But now it's time for you to let it go. The days of closing the door to the junk room or the junk drawer need to come to an end.

So after you are done sorting and cleaning, what did you actually achieve? Well, first, everything is now clean. And the items that you decided to keep are organized and have been put in their own "sacred place," which simply means that everything should be put in its proper place. Tables, desks, furniture, and floors should be clear of clutter. Clothes folded and stacked in the chest of drawers or hung neatly in the closet. Shoes stashed out of sight or right by the door. The loose photos that are found in drawers can be organized into albums or scanned onto your computer. The books can be sorted and reorganized on their shelves, and all the knickknacks and extra papers can be put in their special places or filed away. You get the idea. The things that you no longer want but that are still in good condition can be boxed up for a local charity. It always feels good to help those in need, and it helps you out at the same time.

All old newspapers, magazines, unused gadgets, cards, and the rest of the clutter that you collected should be immediately thrown out. All the possessions that you are left with should be things that you use, that you need, or that have a financial or sentimental value. If you are looking at something and saying to yourself that you will figure out what to do with it someday, you are probably done with it now. Toss it either into the garbage or into the charity box; someone else might need the object more than you do. I know I am repeating myself, but too much clutter leads to blocking the flow of energy. Truly, less is more.

Now, the reason why it is so important for you to be so hands-on with this experience and not hire someone else to do the work is that you will mentally be able to see that you are creating a clean and clear atmosphere. It will leave a strong impression on your subconscious and perhaps force you to think twice before filling up the place again with more stuff. After the physical cleaning, you can work on the psychic self-defense aspect. Think about it. First you bathe and then you select the perfume or cologne to wear.

Once the house is clean and clear on the inside, you can then visualize the sprinkled salt all around the outside of the house, forming a wall of white light. Imagine it growing high into the sky and down deep into the earth. **Know that this wall of protection**

is so positively charged that it keeps in the love and positive energy and pulls out and magnetizes the negatives from the environment within.

For the next part of the cleansing, make sure to get a deep ashtray to burn the sage in, so you won't have ashes falling on your freshly cleaned space. Shortly after doing this exercise, you may want to burn a scented candle or incense, depending on whether you like the lingering smell of the sage or not. After you gather the ashtray and the sage, you will need to make the salt solution for the spray bottle. Mix three tablespoons of sea salt with water to fill your bottle. Okay, ready? Here we go.

Carry the tools with you to the lowest part of your home. You'll begin working there to cleanse from the bottom part of the house to the top, basement to attic. If you live in an apartment, only do the area that you live in. The hallway is also an option if you so choose, but I would check with your neighbors and landlord first, as the smell of the sage is strong and you may also unintentionally set off smoke detectors! It might not be a smart idea unless you get approval from everyone who would be affected. Spray the salt mist and saturate the air in each corner of the room, while paying very close attention to all windows, doorways, and archways throughout. You don't want to make the walls or floors wet; you are focusing on the energetic field around them, so use the sea salt mister more like an air freshener. Then you should light the sage. And then gently, and I mean gently, blow on it to make embers. Keep it smoking throughout the entire exercise, but take care that the embers stay in the ashtray. Force the smoke that the sage creates into all corners of the room by using your hand or a feather to draw it up and out. Focus on all the doors and windows; make sure the smoke reaches all of them. If there is a window or door to the outside in the room, open it a bit. This gives a wall of protection an opportunity to pull out the negativity that you are breaking up. If there is no window or door to the outside, just leave the entrance open so that you can "see" the energy leaving. Watch it move up to the first level and go out an open window. You may want to designate one window or door for the exit of energy for the entire house. While you are performing the task of smudging, repeat the following either out loud or in your mind:

"I break up and release all negative and stagnant energy in this place. May peace, light, and divine love protect us and be ever present."

You should repeat the statement continuously. Every room, corner, wall, and floor should hear this statement. *"I break up and release all negative and stagnant energy in this place. May peace, light, and divine love protect us and be ever present."*

Remember that the way you program your aura is to imprint your own positive pattern of energy upon it. You are creating a more peaceful atmosphere in which to live and work. Do this for each room in the house. Allow your intuition to also guide you. Be open to the experience and follow your instincts. If you feel one room needs a more thorough clearing or cleansing, spend more time working in it. I would suggest doing this clearing practice on a regular basis for rooms that have a lot of activity, such as the kitchen, living room, and your office, especially if it is to be used for doing energy or therapy work.

HOUSE CLEANSING RECAP:

- Cleanse and protect the outside of your home by sprinkling the perimeter with sea salt.

- Clean your house and throw out all clutter.

- Pay extra attention to closets and spaces that hide clutter.

- Reorganize what remains.

- Create a special, "sacred place" for all the things in your life.

- Cleanse the inside of your house by spraying sea salt solution everywhere.

- Purify and protect the entire place by smudging with sage affirmations and prayers to assist you in your smudging.

- Visualize a wall of white light protection blocking out negativity and keeping positivity in.

This will leave you with a lighter and more peaceful area to live and work in. Once you have successfully accomplished your house cleanse, take a shower immediately and perform the energy shower exercise of protection. After your shower you have completely finished the cleansing and protection process. Congratulations! The first time you do this ritual it will most likely be difficult and time-consuming, but it will get easier and require less effort when you do it regularly.

Sitting Water Exercise

The next method of psychic self-defense is a quick fix to any area. This simple exercise is great for an office or one room in the home. Place a large glass of water or a large open bowl of water somewhere in that space. Just let it stay there. Maybe it will sit on a desk, a conference table, or a coffee table. The water attracts the negativity of that space, which can be seen in the form of bubbles forming in the glass. This exercise is probably one of the most interesting experiments to watch. On evenings when I'm seeing clients, I leave the water on my desk. I have found that on nights when I have encountered a lot of negativity, there are a greater number of bubbles created in the glass. It is really fascinating and amazing to observe the change. At the end of the day, you must flush the water down the toilet. Under no circumstances should this water be consumed by any living organism—no person, pet, or plant.

> **Don't forget:** Another source of psychic self-defense vital for your protection is prayer. The power of prayer is significant. Please use it with all defense exercises.

White Light Traveling Exercise

Statistics tell us that one of the most dangerous modes of transportation is the vehicle that most of us use every day: a car. Fortunately, we have airbags and seatbelts, and we are taught defensive-driving techniques. Whether you are the driver or a passenger or are concerned about someone in a vehicle that you are not in, use the white light energy.

Paint a bright, white light all around the vehicle. If it is difficult to visualize this image, come up with something that makes it easier. Maybe you can imagine the white light coming from the sun and that light will surround the car. Or maybe there's a big white light bubble that you can visualize around the car. Once you are able to see the light around the vehicle, repeat: *"I encircle the vehicle in the white light of God's love and divine protection. All those traveling within it are safe and protected."*

This could be adapted and used for all types of transportation. I use the white light method and say a number of prayers when I first settle into my seat on a plane: *"I encircle this plane in the white light of God's love and divine protection. Nothing negative will affect the pilot, passengers, or the plane. We will take off, fly, and land with an uneventful safe flight."*

Deflecting Mirror Exercise

Another psychic self-defense technique is called the "mirror exercise." Mirrors are a source of reflecting not only an image, but also energy. They are another way of keeping unhealthy energy away from you. If you know that you are going to be around someone who is launching a negative attack or in a situation where you want to ensure your own energy protection, you can visualize mirrors all around you facing out to deflect the energy back to the sender and to keep it from reaching you.

SUMMARY

I hope that the techniques I have given you prove effective and valuable in your everyday life. They are only a few of the psychic self-defense exercises that are available for you to utilize. The most important thing is for you to use them! Remember, these are methods that I practice regularly and find very helpful in both my personal and professional life. If these particular exercises do not resonate for you, you can learn about many more in books and on the Internet.

11

PSYCHIC TOOLS
in the WORKPLACE

The Oracle Needs to Pick You.

When you are first developing your abilities, the natural course of action is to learn how to harness and control them. Once that process is achieved and a regular practice of meditation and prayer is established, the next step usually involves trying to utilize your skills in some way. My goal, as you know by now, is not to teach you to do readings professionally, but to help you apply your intuitive skills in your daily life, make smart choices and decisions, and evolve into the best possible YOU. Now if doing professional readings is a personal goal for you, then it's necessary for me to remind you once again about the important ethics you must always adhere to when doing this work. I just want to reiterate that you assume a *huge responsibility* the moment you decide to do a reading for anyone. In fact, even as you embark on developing your abilities or begin to do any type of psychic work, you need to remain always mindful of your intent, humble in your attitude, and pure of heart.

I asked a question in the beginning of the book, and now I bring it up again. *Why are you interested in developing your psychic abilities?* In my opinion, the answer to that question should be at least one of the following:

- I am having or have had a series of experiences that is forcing me to explore the source of my psychic abilities at this point in my life.

- I am feeling that I want to better understand and control my abilities in order to be a more complete person.

- I have suffered some personal losses over the years and I need to know that there is more to this world than just the physical body.

- I feel and *know* that I am meant to use my abilities to help others.

I personally believe that everyone who is seriously considering working on psychic development should feel a little of all four of these responses to some degree, even if the person is not intentionally thinking of ever attempting to do a reading. However, if you are planning to do sessions or contemplating becoming a professional, the ethical responsibility of wanting to help others *must* be the driving force. Otherwise I would question your motives. Helping others should always be considered the primary goal; otherwise, don't do the work. Period.

After you've spent considerable effort on understanding motivations, doing personal programming, studying metaphysical philosophies, and developing your abilities for a while, give yourself the opportunity to explore some methods for divining information. These divination tools, or *oracles,* act like keys to the Universe and to your subconscious. I don't want to give you a set formula and state that you should study tarot, numerology, and astrology in that order or that you need to learn all the methods that I mention and ignore the ones I don't. What I really want you to do is to begin to open up to the possibilities and then just let the process happen. Actually, I really feel like **the divination tool needs to pick you.** First, ask your Guides for assistance and you will *know* soon enough which subject you should study. Go online and do some research and see which psychic tool calls out to you, or go to a New Age bookstore and let the right book grab your attention to the point that you can't put it back on the shelf. You may find several tools fascinating but usually there is one that tends to stand out from the rest, and that one is *yours.* As you grow in your development, you may wish to learn about others and you will be able to integrate each one of them into your work.

I have already covered the science of astrology in an earlier chapter (see Chapter 4) so I did not include it below, but I want to stress that I think it is a valuable tool for self-understanding and growth as well as a very useful tool when working with clients. Many astrologers don't consider themselves "psychic," but in their reading of the charts they end up giving out some pretty amazing information that isn't found in the standard interpretations alone. On the other hand, many psychics will start with an astrological chart as a jumping-off point and see things that have very little to do with the planetary placements at all. I strongly believe that a rudimentary understanding of astrology will benefit you both personally and professionally. I also think it is beneficial for people to consult a reputable professional astrologer at least once in their lifetime to get a true understanding of their natal chart and how the cosmic forces affect them personally. It can be a life-changing experience and well worth the time and expense.

The rest of this chapter introduces some of the psychic tools that you may choose to learn more about in the future. I just want to mention a few of them to you, providing enough explanation to pique your interest and perhaps point you in the right direction. Please know that there are many tools (forms of divination), and I have selectively chosen the ones below for my own teaching purposes. It is imperative that you find the right tools that resonate with *your* personal development so that you can use them to enhance your intuitive skills.

NUMEROLOGY

The basic foundation of numerology is the study of numbers, their vibrational frequencies, and the corresponding meanings. It is by learning the meanings of the numbers' vibrations and how those meanings are interpreted that helps the numerologist understand your personal composition and makeup. Numerology provides insights into a client's personality characteristics, explains life lessons to be learned in this lifetime, and illuminates the present spiritual path he or she is currently working on. This ancient method of divination may also be prophetic when used to unlock your abilities. You may use some of its elementary aspects to glance at a person's life and energy or delve more *deeply* by doing charts as well.

Everything dealing with numerology has to do with numbers and the cosmic vibrations attached to each one. There are several different numerology systems, but the two I studied when I began my journey of development were the Chaldean System (also known as Mystic Numerology), which is one of the oldest schools of numerology, and the more popular Pythagorean Method. It's ironic that the sixth-century BCE Greek "Father of Mathematics" would also be considered the "Father of Modern Numerology," considering that most mathematicians of our day would scoff at the use of numerology. But Pythagoras was a master of numbers who also studied the hermetic sciences for many years before he founded his society in Greece. He taught both scientific and metaphysical theories of numbers for almost forty years. One day I believe that all the academics will finally catch on and realize that Pythagoras was right about more than just his mathematical theories . . . there is something important to be gained in learning the cosmic energy of the numbers as well. Some day mathematicians will be writing books on the study of numbers, their vibrations, and how they can be measured for personal growth. That is a personal prediction! My grandchildren will probably be grandparents by that point, but it is an exciting concept to consider, nevertheless.

We will choose the Pythagorean Method for our numerology system since it is the one most commonly used, especially in the Western world. **You will be working with the numbers 1 to 9 so keep in mind that every number larger than 9 is always reduced through addition to a single digit for interpretation.** For example, 13 is 1 + 3 = 4 and 369 is 3 + 6 + 9 = 18 and 1 + 8 = 9. A numerologist will take your birth date and your name as they appear on your birth certificate and calculate your five primary numbers plus your attitude number for a complete reading. From those two basic bits of data, the numerologist can immediately start to understand your personality and unravel some of your life lessons, as well as recognize current issues you may be facing. Numerology can also give you a quick and easy way to get a handle on the synergy you have with someone else, as well as help to predict the future.

Name Number Exercise

The Pythagorean numerological chart below shows you which number a specific letter of the alphabet corresponds to in order to give you the vibration for that letter and the numbers needed to interpret names. To calculate your *Name Number,* also known as your *Expression Number,* you would use the name on your birth certificate. This number reveals your overall personality.

Here's a quick example: **Mary Day would be 4 + 1 + 9 + 7 + 4 + 1 + 7 = 33 and 3 + 3 = 6. Thus, Mary Day's Name Number is 6.**

Now go ahead and try it for yourself. Remember to use the name on your birth certificate and to reduce the number down to a single digit.

Carol Dissauer = 55 = 5 + 5 = 10 = 1 + 0 = 1 (handwritten)

PYTHAGOREAN NUMEROLOGICAL CHART

1	2	3	4	5	6	7	8	9
A	B	C	D	E	F	G	H	I
J	K	L	M	N	O	P	Q	R
S	T	U	V	W	X	Y	Z	

Carol Digman = 49 = 4 + 9 = 13 = 1 + 3 = 4 (handwritten)
Birth Name (handwritten)

Evan Dissauer = 43 = 4 + 3 = 7 (handwritten)

Now let's learn some of the very basic meanings for the numbers.

One

The number ONE is the first number in the series of numbers from one to nine. That means that it represents the first of something or new beginnings. It is the number of "self" and refers to the thinking mind. When you interpret the number one person you may consider the following positive aspects: a pioneer, a planner, independent, proud, self-confident, imaginative, and courageous. The negative traits include: uncompromising, aggressive, selfish, weak, critical, egotistical, and impatient.

Two

The number TWO refers to the duality of issues. It is most identified with the yin and yang and relationships of all sorts. The positive aspects include: a mediator, considerate, balanced, grace, loyal, adaptable, diplomatic, and calm. The negative expressions include: moodiness, a follower, indecisive, lonely, needy, insecure, fussy, and manipulative.

Three

The number THREE is a very expressive and sociable vibration. It is all about creativity, expansion, and growth. On the positive side of the equation: outgoing, funny, optimistic, lucky, entertaining, fertility, and abundance. On the negative end: shyness, scattered, deceitful, superficial, extravagant, and lacking in direction.

Four

The number FOUR has a grounded and cerebral vibration. It represents the foundation of all issues, the earth and the material world. It requires sense, reason, security, and structure. The positive attributes include: trustworthy, systematic, orderly, stability, builder, material success, practical, and down to earth. The negative traits include: impatient, rigid, stubborn, lazy, chaotic, softhearted, and legal difficulties.

Five

The number FIVE defines change. It is like hurricane energy, full of force, and helps to break away from the norm. It is a very active number that needs freedom and room to breathe. It favors communication, transition, and education. Positive expressions include: flexible, fun, romantic, curious, drive, intelligent, adventurous, and loves variety, travel, and escape. The negative attributes include: irresponsible, unstable, bores easily, mischievous, difficulties with authority, risk-taker, demanding, melodramatic, and restless.

Six

The number SIX resonates with an empathetic vibration. Its primary concerns are a sense of responsibility and service to others, relationship issues, and emotions in general. It is tribal, communal, and family-oriented. The positive messages include: love, harmony, peace, home, nurturing, altruistic, magnetic, managers, and compassionate. On the negative side: self-righteous, jealousy, interfering, codependent, and stubborn.

Seven

The number SEVEN is a higher vibration of the number one. It is about working on the self and questioning all things that pertain to it. It is the number of the mystic, prophet, or teacher concerned with spiritual growth. On the positive side: introspective, reflective, intuitive, discovery-oriented, intellectual, and tends to love nature. Negative traits include: deceitful, sarcastic, reclusive, mysterious, superiority, and cynical.

Eight

The number EIGHT is the most karmic number in vibration. It thinks primarily of attaining goals and making progress. It is all about ultimate success, power, and achievement. Positive attributes include: honest, responsible, ambitious, authoritative, successful, energetic, financial and material prosperity, goal-oriented. On the negative side: relentless, headstrong, tense, narrow, power-hungry, emotionally weak, financial problems, and gambling issues.

Nine

The number NINE is the ending of the cycle and it indicates a sense of sacrifice and finality. It brings to an end the issues that have been evolving. It is the number of the humanitarian and a natural leader, forcing us to strive to be our personal best while we are in the physical body and attempting to take us beyond our earthly existence. The positive expressions include: perfectionist, unconditional love, artist, writer, sympathetic, possible material and spiritual prosperity. If negatively expressed: too much love of self, martyr, overachiever, sullen, jack-of-all-trades but master of none, demanding approval, and unspiritual.

PERSONAL YEAR

One of the things about numerology that I personally like to look at (pardon the obvious pun) is called the *Personal Year Number*. It is a yearly vibrational pattern that lasts a year, from birthday to birthday; not the normal calendar year (unless you happened to be born in January). My birth month is October, so my personal year goes from October to October. The Personal Year Number depicts the "energetic setting" for that period of time. The way to derive this number is explained in the following exercise. The reason why I find this number particularly helpful is that it tells you a lot about what your client is dealing with at the moment, and you also can quickly understand the client's recent past and projected line of probability based on this current of energy. It may help you to predict time more accurately during a reading.

When dealing with prophecy and energy, time is somewhat irrelevant. As you know, free will is obviously a factor for the person you are reading. When you are psychically seeing something and you feel like it will transpire soon, that can be two years from now in reality. So if you're in the middle of a session and you sense that there is going to be some substantial life changes happening around the client, but you aren't sure when they will actually occur, *calculate the client's personal year number.* It is also very helpful when projecting people's future because it gives you windows for their opportunities. Think about a personal year number as a room in a house. Each room represents one of the numeric vibrations, but for our purposes, we will call it by the normal name: kitchen, bedroom, bathroom, etc. Each one of those rooms is programmed for a purpose. You cook in the kitchen, bathe in the bathroom, sleep in the bedroom, live in the living room . . . you get the idea. You know that if you were to "see" someone standing in the kitchen, it immediately indicates the potentials of what can happen within the confines of that room. The personal year number works in a similar manner. It may help you to pinpoint timing opportunities more precisely during a session. If you see that there is a **Five** personal year coming up for your client and you know that five is the number of change and transition, then it gives you a good idea as to when a particular event may take place.

Personal Year Number Exercise

So let's find out your Personal Year Number, so that you will be able to eventually help your clients discover theirs. First, write down the month and date of your birth, using numbers, not words. So, for example, if your birthday is March 5, you should write it like this: **3-5.** Since you are only interested in the personal year number right now, you don't need your birth year for this calculation. For the Personal Year Number, you will only be working with the **birth month + the birth date + the last year the birth date occurred in.**

The Universal Year is the current calendar year. Now to figure out your personal year, you must use the year that you had your last birthday in. What makes this sound confusing is that you must think about where your last birthday fell in comparison to the present. It might be in the previous year, not the universal year. The reason this is important is because you are trying to figure out where you are *now.* To explain this concept, we will say that it is currently January of 2010 and your birth date is March 5. Therefore, your last birthday occurred in 2009.

Carol
$7 + 1 + 2 + 0 + 1 + 3 = 14 \quad 1 + 4 = 5$

Write it down as follows: **3 + 5 + 2009.** Add it all across like this:

3 + 5 + 2 + 0 + 0 + 9 = 19

Then you will add the individual numbers in the sum:

1 + 9 = 10

And don't forget to continue to reduce it to one single digit:

1 + 0 = 1

This tells us that you are in a **One personal year from your last birthday until your next.**

One can be interpreted as the year of new beginnings and opportunities for fresh starts, and it's a time to work on independence and individuality.

Because we go in a natural progression, your next vibration will be a two personal year, and then a three, etc. **Now go ahead and calculate your own personal year number following the same formula and then use the basic definitions of the numbers listed on pages 192–94 to interpret what it means for you.**

Evan
$7 + 1 + 3 - 1 - 9 - 8 - 9 = 23 \quad \sim \quad 2 + 3 = 5$

This is how a numerologist starts to peel away the layers of people's personality, their soul's urge, and the lessons they're here to learn. This introduction is just scratching the surface and giving you a glimpse of what you can do with numerology. It is just one of the keys available for your development, and a very handy addition to your psychic toolbox.

By now you know I don't make recommendations lightly, but I honestly don't think there is a better numerologist currently living on this planet than Glynis McCants, famously known as the "Numbers Lady." Glynis really is a modern-day Pythagoras. She is the author of several books on numerology and has made this ancient science her life's work for over twenty years. Learn more about her and the ancient science of numerology at my website **www.InfiniteQuest.com.**

PSYCHOMETRY

Psychometry is one of my personal favorites in my psychic toolbox. The word originates from the Greek translation of "measurement of the soul" and there are two possible types: objective and subjective. In *objective psychometry*, you are able to read the history, origin, and energy of a particular object. In *subjective psychometry*, you hold an object with the intent of picking up the energy of the owner.

In my private practice I use this tool all the time. I will ask to hold onto an object that belongs to my client. I make sure that it is something that only the client wears or uses, as I don't want to be picking up vibrations from another person's life or energy during the session. Unless you are doing objective psychometry, estate jewelry should never be used, or anything borrowed from someone else. **A medium**

should never look at photos or touch the jewelry of a person who is crossed over, since that will interfere with an actual connection to the Other Side. Now some people will argue with me on this point, and it won't be the first time, but it's a nonnegotiable one for me. The bottom line is this: we are all energy and vibrations. Energy is imprinted on photographs and articles of clothing or jewelry that people wore—the energy is still there. The mediums who know their craft need only tune into the actual energy of the person in order to communicate directly with that person, without any props. A psychic who might want to be a medium can accurately tune into the energy and facts of that individual by picking up the energy imprint off the items, but that is not a conversation with the Afterlife; it is a psychic giving you their perspective on a dead person.

Let me make my point this way. If I showed you a photo of my family vacation to Disney World in which we are all standing and smiling in front of Cinderella's Castle, you would be able to discern immediately where I am, what I am wearing, the weather, my mood, who is with me, and so on. But you are not hearing me directly tell you about my trip to Disney World. This is what the psychic who is giving you all kinds of information about your grandfather while holding his watch is doing, which is fine as long as the pyschic isn't claiming to be a medium, talking to the person on the Other Side. Unfortunately, some readers will often mislead their clients in this manner. It is a very common practice that psychics will often fall prey to in their development. Throw in the perceived glamour of being a medium and the Inner Monster's desire for fame, in whatever form the psychic wishes it to manifest—combined with societal expectations—and it becomes a heady mix that exacerbates something already quite complex by itself.

Don't misinterpret my tone—I want you to know how excited I am that you are reading this book and that I have this amazing opportunity to teach and guide you on your spiritual path. As I have said many times before, this work is my passion, and raising the awareness for these messages of empowerment and responsibility while also possibly shaping other potential "spiritual warriors" reading this book ...it is an overwhelmingly positive experience. I only wish that I had this kind of resource available to me in such a detailed and direct way when I was first starting my development. All right, I digressed enough. Back to work!

Using Psychometry Exercise

The very first step before starting psychometry or any other psychic activity is that you must always initiate your psychic self-defense techniques **(SHIELDS UP)** and allow yourself to enter into a meditative state. Then, and only then, take the object and hold it in your left hand. You may also hold it up to your third eye chakra (forehead). Some people feel that they can see the information more clearly by placing it by the third eye; you will quickly learn what works best for you. Close your eyes and allow your body to relax and concentrate on what you are seeing, feeling, and hearing, and remember that the smallest bit of information is important. You are learning to recognize how you interpret symbolism and what things mean to you. Write down all of your perceptions. *Everything counts.*

In general, psychometry is an amazing way to really tune into a person's vibration. **As soon as you hold the object, just allow yourself to be in the moment. Whatever it is that you receive, you should immediately say or write down.**

When you start practicing psychometry, I recommend using large metal objects like watches and bracelets. I have found that clothing is a bit more subtle in feeling for beginners, as are wood and paper items. The heavier metals seem to carry a stronger vibration, and in order to tune in, the louder the better, right? Once you have practiced this for a while, you can try to "read" all sorts of fun things like magazine articles, photos, and letters. You might connect with something that is currently taking place or something that recently happened. Each success will build your confidence and validate your development, and it can also be a starting point for your intuitive ability, coupled with your Team, to give future insights as well. Just practice as often as you possibly can, write everything down, and observe the results. If you feel that this is a tool that works for you, you may utilize this technique to "connect" with someone when beginning any psychic session. Once you have unlocked the door to the client's energy, you can put the article down, as it has done its job, and the energy should continue to flow.

BILLET READING

Billet reading is an extension of psychometry. Often you will see psychics using this method of divination in a group setting, where they will answer questions that are in previously sealed envelopes. My preference is to work with photos instead as it allows the readers to stretch their intuitive skills without any constraints. You need to use photos of people you don't know, and you must not look at them prior to the reading. Place them face down on a table in front of you, or you may want to have them put in sealed envelopes before you touch them. The best way to do it is to have your friends give you snapshots of family members who are alive, preferably photos that show only a single person in the shot.

Take one photo at a time and keep your eyes shut. You can just lightly place your fingers or hands over the back or front of the photo if you like and then try to describe how you feel and what you "see." I love to do this exercise in my workshops as the results can be literally astonishing. Like most of the psychic tools, billet reading takes a bit of practice, but as you develop confidence in your abilities, you will improve at your readings.

Note of Ethical Responsibility: I repeat—it is very important that if you are working as a medium, you never use photos or any articles of people who have crossed over in order to try and connect with them. You may accurately pick up factual information about the individuals, which is a very different experience from actually communicating with them.

TAROT CARDS

Cards are my first preference and "go-to tool," as well as my "first love" where divination is concerned. Any deck of cards will work for me. In fact, I am in the process of designing my own deck, which will combine my knowledge of energy, metaphysics, and the Afterlife with a traditional tarot design and appeal.

When I first started working with cards in my teens, I was taught by an aunt how to do readings with a Spanish deck of playing cards. Then I experimented with Italian, German, and Chinese cards, as well as a regular deck of playing cards. In fact, the deck of cards we all use for games is believed to have derived from the tarot. I finally learned how to use a traditional tarot deck once I began my studies with my teacher, Sandy, at the age of fifteen. The tarot is one of the best tools in my opinion for developing your skills and opening up to your intuition.

First things first: it is pronounced *ta-roe* or *tar-oh;* please don't rhyme it with *carrot.*

The tarot is probably the most effective tool to use because almost all of the decks have illustrated cards that help the reader to tell a story. There are so many different styles and types of decks available now that you will easily find one that fits your personal tastes and *feels* right to you. The history and origins of the tarot are greatly debated, but there are definite links to the ancient religions and philosophies of the Hebrews, Egyptians, and Greeks. In fact, there are many myths and legends surrounding the tarot that add to its mystery and beauty. The first decks depicted in European museums date back to the fourteenth century, with Italy, France, Spain, Germany, Switzerland, and England all playing a unique role in creating decks and spreading the use of the cards. However, it is clear that the Gypsies or Romany are the ones who made fortune-telling with the cards wildly popular as they traveled through Europe and along the Mediterranean shores, but the cards also undeservedly developed a negative reputation by association because of anti-Romany prejudice and discrimination.

In essence, tarot cards are archetypes of the human experience that, when combined with your intuition, help to unfold ancient wisdom in a modern world. When utilized in a card layout (spread), these mystic cards begin to illuminate what is happening in the client's life and can depict what some of the current lines of probabilities are for the person's future. All the cards have detailed illustrations that, when read in a chosen spread, tell a complex story that the reader interprets to the client sitting across the table.

If you are serious about using tarot cards, I recommend that you first purchase a set of cards known as the *Rider-Waite* deck, which is the most widely recognized of all the decks. Almost all the books that are written for studying tarot use the *Rider-Waite* for their interpretations so it will be easiest to first learn with these cards before picking up another deck. The seventy-eight cards of the tarot consist of two sections: the Major Arcana and the Minor Arcana. The *Major Arcana*, meaning "big secrets," contain twenty-two cards of life, and the *Minor Arcana*, meaning "smaller secrets," make up the other fifty-six cards in the deck. The Major Arcana represent in archetypal symbols a human's journey through life and often refer to the workings of fate. The Minor Arcana are divided into four suits, just like our regular playing deck: the wands, cups, swords, and pentacles. Each one represents one of the four elements: fire, water, air, and earth. Each suit has an ace, a set of numbered cards from two to ten, and four court cards (Page, Knight, Queen, King). The direct relationship between them is as follows:

THE WANDS: THE ELEMENT FIRE (CLUBS)

THE CUPS: THE ELEMENT WATER (HEARTS)

THE SWORDS: THE ELEMENT AIR (SPADES)

THE PENTACLES: THE ELEMENT EARTH (DIAMONDS)

A tarot deck should be kept in a special place that can absorb the energy of its owner. I also recommend that it be kept in some type of natural container, like a silk scarf or cotton cloth bag, or wooden box. When you first acquire a new deck, it is suggested that you sleep with it under your pillow for a few nights. This is not so you have restless nights of sleep, but to allow the cards to pick up your energetic vibrations. It is also a good idea to handle the cards as much as possible by just shuffling them over and over . . . but not like you are about to deal out seven-card stud; just riffle them together. This will not only get your energetic imprint all over the deck, but also ensures that you are mixing the cards really well. It's important that the cards feel comfortable in your hands and are not stiff, so even if you are just sitting and watching television, go ahead and shuffle the cards for a bit.

When you are doing a reading with your tarot cards, have the sitter—also known as the *querent*—shuffle the cards while concentrating on their own energy. Some readers don't like to have the querent even touch their cards, as they want to be the only person handling the deck. I personally prefer to have my clients do the shuffling so that their energy is reflected in the readings. There are many card spreads that you can use for readings, and you should practice working with a few different layouts to get a feel for the cards and to discover which ones resonate with your development. One of the most popular spreads is the ancient *Celtic Cross* layout, which originates from Ireland and traditionally consists of ten cards. It is written about in just about every tarot book, and you will see most tarot readers using some sort of variation of it when they give a general reading. I have used it for so many years that over time it has morphed into my own personal version, which may read very differently from a tarot study guide but is what works best for me. You will also personalize your reading methods as you grow in your development. However, it is always wise to start with the basics—which you learn either from a teacher or by studying on your own—and practice a layout until it becomes familiar; then you can gradually modify it to fit your style of reading.

Here is an example of what I do for a tarot card reading, which is loosely based on the Celtic Cross spread, but uses eleven cards for the basic layout as follows:

1. The Querent/ also known as the "Significator"
2. Now/ what is currently going on
3. Future/ the next three months
4. Foundation/ basis of the situation
5. Future/ six to nine months
6. Distant Future/ next couple of years
7. Immediate Past
8. Home/ environment
9. Immediate Future/ next two weeks to four weeks
10. Hopes and Fears
11. Final Outcome

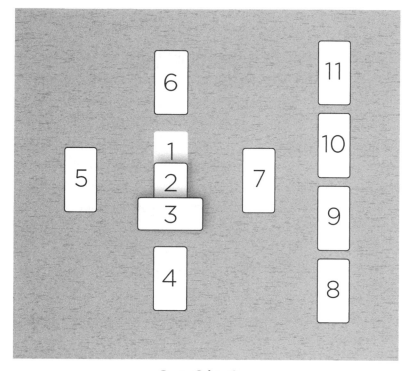

Basic Celtic Cross

After reading the first set of cards, I add another layer of cards over them to continue to develop the story, and often times add a third layer to answer questions or to flush out more meaning. Again, keep in mind that this is a variation of a theme that works for me personally. It is not so much linear as intuitive, since I let my Guides tell the story through the cards. When you are first beginning to practice tarot, you should start with the basic spread as it is taught to you and learn the cards and their meanings first; the rest will follow in due time.

When doing any type of layout, if the cards are placed right side up **(character head at top)** they have one meaning, while if they are placed reversed or upside down **(character's head at bottom)** then the meaning is usually either the opposite or lessened to a certain degree. Simple yes or no answers can also be obtained when using the cards, and some spreads can be as little as one, two, or three cards. Don't be intimidated by the symbology; just like everything else in regard to your development, the more you practice, the more comfortable and confident you will become in your abilities.

A PRIMARY TOOL

The tarot cards are my personal recommendation for people who are serious about developing their abilities or doing readings. The tarot is a visual method that helps to awaken your intuition gently, but with precision. It enables you to quickly unlock the energies of your client. The illustrations on the cards help you to zero in on details that you might not initially be able to get on your own.

Tarot is not a divination method one learns overnight. You must take the time and effort to study all the meanings of the cards, both upright and reversed. My method of teaching the cards is slightly different from what you will read about in most books on tarot. Whenever I speak of symbolism in my lectures, I always introduce the concept of *"frame of reference."* For example, I will ask ten people to tell me the first thing that comes to mind when I say *apple*. I usually get eight, nine, and sometimes ten different responses out of that group of ten! Now with the tarot, we are talking about seventy-eight illustrated cards with amazing details on each one . . . imagine the number of frames of reference possible! For the tarot to work as one of your psychic tools, you need to make sure that you know what each card means to *you*, not just what everyone else tells you it means.

Create Your Own Tarot Book Exercise

There are a few things you will need before you can begin studying tarot with this exercise. Purchase a large composition notebook or a loose-leaf three-ring binder in which you can insert two hundred blank pages of paper. Buy **three** decks of the *Rider-Waite Tarot.*

One you will use for actual readings, and the other two will be for study purposes. I recommend purchasing the larger-size card version of the *Rider-Waite* to use for your two study decks.

On each page of the notebook you will tape in a card from your two study decks, one card per page. Use the first page of the notebook to personalize your book, either with a picture, an affirmation, or just your reasons for learning tarot. Then tape in the first card from one deck on the left-hand page in an upright position, and on the right-hand page the exact same card from the second deck should be taped upside down (reversed). For example, tape in the Magician card upright on the left side and tape in the second Magician card reversed on the right side. Do the cards in the order they came in from the box (0 to 21, The Fool to The World), without shuffling them, so that the Major Arcana cards (trumps) are done before the Minor Arcana cards. After you tape in each card, write underneath it what you feel that card is telling you. **Write your own meanings.** Don't struggle; gaze at the picture and just write your impressions and ideas about the card's message, leaving space for later notes. And do this for all 156 meanings. Yes, 156. Remember there are 78 cards. You must do this for each card, both upright and reversed, which is why you need two decks to create your book. Make sure to save room for adding further notes later on or a way to add pages for each card. The reason why this exercise is so important is that the cards have to speak to you while you are doing a reading. Each card will elicit a feeling or thought or suggest a situation that will combine with your client's energy and your Team to tell the story. You have to learn how to trust this intuitive process and understand that it takes time and perseverance to truly learn tarot.

After you have created your personal "Tarot Book of Meanings," I want you to look through the many books written about tarot either online or at your local New Age bookstore. There are hundreds of them, but don't let that overwhelm you. As always, the books that will resonate with you will jump out at you. I am a fan of the tarot books written by Eden Gray, who is considered the "Godmother of the Modern American Tarot Renaissance." But as I have mentioned before, Sandy Anastasi has been my only true teacher. Sandy's book, *Tarot Reader's Workbook: A Comprehensive Guide from Beginner to Master*, is a must-have addition to your library if you feel drawn to working with the tarot. One of my favorite development stages was studying "Basic Tarot" with Sandy every Saturday morning when I was fifteen. Week after week new worlds of understanding were opening up for me, and in so many ways *this book* that you are reading now is inspired by her teachings twenty-five years ago.

When you are studying books about tarot, take the time to write in your tarot notebook the various authors' interpretations of each card right below your personal description of each card . . . yes, each card. This will be your one-of-a-kind textbook for learning the tarot. Please leave room for your list of meanings to grow, because I promise you they will, and not just from reading more books on tarot. When you begin doing readings, you will look at a card one day and launch into a story that you have never spoken of before. When that happens, you should record that new meaning in your notebook as soon as possible. Your "Tarot Book of Meanings" will be an invaluable and irreplaceable tool for understanding how tarot works for you and your Guides.

When you use the cards to do a reading, the cards will be influenced not only by what you're seeing from them, but in relation to the other cards that are surrounding them. Some cards can intensify another card's meaning, while others can minimize it. But every time that you look at a layout, you should always be able to see something different. And as your skills develop, you will feel more confident in your readings, knowing that the cards are unlocking your intuition in a very special way.

As a metaphysician, I am not allowed to tell you exactly what path to follow or what tool you have to use for your development; therefore I can only strongly suggest certain methods and share my personal insights and experiences. So I am "strongly suggesting" and encouraging you to embrace the tarot as one of your primary keys for universal awakening. Like astrology, its comprehensive and didactic approach to our human experience is revelatory.

SCRYING

The next oracle of divination I want to share with you is called *scrying*. It is more familiarly known as gazing into a crystal ball. It comes from the word *descry*, which means to "catch sight of" and "to discover by careful observation or scrutiny." Scrying is an ancient practice that is found in cultures across the world. Ancient Greeks and Celts practiced scrying using beryl, black glass, polished quartz, water, and other transparent or light-catching objects. Nostradamus is believed to have employed a small bowl of water as a scrying tool into which he gazed and received images of future events. The bottom line here is that scrying is all about focusing. When you sit down to look into the crystal ball you're not tuning into the supreme satellite dish network of the universe; you're giving your conscious mind something to work with so that your unconscious mind can act as a slide. It slips the information into the forefront of your mind and you acknowledge it.

Here's the cool part: you don't need to run out and buy a crystal ball—get a glass of water and stare at it. Scrying stimulates your own psychic ability. But you must remember that you will need to interpret what it is that you are seeing in your own frame of reference. Other objects you can use for scrying are a large puddle, a pond, a pool, shiny surfaces, metal, and unpolished quartz crystal. There are some who believe the art of scrying is not limited to the use of reflective or translucent substances only, but includes other media, such as smoke, clouds, olive oil, and tea leaves. Scrying has been used as a means of viewing the past, present, or future by letting the reader "see" relevant events or images within the chosen medium. It's always a treat going out to a restaurant with my friend Char Margolis, because when the water is delivered there are free readings for everyone at the table!

DOWSING

Dowsing is a divination method that is utilized most commonly to locate water or oil in the ground. It is known as the "art of finding hidden things" and is thought to date back at least eight thousand years. The person who is doing the dowsing, known as the dowser, usually works with a dowsing stick, a divining rod, or a pendulum. Dowsing is based on the theory that all things, living and inanimate, possess an energy force or magnetic power. The dowser concentrates on the hidden item and attempts to psychically tune into its vibration, and the magnetic connection in turn forces the dowsing rod to move in the item's direction. The dowsing tool may act something like an antenna for tuning into the energy of the buried object. Currently, dowsing is used to find water for wells, mineral deposits, oil, buried treasure, archaeological artifacts—even missing people. Albert Einstein was fascinated with dowsing. He believed that it was likely a phenomenon related to electromagnetic energy. Just as birds somehow migrate by following the earth's magnetic field, dowsers react to energies that are unseen and still not fully understood. How the dowsing technique was first discovered is unknown, yet those who practice it are unwavering in their affirmations that it does work.

I CHING

The *I Ching* or Book of Changes is an ancient Chinese book of spiritual wisdom consisting of sixty-four main hexagrams and their permutations, which one consults after tossing either yarrow stalks or coins to obtain answers and information. Envisioning the children's game of pick-up sticks is an easy way to picture how it works. The I Ching is one of the oldest forms of divination and is the most popular oracle in Asia, based on its uncanny ability to provide detailed spiritual insights. This method of reading how the sticks or coins land in their arrangement can give you a universal message attached to what is going on around you now or what is coming up in the future. It can be used as a divination tool or just as a source of inspiration. When you understand how the principles work, even plain pocket change can be used to read the I Ching.

RUNE CASTING

The last tool I want to introduce is the *Runes*, which are often associated with Viking culture and mythology. They originated as an ancient Germanic alphabet used for writing, divination, and magic. Norse mythology tells how Odin hung from the world tree for nine days and gathered up the runes when they appeared below him. Runes may be made from stones, clay, or wood and they have glyphs etched or painted on them. Some practitioners like to create their own set of runes; however, they are readily available for purchase in New Age bookstores and online, so it is quite easy to find a set that resonates with you without doing the work of making your own. Runes are often sold in "kits" that include a book for interpretation, or you may choose to buy your stones separately and find a book that will teach you their meanings and how to use them in different spreads. The twenty-four runes (twenty-five if you use a set with a blank rune) are placed in a rune-casting bag. There are many ways to do a rune reading, and when starting out it is always good to try out a few different ways to see what works best for you. One method is to shake the runes up in the bag and then cast all of them out on a cloth and read only the ones that fall face up. Some rune kits come with a special cloth which you can cast the runes on, and the placement of the runes enables the rune reader to interpret their order and significance. You can also just have the sitter ask a few questions and dip into the bag to pull out a few runes and read their interpretation. Truly there are countless variations of how to read the runes, similar to how you can read tarot cards. It is important to find what feeds your intuition and then that is the right method for you. Rune readings are sometimes obscure. They hint toward answers, but you have to figure out the details. This is when the rune caster's intuition becomes paramount. Keeping a rune journal can be very useful for you and your clients. Runes can be used for meditation purposes as well as for readings since they are not meant to predict the future but to give you possible outcomes to consider.

ONE LAST NOTE

A number of years ago, I lectured at a psychic seminar in New York, and Sandra, my girlfriend (now my wife), accompanied me to the event. While I was speaking, she was outside in the lobby browsing through all the pretty crystals, books, tapes, and other metaphysical items for sale. As we were preparing to leave after my lecture, Sandra told me she had bought some "magic wands." Not one, mind you, but many. I teasingly replied with a hint of sarcasm, *"Of course you did."* Then she pulled out her can of magic wands, which were nothing more than fluorescent painted tongue depressors that one can purchase at any health and surgical supply. They were decorated with little wizards and all sorts of magical symbols and words. The instructions for their use said that you should ask a question, shake the can of wands, pull out a few, and read them to receive your answer. Although I laughed at first, I realized that the wands, like any other type of oracle, were just a tool. The point is that when you assign a meaning to an object, whether it be a rune, coin, card, spoon, or, in Sandra's case, a tongue depressor, it acts as a psychic key to unlock the deeper understanding of your life or the life of the person you are reading. Trust your Guides to help you discover the right tool for you, learn how to use it with responsibility, reverence, and humility, and then let the magic begin.

12

WHY AM I
Doing This Again?

DISCOVERING how to be centered and balanced in your
daily life is the key to achieving your spiritual goals.

Guess what we get to do now? We are going to build on everything that we have discussed so far, and as is done in the scientific method, we will replicate and extend the data. At this point in our spiritual sojourn, I will find it necessary to occasionally digress and rant, but my intentions are ultimately about instructing you on how to live up to your highest potential. As I mentioned earlier in the book, I always prefer to first teach the philosophy and theory of intuitive development before launching into application and practice. When my friend and student Jonathan Louis started out on his spiritual path, his goal wasn't to learn how to do professional readings at all. Instead, his desire was to gain self-awareness and personal growth, as well as to become more in tune with the energies of his family. After many years of studying and training, the unexpected result was that Jonathan has grown into one very talented psychic medium. His development mirrored my own in that his personal journey led to his life's work. Once he began doing readings, it was obvious that he had found his professional calling. When something works, why reinvent the wheel?

Even though developing your intuitive skills might not lead you to a new vocation as a psychic reader, it can still most definitely impact your life in a dramatically positive way. Here within the pages of this book I have striven to give you the same format of learning that I gave to Jonathan over the years we worked together. In keeping with my promise to teach you in a similar way, we are now at the point where we should discuss meditation and the chakras. I also want to reexamine the motivations that brought you thus far in the book, as well as the problems that you are likely to encounter if you are not practicing ethical responsibility and humility while walking on your spiritual path. It is crucial for you to understand how important it is to be grounded in a solid foundation of daily meditation and prayer work so that you can avoid the common troubles that would otherwise hinder your development and stunt your growth. It is imperative for you to take the necessary time to practice meditation until it feels like second nature and can be done easily wherever you are and whenever you need it. You cannot expect to do readings without training your mind first, just like if you want to run a race you need to learn how to breathe while jogging and the mechanics of stretching so that you do not injure yourself along the way. You cannot master your spiritual potential without making a true commitment and then following through with the work, or you could bump into trouble around every corner.

MEDITATION

Meditation is enormously important to the process of your psychic development and evolution. It is an essential tool to assist you in creating a life that is *centered and balanced.* Discovering how to be centered and balanced in your daily life is the key to achieving your spiritual goals. Being centered and balanced simply means being in tune with the Universe and God (Higher Power). It is a peaceful and quiet feeling of being settled in your soul, otherwise known as *atonement*—in its definition as a sense of restoring harmony. It helps to understand what atonement means if you break down the word to read as "at-ONE-ment." Atonement enables you to be more aware and in tune with the world of energy all around you. If you become more present in the moment, you are able to look for the opportunities and the magic right in front of you.

I am going to ask you what some people consider a scary question: *Are you happy by yourself?* The goal is to be able to say *"Yes!"* to this question. Unfortunately, many people look externally for answers that are only truly available within themselves. Frequently my clients think that if only that relationship, job, or event would happen for them, then they would find happiness. Honestly, that is like saying if you had a couch you can have a house. The couch may provide additional comfort or pleasure, but the house can exist quite fine without it. *You are that house.* You need to make sure the house has a strong foundation spiritually, energetically, physically, and so on, before you worry about furnishing it. Now back to meditation.

Practicing daily meditation can help you release stress and negativity on a conscious as well as an unconscious level. It relaxes the physical body and teaches the mind to focus for a specific period of time. When you can focus, then it is much easier to visualize—which is the basis for creating your own reality. The foundation for any type of serious psychic or spiritual work is being able to work with energy through meditation and visualization. So there really is no getting around it. If you want to become centered and balanced on your spiritual path, you will need to do some form of meditation. But before you start shaking your head, thinking that you can't meditate or that you've tried and it doesn't work for you, keep in mind that there are many ways to do it and that all it really consists of is a *state of mental relaxation.* The goal is to achieve a level of stillness and peace, similar to a daydream or a prayer. Often, when many people think of meditation, all these different kinds of associations come to mind: strange chanting, flowing robes, shaved heads, New Age music, and so on. But if you haven't noticed by now, I am the least "woo-woo" person you are going to deal with when talking about meditation—or anything metaphysical, for that matter. I sincerely appreciate the many various forms of meditation practiced by others, but most of us don't have the time or patience to devote to sitting in the lotus position for an hour twice a day to achieve this spiritual "oneness" with themselves and the Universe. For average people to be able to practice meditation in an already overly busy life, they have to find a way to fit it into a daily routine, and I know firsthand that if it is not easy to do, people won't do it. You must make a commitment to learn how to meditate and attempt to make it a regular practice. You need to develop patience, strengthen your skills, and experiment with different methods. Ultimately, the right form of meditating is discovered by trial and error, and you as the student must find the method that works best for you.

LOCATION, LOCATION, LOCATION

Okay, so you're willing to give meditation a try. Good. But where should you attempt to do this? The ideal goal is to build up energy in one specific space and location. If you have a room in your house where nobody is going to bother you, then make that your meditation spot. But if you share your house with others and you are not going to be able to shut out the rest of the world at the same time every day, then meditate in the bathroom. YES, the bathroom. It is often the only room in the house that people program for privacy in their lives. Grab a pillow or a blanket, lock the door, and claim the bathroom floor as your meditation space.

Candle Meditation Exercise

Go to the location that you have chosen as your meditation space and sit in a comfortable position. Start by lighting a white candle and staring at it. I recommend a white candle because it represents purity and the white light of protection. Say your White Light Prayer of Protection and just focus on the flame of the candle. Pay close attention to your breathing and try to create a rhythm. Breathe in for a count of four to six seconds, hold for two seconds, and then exhale for four to six seconds. Inhale through the nose and release through the mouth. You can meditate for one minute or ten minutes; it's up to you. Simple and easy. You can do this every day, if possible even twice a day. No rules here . . . just make the time to do it daily, preferably at the same time every day. The cool part about doing this type of meditation is that you can personalize it by adding your own affirmations to the protection prayer and by visualizing your current goals while you stare into the flame. You will be able to build upon this technique as you grow in your development. When you are finished, take one last deep breath, blow out the candle, and thank your Guides for their presence in your life. After practicing this simple exercise for a couple of weeks, you might be surprised at the subtle difference it makes in your life.

An important note on affirmations: Please don't superimpose your will onto anyone else. I like to add into all my affirmations *"If it is in the best interest of all those concerned."* This simple phrase makes it clear that I am not practicing any energy work that would be manipulative or considered "dark" in nature. Remember, I told you the Force was real and always needs to be treated with enormous karmic respect!

CHAKRAS

The human body consists of many centers of spiraling circles of energy, and these energy vortexes are known as the *chakras*. The word *chakra* comes from the ancient Indian language of Sanskrit and translates as "wheel." It is thought that the chakra concept developed thousands of years ago in India within the traditions of yogic Hindu philosophy and the holistic medical practice of Ayurveda. Chakras are the major centers of spiritual power in the human body, circles of energy that balance, store, and distribute the energies of life all through our physical body and along the etheric body. The etheric body (aura) is our nonphysical body or spirit, which overlays our physical body. There are seven primary or main chakra points, with about a hundred smaller, secondary chakras called *meridians*. Each primary chakra relates strongly to a specific part of the body, as well as specific emotional, mental, and spiritual concerns.

The seven main chakra points are linked together in a central column that begins at the base of the spine and goes up to the crown of the head. When we open these chakras and align them properly, we allow our vital life force energy—also referred to as *prana* (in Sanskrit) or *chi* (in Chinese)—to flow freely through our body. The energy then spirals upward through each of our centers. This ascending and spiraling is referred to as "raising our *kundalini* energy." *Kundalini* loosely translates into "coiled" in Sanskrit, and during meditation or yoga, kundalini energy is often visualized as a coiled serpent rising up through the spine. The healthy flow of our chakras is integral to our work with physical, emotional, mental, and spiritual energies. The chakras are the core of an energy network that affects every aspect of the individual.

Let me explain this in another way. A car needs gas for fuel, right? The body needs food for fuel as well. But the electromagnetic part of our physical body, our central nervous system, is wired with this chi or prana. If we make sure that all of our energetic circuits are operating, the machine works better. Think about a computer and how we get frustrated with it because it is not downloading fast enough or doesn't power up quickly. In our attempts to improve the speed, we clear our temporary files and cookies from our cache, or we defrag the system if it seems sluggish . . . all in the hopes of making it work more efficiently. Our energetic self is very similar in its energetic makeup to a computer. Every so often we need to clear it out and reboot; working with our chakras helps us to keep the hard drive of our soul operating at its peak potential.

The main goal in learning to work with these vortexes of energy is to foster integration of all aspects of our life to create a more holistic human being. The elements in our physiological system work with each other—our spiritual network should complement them also. When we actively start understanding the chakras and really begin working to open them up, we are taking all of the aspects of our being and aligning them in a harmonious state.

The chakras are the gateway for our spiritual selves to manifest through our physical reality. Our thought processes unfold into the body, mind, and soul connection. When we live in an emotional state that creates disharmony, disappointment, and dissatisfaction with ourselves, the potential is for this negativity to then overflow and manifest into disease. Ayurvedic medicine utilizes herbs, massage, yoga, meditation, and food to balance and heal our prana in the belief that physical illness can often be caused through a nonphysical reality. Therefore, the opposite theory would be true also. Maintaining a healthy mind and spirit helps to maintain a healthy physical body. It is refreshing to see that the Western health-care industry is now waking up to this mind-body-spirit concept. A patient's care should not solely consist of treating the physical body; it should encompass an integrated approach to help heal the whole person.

When I first started working with chakras, I envisioned inventing a chakra meditation apparatus. Basically, imagine a surge protector, but instead of outlets, it would have seven colored light bulbs that correlate to the chakra colors. I would then be able to sit in a dark room and turn on the color of the chakra bulb that I wanted to focus on and literally would be surrounded by that color. Unfortunately, I never actually got around to creating it. However, when I launched my website, www.InfiniteQuest.com, it was the first thing I asked the programmers to design. We came up with a wonderful easy way to practice chakra meditation that provides music written specifically for each center along with the corresponding color to use for visualization. If you are just beginning to work with your chakras, this online meditation would be great for you to try. One of my favorite chakra meditation videos is Shirley MacLaine's *Inner Workout*, released in 1989. Shirley takes you on a relaxing journey through the seven chakras, and the video has remained so popular that she recently released a DVD version titled *Inner Power: A Journey Within*, available at www.shirleymaclaine.com.

THE SEVEN CHAKRAS

I want to give you a brief overview of each of the chakras so that you can start practicing some of the meditation exercises right away. Obviously, if you are interested in learning more about working with chakra energy, there are many fantastic books and tapes to help you explore the subject further.

First, start by imagining an outline of the human body. Nothing fancy, just a simple outline.

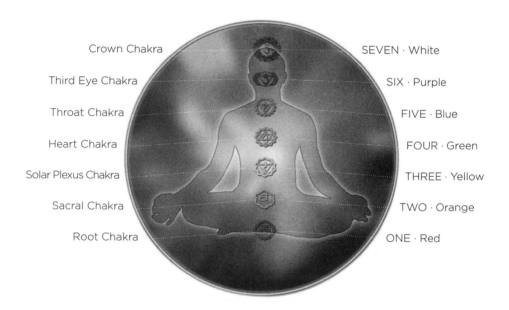

Crown Chakra — SEVEN · White

Third Eye Chakra — SIX · Purple

Throat Chakra — FIVE · Blue

Heart Chakra — FOUR · Green

Solar Plexus Chakra — THREE · Yellow

Sacral Chakra — TWO · Orange

Root Chakra — ONE · Red

THE FIRST CHAKRA is the base or *root chakra*. It is located at the base of the spine. It's identified with the color **red** and the element of fire. The first chakra is the foundation of the physical body and assists in keeping us grounded to the earth. It helps us with the flow of our life force energy into the physical body. It is also associated with the survival instinct and self-preservation. It is known to affect the kidneys, adrenals, legs, bones, spinal column, and colon.

THE SECOND CHAKRA is the sacral plexus or *sacral chakra.* It is located in the lower abdomen to the navel area. It is identified with the color **orange** and the element of water. It is referred to as the instinct zone and is connected with the fight-or-flight scenario. It influences our sexuality and sensuality and how we assimilate and process food; it is the source of creativity and inspiration. It is known to affect the sexual organs, spleen, liver, kidneys, and bladder.

THE THIRD CHAKRA is the *solar plexus chakra.* It is located below the chest and above the navel area at the base of the rib cage. It's identified with the color **yellow** and the element of fire. The third chakra is referred to as the personal power center. It works with aiding digestion, metabolism, and our nervous system. This is where we feel that gut instinct and sense the butterflies in our stomach when we are nervous. It is here that we work with understanding our willpower, self-control, anger, and how we deal with authority in our lives. It is known to affect the pancreas, nervous system, gallbladder, muscles, liver, stomach, and adrenals.

THE FOURTH CHAKRA is the *heart chakra.* It is located in the center of the chest. It's identified with the color **green,** but I also like to add a swirl of bright pink as a personal preference. Pink roses have always been a symbol that I have seen to represent love. So when I meditate on the heart chakra (love energy), I like to drop that color into the traditional green. The heart chakra is associated with the element of air. It is also referred to as the heart and emotion center. It influences the intuitive faculty of clairsentience, or clear sensing. It helps us to get in touch with nature and connects us to the plant world. It deals with the different aspects of love in our lives, giving, receiving, losing, and acquiring. It helps us to balance our emotions and works with acceptance of these issues in our lives. It is known to affect the heart, thoracic area, lungs, immune system, and circulation.

THE FIFTH CHAKRA is the *throat chakra.* It is located at the base of the neck in the throat. It's identified with the color **blue,** the element of earth, and is referred to as the communication center. It works with all types of communications and vibrations. The fifth chakra deals with issues of self-expression both in writing and speech, truthfulness, self-belief, dreaming, and out-of-body experiences. It is associated with the intuitive faculties of clairaudience, or clear hearing, and clairambience, the ability to pick up information through taste. It is known to affect the thyroid gland and other glands of the throat and mouth, teeth, and the immune system. It occasionally affects the ears and upper respiratory system as well.

THE SIXTH CHAKRA is known as the brow or *third eye chakra.* It is located in the center of the forehead between the eyebrows. It's most often identified with the color indigo, which is a very dark blue. However, I am going to suggest that you visualize it as **purple.** Please note that if you have studied the chakras before reading this book, you already know that some of them have secondary colors. I choose to create more of a contrast between the sixth and seventh chakra to aid in the visualization process and make the meditation as uncomplicated as possible. This is what works for me; neither color is wrong. If you are already very comfortable using a particular system of connecting with the chakras, by all means there is no need to change it. On the other hand, you might like to try my method and see how it feels for you. Sometimes a subtle shift can make a big difference.

The sixth chakra is referred to as the psychic center and is associated with the element of water. Many cultures depict the third eye as a triangle in the forehead with an eye in the middle. It works with aiding vision in different aspects of our lives, while it influences our dreams, imagination, intuition, concentration, and wisdom. Our perception perimeters are created here and it helps us to define fantasy from reality. It impacts the intuitive faculties of clairvoyance, or clear seeing, as well as clairalience, the ability to receive impressions through smell. It affects our upper glands, central nervous system, brain, and the mid-facial region, including our eyes, nose, and ears.

THE SEVENTH CHAKRA is the last chakra, and it is known as the *crown chakra*. It is located at the top of the head. It's commonly identified with the color purple, but I prefer to visualize **white** to create a stronger contrast in the colors of the chakras, and because white symbolizes divinity and purity. The seventh chakra is referred to as the spiritual center and is associated with the element of fire. It is where we can create our link to our Spirit Guides, our Higher Self, and God, to become one with the Universe. It works with all issues pertaining to our spirit and how it blends with our earthly personality. It physically affects the head, the pituitary and pineal glands, and all parts of the brain.

CHAKRA MEDITATIONS

I have been sitting here staring at my computer screen now for about fifteen minutes trying to figure out a way to explain how to do a chakra meditation in a book. I have just surrendered to the reality that I can't go about it in the way that I have normally taught it for decades, since I have always done it verbally either in classes, tapes, or videos. So with the limitations of the printed page in mind, I am going to give you a couple of analogies to help you visualize a chakra meditation that I can't talk you through by words alone. I am counting on you to stretch your imagination and give these visualizations a serious effort. I need you to feel as if the colors of the chakras are not just all around you, but actually permeating every cell of your being while you're meditating and breathing throughout each exercise.

Visualizing Your Chakras Exercises

Here are a couple of techniques to help you to quit thinking about the chakras and start experiencing them instead. The first one involves stretching your imagination and thinking of gemstones like large-sized caves of color. Close your eyes, take three deep breaths, and imagine yourself stepping into giant, vividly colored gemstones. What would your world look like if you were standing inside a gemstone that matches the color of each individual chakra? Spend time lingering inside each one, focusing on the color and vibration, while breathing its essence in with all of your being. Bask in the light of each gemstone and let it fill you with a sense of peace before moving onto the next one. Make sure you proceed in the order of the chakras: First, a magnificent **Red Ruby;** second, a bright **Orange Mandarin Garnet;** third, a light-catching **Yellow Topaz;** fourth, a sparkling **Green Emerald;** fifth, a beautiful **Blue Sapphire;** sixth, a soothing **Purple Amethyst;** and finally, seventh, an incredibly brilliant **White Diamond.** Surround yourself with each color and soak up the feeling of each one before ending the meditation by encircling yourself with white light. Take a moment to journal about what you experienced while visiting each gemstone and how you felt once you finished the visualization.

Here is another helpful meditation exercise you can use for working with your chakras. Imagine that you are stepping into a glass elevator that takes you up seven beautiful floors. As the doors of the elevator shut and you turn around to push the up button, you feel the warmth of the rays of the sun shining through the walls and watch how they illuminate each level with the corresponding chakra color. As you begin to ascend, you look up through the glass ceiling and see a cylinder of colors; each color has its level and swirls and spins into the next color. The first floor correlates to the first chakra and the color **red.** Let yourself breathe in the color red and focus on the spiritual journey you are taking. Once you feel the color permeating throughout your being, take another deep breath and notice that as the elevator moves upward you are now floating through the second color, **orange.** Take a moment to experience orange to the point that you feel like you are the color orange. Look down through the glass bottom of the elevator and see where you started and how the colors spin and merge. Then gaze up again to see where you are heading and watch how all the levels of colors twirl and dance. Let your eyes follow the swirl of colors as you travel to the next floor where **yellow** begins to surround you. Soak in the brightness and lightness of yellow. Keep breathing and feel a sense of joy as you take this incredible ride through the colors. Continue this meditation by experiencing each intensely beautiful color of the remaining chakras: **green, blue, purple,** and then finally ending at the top with **white.** As you ascend, try to become one with each color while you pass through it. Once the elevator stops, linger for a moment to notice all the colors spiraling upward, below you, and all around you, before stepping out onto the last level, the white floor. You are finally at the top and are now able to connect with God and your Higher Self! Breathe in this white light and let it wash over you, shining completely through you. Take as much time as you need to feel a true sense of peace. Then make sure to surround yourself with white light before heading back into the elevator and floating peacefully down to consciousness to end your meditation. Don't forget to jot down in your journal any feelings you felt during and after the exercise.

Practice both of these visualizations a few times so that you can discover which one works the best for you. As you can probably guess, there are many ways of meditating on chakras. After you are capable of doing these two exercises without much effort, be creative and experiment with your own version so that you find the way of working with your chakras that resonates the most with

you. And as with any type of meditation, the best advice I can give you is to practice, practice, practice! I promise you that the rewards will follow.

If you find that you are having difficulty visualizing one of the chakras, you must immediately try to figure out what energetic blockage in your life might be causing this difficulty, and attempt to clear it. For example, if you are having a problem with communication in any sort of way, you might have a blockage in the throat chakra and you won't be able to see the color of blue. It might appear murky or gray, or you might not even feel any color at all. Pay close attention to what happens during your chakra meditations as you could receive valuable clues on where you need to spend time taking care of yourself, either physically or energetically.

ETERNAL STUDENT OF THE UNIVERSE

One of the amazing things about developing your psychic abilities and spiritual empowerment in general is that everything is so interconnected. Once you start studying and listening to your Guides, you will become more and more aware of all the various facets of metaphysics and how the learning feels never-ending—and it should feel that way! *If you ever get to a place where you think you know everything, you have failed.* You should always be a student of the Universe and its processes throughout this incarnation and the ones to follow. If you stop asking questions, there may be a bigger problem at hand. But keep a close watch on your ego and please just accept the fact that **there will always be someone who knows more and is better at your job than you.** The benefit of that statement allows you the luxury of never getting sedentary in your learning. I love to talk with colleagues about their perspectives and teachings and to continue to read new books that are published on metaphysics and psychic work. If you can understand that you are only competing with yourself on being the best YOU possible and not against anyone else, you will be able to force the Inner Monster into respectful submission, where it belongs.

Of course, I have to take this opportunity to remind you once again of the importance of psychic self-defense. Every meditation you do should always include achieving protection as a goal. NEVER ever attempt to do any energy work without first protecting yourself. Do not become lazy about it because it's not worth the potentially negative consequences. Start your day with a protection prayer and make sure to continue self-defense throughout the day so it becomes a constant good habit.

READING THIS BOOK DOESN'T QUALIFY YOU TO BE A PSYCHIC

We are all psychic beings by nature of our birth. As I have said previously, just because you are intuitive, it doesn't mean you should do readings. You might have the ability to draw, but it certainly doesn't qualify you to be an architect. I use that analogy because you can understand the futility of building a structure that is not designed properly—it will collapse. People who watch professional race car driving on television and then get into their cars and speed out on the roads can do irreparable harm to themselves and others. Hopefully, the police catch them before they do. The difference is that in my line of work there are no cops to protect the average person from falling prey. So that is why I am being so blatantly direct with my feelings about the concept of professional ethics. I will not apologize for repeating this statement over and over again like a broken record. The responsibility I feel toward my work is immensely heavy and I only want to inspire and educate everyone with information that raises the planetary vibration as a whole; I'm not writing this book to elevate individuals' egos and their sense of self-importance. Confidence in your abilities is one thing; thinking you are better than someone else and acting without humility is an entirely different story that damages the credibility of the entire psychic profession.

Just last week during a small group event in Long Island, I encountered a woman who fell prey to a "professional psychic medium." This so-called medium told her that her dad was "Earthbound" and that was why the psychic wasn't able to make the connection with him. I wanted to scream right in that moment! I am so tired of dealing with the false information and emotional manipulation that people are experiencing at the hands of the Inner Monsters of "professionals" or even just their lack of ability, knowledge, and ethics. The Better Business Bureau would investigate a car mechanic who kept selling faulty car parts to customers, but no one is there to stop a "psychic" from taking someone's money and then hurting them emotionally with untrue information.

Fortunately, I was able to rectify the situation for this particular woman by bringing her father through and showing her that he was okay on the Other Side. I used the woman's experience as a teaching tool for the entire group. I explained to everyone that night about the absolute need for ethical responsibility in a medium and how to discern if mediums are giving you false information or letting their ego run the show. The woman responded to my rant by saying, *"You should hear what she said about you."* That statement alone is vile; why would that psychic feel the need to attack my work? It would be one thing if I walked around telling people how I am 100 percent accurate or that I am the best psychic on the planet—*then* it would be a viable attack. But by reading this book alone, you should know that I am a proponent for the work of mediums and psychics but not for John Edward. Otherwise, I would discuss my work only and not be bringing light to other practitioners, nor would I have started an online metaphysical network that celebrates over fifty contributors who help raise spiritual awareness.

The reason why I want to address this issue again and again is simple. There are people who will be doing this work and their personal motivations will not be anywhere near where I want yours to be. If you fall victim to this type of Inner Monster energy in the future, it's nobody else's fault but your own because now you have been informed in no uncertain terms that it's out there and that you should avoid it.

Stay away from people who claim they are coming from the right place when they are not. It reminds me of the final book in C.S. Lewis's *Chronicles of Narnia* series, *The Last Battle,* when the donkey dresses up as the lion Aslan so that he can fool those who will listen. When I asked the woman in Long Island if this particular psychic teaches classes and had advised her to attend, she responded with a surprised, *"Why, yes."*

"Shocker. Of course she did," I sarcastically replied and shook my head.

> **When someone tells you that you are "psychic"** and you should enroll in her class, RUN. But if someone says that you are psychic and, without any self-promotion, gently points you in the direction of how you can learn more about developing your abilities, ask if THAT person teaches a class. Do you understand the difference? It may seem subtle, but it's not.

Later on that same night when I was reading other members of the group, I heard the name Martha clairaudiently for someone else in the room. The same lady piped up again and said, *"That same psychic told me that I was MARTHA in a past life."*

"Right . . . something else she couldn't validate and you can't disprove" was my response. Time to move on.

UGLY EGO

If not guided properly, the psychic ability of an attention-seeking person can fall into a place that is energetically unattractive, lacking grace and humility. People can become harnessed by the braces of their own desire to utilize their intuition for personal gain, even if it is quite amazing in its potential. I call this the Ugly Ego standpoint. If psychics honor the work and the processes involved, they as individuals would also be validated in the process. But when they are trying to say *"Look at me!"* in any way, they have failed themselves and the work, and if they are doing readings, they are most definitely failing their clients. It is that ego-driven bullet of energy that creates perpetual negativity for all those it encounters.

For centuries, mediumship and psychic work in general have carried a backroom, gypsy fortune-teller, carnival-like vibe that has often attracted people who are looking to take advantage of those who are vulnerable and seeking guidance. Thankfully, over the past thirty years this work is becoming more mainstream and the prevailing attitudes are changing because people are starting to take it more seriously, partly due to the study of quantum physics. People are finally catching on to the validity of the work of ethical and professional psychics and also the concepts of how energy works. However, the subject matter will always attract people who are looking for something else to help define them. Many people wear this world of energy like a child walking in her mom's shoes. That is why it is so important that we have the shoes made for you, by you. You can't *act* like you are psychic or living a psychic lifestyle; you have to be it for real, sincere and straight from the heart. You can be no one else but you and can use only the abilities you have at your disposal. If you are not born a medium, you are not a medium. If you are just starting out developing your intuition, you are not ready to give readings. It's really no different than an actor on television playing a doctor; he can't perform actual surgery. He would need all the training a real doctor needs before even looking at his first patient. Remember, the same holds true with psychics. There are no shortcuts to becoming one, no matter what anyone else tries to tell you.

I have witnessed so many talented people, ranging from novice to professional, who allowed their ego to get in the way of what they are doing in regard to this work, and I have seen firsthand the negative consequences of their actions and choices. That is why I refer to it here as Ugly Ego. At some point the Universe will set up a reality-check moment, something akin to a pie in the face energetically, and it's not pretty. My colleague Suzane Northrop calls it a "rug-pulling party," and I refer to it as being "slammed." Nobody is exempt from their own karmic bullets, and throwing a pity party only makes it worse. The sad part is when people don't take responsibility for their actions and play the victim instead, further perpetuating the same negativity. **Don't ever forget—whatever you send out energetically will find its way back to you.**

THE HUMBLING

I always say that I have a healthy respect and reverence for my Guides and a slight fear of them as well, and I recommend that you should feel the same way about your Team. When I tell you that they are not messing around, I mean it. My Guides don't care what I might personally want to happen; I am just a pawn on this chessboard of life for them to utilize to teach their message of love and empowerment. I consciously agreed to this arrangement and "the boys" are going to hold me to it. If I were to continually get in the way of their goals of raising spiritual awareness, they would stop working with me and move on to another "pawn" who would be more willing to cooperate. If my personal desires can develop as a by-product of what

I am doing, then it is a bonus. But if my ideas go against the process of what's right for the work, a "slamming" will happen. The slamming would continue to be a theme until my Guides decided that I was not listening any longer and they would move on. Don't get me wrong; I would still have Guides working with me—we all do—but not the higher-evolved ones who have been assigned to me for doing this particular work of mediumship and teaching.

My Guides have been training me with this humbling energy since I was a boy. I can remember many moments in my youth when I started to show off in some manner and the outcome was always embarrassing to me. Whether I was busting out a dance move at a family party and ended up breaking a mirror, or doing tricks when roller-skating or riding my bicycle with my friends, the negative result of showing off (ego at large) was embarrassingly painful to me and sometimes even involved some physical injury as well.

At my school's eighth grade talent show, I was featured as the headliner playing the first movement of Beethoven's "Moonlight Sonata," and I felt exceptionally full of myself. The auditorium was so hot and packed with attendees that they had to open the doors in the back of the house. This created a lovely wind that right in the middle of my performance invisibly turned the pages of my sheet music. I watched page by page turn and close in front of me, and all I remember hearing was my mother gasp in the front row. Lucky for me, I had the music somewhat memorized and knew how to cut it short so only another musician would have known what I did.

I think the greatest humbling I ever received was when I was about twenty years old. I had already been working as a medium professionally for about five years and I was on my way to a mall with a friend. He was driving and I was complaining that I didn't really ever have the normal teen life that most kids had; while they were partying, I was doing séances. I was just venting to a friend and letting off some steam, saying stuff like I wish my abilities would just go away sometimes. That night I had a group of eleven people coming to see me to connect with the Other Side. I gave my normal introduction, but when the information should have started to come through, I wasn't able to receive anything. Nothing. After sitting there for about fifteen minutes, with nervous sweat dripping down my back, I asked my Guides, *"What is going on here?"*

They immediately played back for me the conversation that I had with my friend earlier that day as if they had been riding in the back seat of the car. They made me feel like I didn't appreciate the abilities that were bestowed upon me nor the responsibility toward the people who came to see me. As soon as I humbled myself and acknowledged learning the lesson they taught me, the information started flowing and the group event continued without a hitch. The lesson was learned and imprinted in my brain. I recognized it was my job to pass on the information to help and heal the people whom the Universe was putting in my path. It was not me, John Edward, who was doing the reading; I am just the vessel and instrument being used. I got the message loud and clear that night and never forgot it since.

The point is that I remember all of this vividly to this day. This energy carried forward into my psychic work as well, where my Guides have humbled me to their processes and made me realize that I can't look at my work as being about *me* the person. I am just the messenger. Please understand that I am not preaching; instead I am sharing the pitfalls that are lurking both personally and professionally, to prevent you from needlessly plunging into them.

THE DARK SIDE

Honestly, I really hate having to discuss the concept of *the dark side* in this book, or at any other time for that matter. For many years I consciously didn't focus any of my attention or energy toward it, as I felt it unnecessary to give it any power by feeding into it in any way, shape, or form. When people would ask me questions about negative energies or entities on the Other Side, I would acknowledge their existence but not go into any detailed explanations. However, I would be failing you as an earthly guide if I did not warn you about them on your journey. I discussed this topic briefly in Chapter 9, but I think it's worth taking it a bit further now that you have more of an understanding of how psychic self-defense works.

I don't want to call them "evil spirits" because that term conjures up some ridiculous horror movie depictions. Please think of them as what they really are . . . tricksters or gremlin-like energies. I don't want you to have to sleep with the lights on for the rest of your life in fear of possession; instead, my goal is to raise your awareness of their existence and motivations so that you sleep with your psychic self-defense alarm on. Always remember that **awareness leads to action.**

The true credit for forcing me to address these energies at a deeper level goes to my good friend, Char Margolis. She heard me gloss over the topic of negative spirits one night when I was a guest on *Larry King Live.* Again, it's not that I was blind to their existence; I just didn't want to energetically feed into the fear by talking about them, nor did I want to create a freak-out on an international TV show. I acknowledged their presence, but said I didn't want give them any power. And as a general rule, I still don't.

The bottom line is that there are positive and negative energies in the world on both sides of the veil. But I am still to this day more fearful of the negatives in the physical world than on the Other Side. When was the last time you saw a spirit shoot someone? It was people who flew planes into the World Trade Center, not spirits.

That being said, it was Char who drove this message home relentlessly, pushing me to review and revisit situations that were happening around me. Simultaneously, my teacher, Sandy Anastasi, sent me an e-mail that had nothing directly to do with me; instead, it was an e-mail exchange between her and her assistant about negative energies. When I told her that she had accidentally sent me an e-mail that was not meant for me, she replied that she had sent it on purpose because her Guides said that I needed to read it. Here's what she wrote in that e-mail:

> The currency of the physical world is money and that is what we utilize to live, but the currency of the Other Side is energy. The bad guys or lower-level entities like to prey and feed off of our energy and keep the light from evolving. They don't want the level of the planet's vibration to evolve because *they* won't be able to control it if it does. They act like tricksters who can prey on our fears and that can generate energy for them. We have to have a healthy sense of suspicion about life's situations, and raise our awareness to their existence so that we can block out their presence consciously. The hard part is that the negative spirits will always attempt to use those who are closest to us as they are our weakest links and make us vulnerable because of our love for them. It can be our mother, father, spouse, child, or best friend. You have to be aware that the dark side exists within the realm of energy we all live in.

This message is a powerful one and is worthy of reading a second time just so it sinks in. Keep in mind that it was part of a personal dialogue between Sandy and someone involved in working with the Other Side, and she sent it to me clearly because I needed to read it at the time. I am sharing it with you because I want you to understand that you don't walk out into the middle of a battlefield with a deck of tarot cards and an astrological chart to solve the world's problems with your intuition. You can't naively walk into a war zone thinking that your newfound abilities will disarm the evil at hand. You need to be aware that people want to pull you into conflict and you can always opt for a different resolution. Be smart; you must protect yourself accordingly or choose not to go into battle at all. Understand? I know it seems as if I just contradicted everything I have written up until now, but I assure you it is just a continuation of the same message. You would not walk through a seedy part of any city at 3 a.m. sporting all your jewelry and a handful of cash—instead, you exercise judgment and assess certain realistic risks in order to maintain physical safety. You must do the exact same thing on an energetic level.

I want you to know that by not protecting yourself properly and by allowing your Inner Monster to take the lead, you will encourage and allow those negative energies to develop a parasitical relationship with your energy, work, and even your personal life. It is the reason I don't advise people to use "witch boards," boards that are sold as games to connect with the spirits. The boards attract lower-level vibratory predators in the same way a pedophile preys on kids on the Internet. You might receive accurate and friendly information at first to pull you in, but then the message shifts to be what the negative entity wants it to be about. It might be to create strife and havoc in order to keep you off balance. Again, I am not discussing this topic to alarm you or give you a scapegoat for every little bad thing that pops up in your life. I mention it because the dark side is a real and viable energetic issue that you will deal with on some level.

So what do you do about it? Just be alert to the fact that the negative world exists, but don't go looking for trouble or feed into the fear of it in any manner. The same way that a doctor checks a patient for certain symptoms to diagnose a condition, you need to be aware of what the symptoms could be when you are under any type of psychic attack. Those symptoms are anything that can put you out of balance and harmony. To be proactive is to be protected. If you fortify your aura to make sure that you can't be affected negatively, and if you are coming from a place of love of self—not fear of the dark side, you will be able to handle whatever comes your way. If you consciously choose love over fear in your actions and your attitude, the negative entities can't win. They won't be able to penetrate your shield of love.

I know that you are wondering why I am putting this material on dark energy here and not in the chapter about psychic self-defense. It's simply because I wanted to do what I said in the first paragraph of this chapter, replicate and extend the information. I didn't throw in the entire "Darth Vader" topic at once because I wanted to give it to you in small bites. I am including it here as one of the downfalls that so many people experience because they allow this negative energy to infiltrate their everyday lives simply because they don't protect themselves. For the metaphysician who does readings, the chance of being infected is taken to a whole other level. Honestly, I would say more on this subject if we were in person and I could read how you are receiving my message. But it is so important to me that you don't get caught up in the fear realm that I am going to stop here. **Don't let fear get in the way of your spiritual journey.** But do remember that, just like any time that you are traveling somewhere unknown, you must be aware and prepared at all times.

Reading this book won't make you psychic. Doing the exercises in this book won't teach you how to talk to the dead or put you on the path to becoming a professional medium. What I can tell you is that the goal of this book is to raise your awareness of the worlds of energy that you have perhaps only perceived up until now and to enable you to go much further in your spiritual journey. Reading this book will give you a deeper understanding of the new realities of this energetic Universe. By choosing to take the "red pill" in your metaphysical endeavors, as Neo did in *The Matrix,* you must become more responsible in your decisions, thoughts, feelings, and energies. You also will become acutely aware of how energy ripples out into the world we live in and has such a critical impact on others. I am trying to teach you the importance of keeping your ego in check while also completely honoring what you feel and not what you fear. I sincerely hope that you learn how to have just enough ego to allow you to trust the magnificence of the Universe you live in while remaining centered and balanced, instead of feeding the Inner Monster. Ultimately, this book's message is to empower you to recognize your universality in connection with a Divine Source and how to reflect it in your development.

There are moments that take place for all of us when we are forced to examine what our potential outcomes might be depending on the choices we make. We assess what is happening and how we are feeling and often we can see only the downside of a situation. Our perspective is intrinsically shaped by our past and helps us to define our present; it also affects our view of the future. It is normal and healthy to weigh all the options and explore every opportunity or potential, both negative and positive. Unfortunately, most people can't get past the negative and perhaps even dwell on it purposefully, afraid that they will set themselves up for future disappointment by thinking about the positive potential. By choosing to act on their fears, people often miss out on having what they so desperately want. It is extremely important to change your programming if you are still hooked on making decisions based on fear. Your spiritual growth depends on trusting your instincts that have love as the primary motivating force. Be a soldier for love and the rest will fall into place.

13

How to Live
with Yourself
& How Others
Can Live with You Too

OUR GOAL is to recognize the world of energy around
us and to be able to make empowered decisions from an
intuitively informed, centered, and balanced point.

In this short chapter, we are moving away from the practical application of development so that I can give you some serious advice regarding your psychic development and how it might affect the people around you. These life-saving tips will stop those nearest and dearest to you from coming into your room in the middle of the night and putting a pillow over your face while you are sleeping. Are you paying attention? Good. Of course, I don't mean to suggest that anyone is going to literally suffocate you, but someone certainly might want to shut you up if you aren't careful about respecting boundaries and understanding limits.

Please remember that your newfound perspective on life is just that—*yours*. This is an extremely important point for you to remember at all times. As you are developing your abilities and experiencing all the aspects of awakening metaphysically, you will become a very excited conduit of information, which is great *for you*. The problem is that you will foolishly believe that people have asked you for your insights and thoughts, when most of the time they have not. Not only is it likely that they didn't ask for your input, but you might unintentionally come across like that self-righteous person who just recently quit smoking and is now expounding the dangers of smoking to everyone, including those who still smoke. Or like those people at the office who are always discussing their own personal opinions based on their religious views or politics. Your intentions may be altruistic, but your enthusiasm about your spiritual growth and what you are learning will literally ignite the principles of fear (and/or loathing) in those around you.

This is dangerous territory, my friends, very dangerous. You probably won't notice the suspicious looks that your family and friends will be giving you, and you might even mistake their questions as genuine interest in the subject matter. But in all likelihood, many of them suspect that you have joined a cult and have drunk the Kool-Aid. I cannot tell you how many conversations I've had over the years with individuals who have developed their abilities or embarked on some type of personal empowerment regime—whether it is spiritual, psychical, or physical—about how those closest to them are the least supportive or the most critical.

You would think that a person who is attempting to make a positive change in their life would be rewarded with praise and love. Of course if you are lucky, you have a few people who are always in your corner, cheering you on in your endeavors and wanting the very best for you. But I want to warn you that if you choose to actively pursue your spiritual development, you had better realize that you have just ordered up a main course of judgment with a side order of criticism.

Why? Initially, your family and friends will say that it is out of concern for you. But I truly believe that masked underneath that "concern" are their own issues of fear about seeing you shift and develop into a more spiritual being who is stretching to reach your highest potential. Your personal growth forces them to look at their own lives and suddenly you become a mirror, reflecting what they are not doing. Essentially, your development makes them feel bad about themselves. Hopefully, there are some who are more centered and balanced and they will definitely be sincerely interested in what you are studying and discovering. But others will be fearful and will attack you or your particular area of empowerment, whether it's a psychic tool (astrology, tarot, numerology, etc.), a particular teacher, the books you read, or the psychic world in general—anything that they don't understand and that they see as the root of your change. They will feel an innate need to tear it down in an attempt to show you how bad it is, or they will mock it and you in the process.

I discussed the idea that you would lose some people along your path of development earlier, in Chapter 9, but I feel that it's important to bring it up again. I am not trying to harp on the negative consequences of your choosing this path of development, but I wouldn't be completely honest if I didn't warn you that it may be a painful experience. I don't want to paint an inaccurate picture for you of nothing but sunshine and roses. You are making a conscious choice to change your life and there will be some fallout in the process. You might find that the people whom you love the most are the ones who disappoint you with their lack of support. Old friends you've known for years might fall to the wayside, and family members may distance themselves. It's common to find yourself feeling very alone and isolated as you develop your new belief system and integrate it into your original programming and religious foundational beliefs.

The best-case scenario is that your family and friends are supportive of your development and want to legitimately learn more about what you are doing because they care about you. I was lucky enough to have that kind of loving support, for the most part, on my mom's side of the family. Many individuals who are on a spiritual path are not as fortunate and have been tortured for years for being different. Stick with your convictions and don't let other people's issues deter you from your growth. This kind of alienation or conflict is another reason why practicing psychic self-defense is so critically important. If you have the type of relationship with your mother in which she can express her disappointment with the raising of an eyebrow or the tone of her voice, her disapproval can stop you in your tracks and make you feel wrong about attempting to be the best You possible. Now, please don't take what I am saying as permission to disregard anyone's feelings and use it as an excuse for being foolish by exaggerating what my true intent is in this message. This is not a license to be reckless in your behavior or do anything that is harmful to others. Remember to always operate from the love principle for yourself and those around you. Love is both your best offensive and defensive approach when it comes to relating to others.

It is essential that you learn through meditation, prayer, and psychic self-defense how to maintain your balance and center yourself from a place of love. You need to recognize how to discern the difference between your organic feelings and the feelings of everyone else around you that you may empathically be experiencing. It's crucial that you can separate the two or you will be overwhelmed by the onslaught of emotions.

Once you are doing this work and the positive changes become more and more evident, the new people you meet will always understand your development, as it will just be another part of who you are. But for those who have known you prior to your decision to embark on this path—whether friends, family, or even partners—sometimes your choice to change becomes the catalyst that ends the relationship or friendship. I know this is hard to read and maybe you don't even want to believe it . . . but I have seen the personal loss happen on a number of occasions and I need you to fully understand the price you might have to pay to become a better, more spiritual version of You.

SHUT THE HELL UP ALREADY

As you start to open up your faculties for receiving Universal energy, it is only natural to want to share everything that you are seeing, hearing, and feeling. It is not that you are intentionally showing off or trying to tell people what to do, but you will just know things and have an internal urge to say them. Learn as well as you can to control this impulse right from the beginning. Sometimes "less is more" is a really good rule to live by.

The people who are closest to you will be the target of your psychic broadcasts because they are the ones you love and focus most of your energy on. Some of them might appreciate your insights, thinking it is kind of cool to have their own "psychic friend," but others might be downright freaked out by what you say. In their defense, it can be quite disconcerting if they feel like you are trying to read their minds all the time. Remember, back in Chapter 3 I told you that it is a universal violation to be a "peeping psychic," looking in where you have not been asked to go. The hard part is when you see something painful or difficult for people you care about and you really want to help them through it or even avoid it altogether. *This was a lesson that took me years to learn.* You have to allow people to live their own lives; you must not interfere with their choices. You might think you are helping them by giving them your unsolicited advice, but you might not be in the long run. There is a subtle difference between sharing your impressions versus telling others exactly what is going to happen in their lives or preventing them from using their own free will to experience their life lessons.

Now I know I told you in Chapter 7 that you should share your psychic impressions with people and I am not contradicting that advice. I think it is important for you to pass on any information that you receive for someone, whether it is positive or negative. But I also told you to be extremely responsible in your approach by explaining that you are discovering how to use your abilities and that you could be wrong in your interpretation. You are only a vessel for your Guides and you must be humbly aware of your role at all times. It's how you deliver the message that is so critical, especially when you are new at this work. There's no need to scare anyone or to exaggerate the meaning of the impression. Useful advice such as *"It would be smart to take your car into the shop now to get your brakes checked"* is more acceptable than saying *"You will be in a car accident next week."* You are striving to be helpful, not trying to incite fear. However, it is one thing to share your intuitive message; it's another thing to preach or break into a personal narrative or counseling session. You can't take one image and turn it into an entire scenario without being very certain of what you are doing. There are very fine ethical lines that should not be crossed. You are not a psychologist and can't pretend to be one just because you have an energetic hit about someone's future. As you journal about your intuitive information, make sure you take time to review your motivations for sharing what you have received.

Is it for the good of the other person or is it about you and your newfound "powers"? First and foremost, you have to make sure that your Inner Monster is in check and you aren't just looking to have the *"I knew it"* and *"I told you so"* moments. That is obnoxious. If a person is going through a hard time, the last thing they want to hear is you gloating that you knew it all along. When someone you love needs emotional support, it's better to be a good friend than a psychic at that moment.

The ultimate goal of doing this work is to bring people to a positive place in their lives. Your insights are to help them learn and evolve. **You must never tell people what to do ... EVER!** You would then be taking on the karma for their experiences, and such an act is never ethically responsible, not to mention that it is something that you truly do not want to do for your own sake. If you are not a doctor you should not be diagnosing, as you could cause more harm than good. Now if by chance you are a physician, then your newly developed intuition will only aid and assist you in your practice ... and how lucky your patients would be to have you as their doctor!

The tricky part is learning the timing of when to say something and when to keep your mouth shut. Remember, we are all here on Earth as students of the Universe to learn important lessons in this incarnation and those around you are not exempt from that work. If you interfere with someone's "studies," they will more than likely have to redo the work in some other way because they spiritually need to learn that particular lesson before they can move on to the next one. Now, if your friend asks you why something keeps happening over and over again and you assist them with your insights, that is a totally acceptable way to give guidance and support. If they continue to do the same action or repeat the same pattern, then it is your call as to whether you want to keep repeating the same information or leave it for them to figure out. Sometimes we have to learn the hard way or we never master the lesson at all. There's a fine line between enabling and supporting, and it is up to you not to cross it.

REPEATING MESSAGES

This is a simple tip, but one worth remembering. Pay close attention to the number of times you are receiving the same intuitive information and then repeating the same message over and over again. Your Team will assist you in sensing the flow of information and how frequently it comes through as well the way it is delivered to you, but you can help this process by journaling. This is another reason why keeping a daily journal is so crucial, as you will be able to recognize the patterns more quickly. For example, if you are telling your sister repetitively that the guy she is dating is going to get a ticket for drunk driving and she is ignoring your warning or laughing at you "playing psychic," don't let self-doubt creep in. If you keep seeing the same vision or getting the same impression over and over again, more than likely, it will take place. The repetition of the same information coming through is usually an indication that the situation is imminent. By continuing to share your message, you can at least attempt to assist her in making the right choices. Hopefully, at some point your sister will listen to you long enough to take preventive measures and speak with her boyfriend about the consequences of drinking and driving.

The thing to understand about psychic impressions is that if something negative is coming through from your Guides, the only reason why you would be receiving the message is to help to prevent the negative event from happening or to assist someone in dealing with it and the consequences in the best way possible. It certainly won't be told to you by your Team so that you can have the *"I knew it!"* moment. As time passes, when those around you are able to objectively see that your messages are accurate more often than not, you will earn their respect and trust when you share your impressions in the future. But they must come to that belief of their own accord, not because you forced them into acknowledging it. No matter what the circumstances are, no one really likes to hear *"I told you so!"* even if you did. **Don't forget that you are just the instrument, not the music.** Keep the ego in check and others will appreciate your humility as well as your insights.

PAYING ATTENTION, NOT PRAYING FOR ATTENTION

Once again I am going to address the "Inner Monster," which will rear its ugly head whenever it gets the chance. Think of it as a hunger of sorts. It is a real craving and you must systematically choose how you react to it every single time. You can give in and have a moment of immediate gratification, only to suffer the consequences soon afterward, or you can demonstrate some conscious self-restraint and make a choice that you can be happy about for a lot longer. Just be aware that your goal is to pay attention to the Universe in order to live the best life you can live. You can be responsible only for driving your car; you cannot be responsible for driving anyone else's.

When the hunger pangs of the Inner Monster kick in, people who are developing their abilities will sometimes convince themselves that they are paying attention to their Team, but they are really trying to create opportunities for attention instead. It is one thing to receive a message from the Universe; it is another thing altogether to try to force something so that you can be "right." Once again it is always important to isolate and understand your true motivation when you are doing this work. Are you seeking attention from those around you? Stop and check yourself if that is the case. Fame, money, glory, validation . . . none of these are ethical goals for furthering your psychic development. Are you hearing how hard I am hitting this point? I don't call it *spiritual development* for no reason. Think of your psychic ability as the water department that is channeling all the water to the community. You need that water to be "protected and pure." If it is contaminated in any way whatsoever, there are dangers to the well-being of those who come into contact with the water. Your energy needs to be pure and to originate from the source of love, not fear or ego, for it to be healthy for those around you to experience. It's that simple and that serious.

Yes . . . We Know You're Psychic

No, I'm not going to berate you about the ego monster here. Instead, I'm going to try to stop you from attacking your family and friends for not listening to you when you are trying to communicate information to them. Without a proven track record of accuracy, they might not take what you are feeling or seeing seriously. It is extremely frustrating when you sense something that is occurring or that's going to happen in the future and you can't get others to recognize it. I assure you if they don't pay attention now, the next time they will be more inclined to listen when they realize that you were right. Have patience with your development *and* with how others respond to it.

LETTING PEOPLE TAKE CHANCES AND MAKE EMPOWERED CHOICES

If this book had a mission statement, "take chances and make empowered choices" would come pretty close to it. **Our goal is to recognize the world of energy around us and to be able to make empowered decisions from an intuitively informed, centered, and balanced point.** If you are doing readings for other people, your task is the same: *to help them, not to decide for them.* If you are doing your job correctly, you will be taking your clients on a tour of the current state of affairs in their life, and with your insights, they should feel positive and confident about their choices and decisions. Many people who seek out a reading will be coming from a fear-based motivational standpoint and will try their hardest to get you to tell them what to do. You must tread very carefully in those situations, which are similar to getting conned by someone in rehab for substance abuse when they ask you to buy drugs or alcohol for them. They don't want to have to make the decision, because then they are responsible for how it turns out. If you choose for them, then you are culpable, and they can place the blame on you if things don't work out the way they want. Instead, **it is your ultimate responsibility to inspire others to use their free will and manifest their own realities.**

The loved ones on the Other Side will come through with information that deals with all aspects of the client's life. If the client is in a negative relationship, they might address factual issues concerning it, but won't give such extreme advice as telling her to get a divorce or quit her job. This holds true for all other matters as well. That choice is up to the individual to make, not the medium, not her loved ones, not the Universe, or even her Guides. It would be unethical for you as a psychic to infer otherwise; you cannot tell a client what to do, only give her insight and support.

And just for the record, since so many people seem to wonder about it, Spirits are not concerned with what I refer to as *"bedroom and bathroom areas."* Seriously, they are not watching you and holding up scorecards like the judges on *Dancing with the Stars* while you're making love. However, a client's loved ones will bring up intimate information to validate their presence, especially when it is a romantic partner coming through. For example, a husband might mention the honeymoon photo that his widow keeps next to the bed or that he is aware that she still says goodnight to him every night before she falls asleep. Additionally, Spirits are often very interested in our physical health and well-being, so that is where they will show concern. As a medium, this is another time when you need to be very careful in your method of relaying information. Let's say your client's grandmother has some medical advice that she wants you to share; of course you should pass the information along, but be responsible and caring in the way you go about it. Your words could gently encourage your client to go to a doctor for a checkup; on the other hand, if you give an extreme diagnosis you could scare the hell out of him so that he ignores the message out of fear. What could be a simple issue may then become life-threatening—it really depends on the way you choose to deliver the message. The subtleties are enormous.

Your insights will be like the waves that ripple out wider and wider when a penny is thrown in a pond, touching and affecting the ancillary lives of the people you read and impact with your information in ways you can't even imagine. As I have already said countless times before, if you choose to give professional readings or even just share your intuitive impressions with those around you, the ethical responsibility is enormous. **What you do and say has karmic repercussions and should never be taken lightly or be pursued for any other reason than to help others.** The reverberations from your instrument as you play the music you are given are widespread and long-lasting.

14

Creating Your
PSYCHIC
ROOM

YOUR PSYCHIC ROOM is a place of

protection, wisdom, and Universal Love.

A few years ago, I received a book in the mail entitled *The Anastasi System—Psychic Development Level 1: The Fundamentals*, written by my friend and teacher Sandy Anastasi. As I sat at my desk and perused the contents of her book, I couldn't help but smile when thinking back to those first classes nearly twenty-three years ago. As I continued to turn the pages, I was astonished by what I was reading. I immediately called Sandy to tell her that I was blown away by the material because the way I taught psychic development was so similar. You know what I had forgotten somewhere along the way during those twenty-three years? My manners. The conversation should have started something like this: *"Sandy, I want to thank you again for your profound insights and teachings so early on in my development. I've been reading your book just now, and it is so clear that your words and lessons have greatly inspired my work: I can hear your voice echoing through mine today."* That is what I *wished* I had said when she first answered the phone. Instead, I think I excitedly exclaimed, *"I can't believe how we teach so much alike! Do you think we have the same Guides?"* I could hear her pause, and then Sandy gently nudged my ego back into place with as much professionalism as possible. She lightly reminded me that of course my teachings would mirror hers; after all, she was my teacher. So here within the pages of this book I want to honor Sandy Anastasi as I help to raise your awareness just like she raised mine.

GO TO YOUR ROOM

The goal of this chapter is to create a metaphysical workplace in your mind, an inner sanctuary used only for spiritual practices. When you were a child, you were probably told to "go to your room" at different times, perhaps as a form of punishment or when your parents just needed some kid-free time. Now, we can consciously choose to do the same thing but for an empowering reason. Just to be clear—this isn't a physical space I am talking about; it's not your bedroom or office. This room is located in your imagination; it is your very own *psychic room.*

This room is very special and you will design it with a guided visualization exercise. How to build a psychic room is something I would normally talk my students through either in person or on tape, but I believe that if you read my instructions carefully you should be able to do it on your own. Review the steps carefully a few times and then give yourself the necessary time to create this inner retreat the next time you meditate. Once you have built the space in your mind, it will be easier to visit each time and you can continue to add to it as you become more comfortable with your inner surroundings. This is a place that you should retreat to when you need to reduce stress, relax, and create harmony. Consider it a sacred space where you can safely work through your issues and find answers to your problems. Your psychic room is where you should meditate and where you will be able to connect with your friends and relatives who are on the Other Side, as well as meet with your Spirit Guides. If you choose to do readings for others, you will only do them while you are working in your psychic room. This inner office is where you will commute daily to work on obtaining psychic information; it is a place of protection, wisdom, and Universal love.

However, there are special rules that must be followed regarding your inner sanctuary. The door to this sacred room will always be locked. Regardless of how many times a day you visit, you will always need a key to unlock the door. You may not enter your room without finding the key each and every time. There is only *one way* to actually obtain the key: you must consciously and symbolically surrender all your negativity.

Another rule of this special place is that you cannot bring anyone in here with you. This is your space. You cannot imagine someone else in here: this is your room, your energy. You cannot bring your clients or friends; even though you must do your readings while working in this space, your clients are not to be seen in this room. Now don't get me wrong; other energies will join you while you are there, but not because you imagine them sitting on the couch or try to create their presence when you arrive. Your Guides and loved ones from the Other Side will drop in on their own volition, when the timing is right. You can't force them to show up by pretending they are around just because you want them to be with you. Your mind will not permit you to bring any other energy, living or passed on, Angel or Guide, into this room. It is up to your Guides when they wish to visit with you. Spending time in your room in a meditative and relaxed state gives your Team more of a chance to connect with you. I hope you understand the difference.

Your room is a place of truth. It is a place where you work on your acceptance of this incredible spiritual journey you are undertaking. You must learn to acknowledge and recognize that whatever happens in this sacred space is supposed to happen, and is not a coincidence or accident. The messages and impressions that you receive are meant for you at this exact time for a specific reason, even if you don't understand it at the time. Don't let doubt, logic, or disbelief block your abilities; have faith, and let the energy flow. If you can really let go and know that you are not creating this moment, then you can start to allow yourself to comprehend that something bigger is actually occurring. It's not a trick of your imagination. You did not make it up. This means that the experiences that you have in this room are not fabrications of your mind. They are not what you hope or wish them to be, but are what is truly happening. It is the working on the acceptance of this important concept that will help you believe in the reality of what is. This is the place for you to honor the validity of your psychic experience.

* * * * * * *

How to Build Your
Psychic Room Exercise

STEP ONE: Initiation

This exercise is a guided visualization. As prevously mentioned, you should read it a few times before attempting to actually do it on your own. You might even want to make a recording of the instructions so that you remember everything. You will be returning often so you can always fill in the details if you forget something the first time around. You will want to give yourself plenty of uninterrupted time since you will have to build the space during this first visit.

The very first thing you always must do before going to your room is to meditate and protect yourself. You can use the glass elevator analogy (see Chapter 12) to ascend to the top of the colored floors of the chakras; when you get to the seventh floor, the crown chakra, and everything turns to white, watch the elevator doors open. As you stand there letting your eyes adjust to the bright white light surrounding you, bask in the warmth and peace that you always feel on this top floor. Imagine that straight ahead of you is a locked door. You are curious as to what is behind this door but don't have a key to open it. The only way to obtain this key is to consciously and unconsciously surrender and release all your fears, doubts, and negative thoughts.

You are absolutely not allowed to have the key to the door until all your negativity has been released. Now look down and notice that on the floor next to where you stand is a large heavy box. You can visualize it as a cedar chest, a big trunk, or a treasure chest— whatever image comes to your mind. This is called your "Negativity Box." Try to lift it and feel how heavy it is . . . so heavy you can't pick it up. In fact, you must use all your energy just to open the lid of the box. Now see and hear it open. Look inside. And as you look inside you see nothing but darkness, as if it is a bottomless pit, endless, reaching to infinity. Now start placing symbolic representations of all the negativity in your life in this big box. You can use whatever images or symbols that you wish; give each one a name as you put it into the box. These symbols can represent a doubt, fear, attitude, person, or situation that you are viewing as an obstruction or negative issue in your life. Please note that these are only symbolic meanings. This will not neutralize the energy of any person. It will, however, neutralize the negative energy in your personal and professional life that you might encounter with that person or situation.

As you cast away all these symbols, which represent the issues that harness your personal and spiritual evolution, it should feel as if you have just sent a part of yourself down the bottomless pit and you can watch it spiral down out of sight. Know that these negative aspects are now gone forever, even if you had felt shackled by them for a long time. See this as an opportunity to let all of your fears and doubts go. You've placed everything that was negative and weighing you down needlessly into your Negativity Box, and now you watch the lid of this chest close with a heavy clang. If you were to try to open it, you would not be able to now: it is locked. It is too heavy to move because you have deposited into it all negativity in order to free and lighten who you are so that you can move forward in your development.

As a result of ridding yourself of all your negatives, something magical has happened—a key has now appeared on the floor right in front of the box. Your key has shown itself to you! Take the key and unlock the door. You will hear the lock click open and once that happens the key vanishes as if it has evaporated. You will need to go through the releasing of all your negative energy every time you want to enter this room.

STEP TWO: Creating Your Room

As you open the door and step into the room, visualize that the white light shining all around you begins to illuminate the inner sanctuary. Now you are going to design your personal psychic room. You will be able to decorate it however you want, but you need to create a few essential elements first. We both need to imagine this room in the same way in our minds so that you can understand where to place the items that I tell you to build. We're going to refer to this room and its walls as if we were looking at the face of a clock. The doorway where you're standing is the six o'clock position. Directly ahead of you, on the opposite wall, is the twelve o'clock wall. The wall to your right is called the three o'clock wall and the wall to your left is the nine o'clock wall.

Please imagine that you are now standing inside your room and you're facing the twelve o'clock wall. Bask in the white light that is filling the room, and let yourself feel the warmth and protection flow through you. Take a couple of deep breaths and know that you are in a safe and beautiful room that will foster and encourage your spiritual development.

STEP THREE: Activation

We have already established that in order to train our psychic abilities we must first recognize, acknowledge, and accept them. We also must give ourselves permission to work with our abilities. You will do that every time you enter your psychic room, but first we have some "building" to do.

Turn your attention to the three o'clock wall on the right. We will now begin to create your *psychic center.* Please visualize that your psychic center is set up like a media center: two floor-to-ceiling speakers that measure about three feet wide and stand as high as the ceiling, and in between them an entertainment console. Imagine a very large high-definition flat-screen monitor sitting on this console; next to it on the wall you will see a phone. On a desk in front of the screen there is a keyboard, and to the right of the keyboard is a notepad and pen. Right by that desk is a comfortable, plush chair; you can make it any color and type of chair that you like best. Please sit down in this chair and take a moment to admire the psychic center you have just built. On the console, to the right of the pad and pen, notice that there is a big switch. Look closer and you can that there are three positions: On, Off, and, in the middle, Standby. Now it's time to flip the switch to make sure that your psychic center is turned on. You might even hear the center hum with a quiet vibration now that it's running. You will always want the switch to be on to actively utilize your abilities and connect with the energies around you when you are meditating, working with a client, studying, or doing protection exercises.

Now I will briefly go over what the equipment in your psychic center symbolically stands for and how you will use it. The huge speakers represent your clairaudient ability. They will help you in receiving auditory messages from your Guides or from those you love on the Other Side. The large screen symbolizes your clairvoyant ability to visualize information and will be where you can receive images, dreams, and pictures. The keyboard represents your telepathic ability and may be used to send and receive messages. Those of you who are not comfortable using a keyboard can work with the notepad and pen instead. Also you may want to practice your automatic writing skills with the paper and pen. The telephone receiver represents communication with your Spirit Guides and also with anyone from the Other Side. It might be easy for you to start the conversation by using the phone as if you were taking a long-distance call. But *you* don't make the call: *they* call you. If the phone rings, pick it up, say hello, and ask who is calling. Finally, don't forget about the chair: think of it as a "chair of feelings" because it can trigger your clairsentient abilities. You may feel warmth, spiritual hugs, and different types of energy when you are sitting in it.

Your three o'clock wall will now be known as your psychic center. You have just built, activated, and turned on your psychic center. It is the place where you can recognize and develop your abilities. Each time you visit your room, you will flip the master switch to On and sit down to work in your chair. You have all the tools you need in front of you and it is up to you to take the time to meditate and see what happens. You can't force the energy, but by showing up daily to connect with your Guides your chances for success increase over time.

STEP FOUR: Healing Space

Now it's time to walk over to the twelve o'clock wall, which we will call the *healing area.* The first thing I want you to visualize is a table similar to one you might see at a doctor's office. But this is a very special Universal Healing Table. You can lie on this table and symbolically receive a universal healing. Additionally, while you remain on the table, you can also visualize someone who is either living or crossed over and direct this universal healing to that person— anyone in your life who is in need of an emotional, mental, spiritual, or physical healing. Imagine a green button on the side of this table. When you press this button, the healing begins. You can feel an all-consuming, warm, healing energy radiating from above and then the Universal light of love and divine healing envelops your body. You can direct or channel the healing energy to others just by thinking of them. You can also choose to say a prayer for them while you are on the table to send them extra positive energy.

After you are done trying out the table, notice that right next to this table there is a healing screen. Think of it like a projection screen, the type that you might see in a classroom. This is the health detection screen. Now in Chapter 13 I made it very clear that at all times you must remember that you are not allowed to use your psychic ability to diagnose anyone. Unless you are a certified practitioner in the field of medicine, like a doctor or nurse, you cannot use the screen or your intuition to make any type of medical claim. This detection screen is simply an aid to help you gain insight into an area of a person's body that might have a potential stress: a block of negative energy, a physical problem, a surgery, or any type of ailment or energy deficiency in the past, present, or future.

The best way to use the detection screen is to imagine writing the name of the person on the bottom of the screen and then step back. As the screen darkens, visualize an outline of the human anatomy on the screen, not in any great detail, just a simple outline. A red light will flash and blink to designate a trouble spot or blockage of energy that needs to be examined further, either currently or in the future. If you notice a particular place in your client's body that is lighting up on the screen, by all means, make sure to mention it. Let the person know that it could be a past, current, or future issue that you are noticing but that you recommend a visit to a medical professional for a consultation. Again, it's all in the delivery of the message. You don't actually know why you are getting the message about that spot, so be very careful in the words you choose when telling your client about it. Do not say, *"You have a heart problem,"* but do share the information in a more subtle way—always accompanied with a suggestion of seeing a doctor if the client has any concerns. Be aware that you could see the heart highlighted on the screen and it could just as likely refer to an emotional pain as a physical one. **Do not play doctor** and put fear into your client's mind without any reason. This blinking light might be showing you past physical issues as perhaps a way to validate other information from the past—in fact, there is a good chance that you may be seeing a past physical issue instead of a present-day one. Share the information gently and approach the subject in a general manner, especially when first doing this type of work. Your client will most likely have more information than you about what you are seeing and can work with your message to determine the next step. Consider the healing area to be a great asset to your room, but always practice this type of psychic work with ethical responsibility, pure intentions, and a healthy dose of practicality.

STEP FIVE: Let There Be Light

Finally, I would like you to turn to look at the nine o'clock wall. The only thing I want you to imagine on that wall is an old window that has been covered up with wood boards crisscrossing in every direction. This window symbolically represents your *third eye,* which is in the shape of a triangle in the middle of your forehead. To be able to gaze out this window would be like seeing out through your psychic third eye. Now go over to the boards and using all your physical strength start to pull them off, one by one. Don't stop until you remove all the boards and discover that behind the boards is a beautiful triangular-shaped window. It has a huge metal shutter, the type that you would see on a submarine. Marvel in the knowledge that this is your third eye window. We will refer to the opening of this window as the *opening of your third eye.*

I would like you to imagine that you have to use both hands on the shutter handles and with all your might push and lift. At first, feel the shutter being heavy and not wanting to budge, and then you slowly start feeling it move. See it lift up like an old shade that hasn't been opened in a long time. When you finally get it open and try to look outside, the most brilliant bright white light floods through the window, almost blinding you and making it impossible to see anything. The entire room is illuminated by this bright white light. This is the white light of God's love and divine protection. This third eye window will always fill your room with light and inspiration, enhancing and strengthening all the work you are doing in this space.

Welcome—you have officially created your own psychic room, complete with all the psychic tools and instruments you will need for your development. Please take a few moments now to design the rest of this room with the furnishings and personal items you feel you need to have to make this place truly yours and a space that you want to return to often. For example, you may choose to add more furniture and some plants, tarot cards, candles, music, books, and artwork. Create an inner sanctuary that will make you feel inspired, comfortable, and safe. Your psychic room should be a healthy and positive retreat that is conducive to your spiritual development and a wonderful place to work.

A WORK IN PROGRESS

Know that as you develop your abilities and evolve as a person, your room will change and grow as well. Just as when you choose to redecorate your home, you might feel like switching things around as your tastes change over time. The items that you place in this room now might need to be moved out to make room for new ones. You may feel that you no longer want that couch taking up space or you may decide to add some new tropical plants. The room will change as you change. Perhaps you will want to replace some of the older photos with new ones, update the books and music, and add more personal touches. Whatever you choose to do, you can make this room feel like the best escape in the world. Maybe your room is like a breathtaking villa in the Caribbean where you can hear the sound of the ocean waves, or perhaps it is a cozy cabin in the woods with birds singing outside your window. Know that you can renovate or redesign your psychic room any time you wish. Let your inner sanctuary be a true reflection of you.

Now that your psychic room is built, you will be able to return here anytime you wish to meditate, connect with your Guides, solve problems, or even just to relax. It is a place of harmony and peace of mind. If you plan on doing readings, you must always visit your psychic room as part of your preparation before seeing your client. By going to your room, you give yourself permission to receive information. You will remain in your room throughout your session so that your Guides can assist your process.

We will cover how to conduct a reading in more depth in Chapter 15, but for now just remember that you are not bringing your clients into your room. You will have already greeted them and chatted with them prior to traveling to your sacred place to do the reading. Once you are sitting in your room, you are in a meditative state and will not be talking with your client as much as relaying your impressions. This is a practiced and subtle skill, and it will take a lot of time for you to understand exactly how it works. You must not rush your development. Most of you are not going to be professional psychics. Listen to your Guides. Once again I want to discourage you from doing readings until you feel **absolutely confident** in your abilities and ready to make this energetic leap. It is not a game; it is serious business.

The best place to try to connect with your Team is in this space. Meditation will be more successful when done in your inner sanctuary. **The more often you visit your room, the easier and faster it will be to travel there,** just like a quick commute to the office. You will always need to drop off your negatives in your Negativity Box so that you can get the key to your psychic room. Once you enter your space, turn the psychic center master switch to the On position and then open the third eye window and know that you're now able to accomplish whatever you came here to do. Sit or work wherever you feel most comfortable or decide is best-suited for your particular goal during that visit. Follow my steps exactly to get started, but once you have done so you might want to mix up your routine a bit, especially at first, so you can see what gives you the best results.

It is very important to know that when you're finished and ready to leave, *you need to shut down.* You don't always want to be psychically on or have your third eye open while going about your daily routine. That kind of vulnerability would not be smart or effective, and it could lead to being energetically exhausted and overwhelmed.

Exiting Your Psychic Room Exercise

Shutting Down

There are a couple of important steps you must take in the process of closing down your psychic room, just as there are things you do when leaving your home or office. First, go to the nine o'clock wall and lower the shutter on the third eye window. Now head to the three o'clock wall where your psychic center is located and flip the master switch to the Standby position. It is critical that you close the third eye and turn the switch to Standby because you don't want to live your life being psychically open or energetically On all the time. That is dangerous for your emotional and spiritual well-being. Take one final look around the room and know that you will be back soon. Now it is time to leave. Don't forget to shut the door behind you. When you close the door, you will hear it click. Try to open it again and notice that it is locked. You can't open the door again without the key. It is important to remember that you cannot trick your unconscious mind. The boundaries and rules for your inner sanctuary have been created and they must be followed in the order given. You will not be allowed to gain access to your psychic room without the key. You will only find the key after you drop off all your negativity into your box. In this way you will never be able to bring your negative baggage into your psychic room, which keeps your workplace a sacred and protected space.

Back to Reality

Now return to the magical chakra elevator that is waiting for you. Enter it and let it slowly and peacefully bring you back down from your meditation. Take a deep breath and be aware of the energy realigning itself in your body. Pay attention to how your body is feeling, become aware of your feet, and wiggle your toes and fingers. Slowly bend your knees up, stretch gently, and feel how your back, legs, and arms feel as you move. Roll your shoulders, neck, and head, letting the energy return to your entire body. Don't rush the process; it is good to give yourself a few minutes to fully come out of a meditative state. Drink a glass of water and allow yourself to reconnect with the physical realm slowly.

As soon as you have completed this exercise, grab your journal and write down everything that you have experienced. Nothing is too insignificant, so whatever impressions, feelings, and thoughts you had . . . put them all down. It is in those first few minutes after your meditation that you will remember the most details, so it is critical to journal immediately afterward. Some of it may not make sense to you at the time; that's okay. Do not get discouraged. Keep up the process. You will be surprised later on when you reread your entries and discover the real messages and meanings in the information. Think of it like puzzle pieces . . . you may not know how it all fits together at first, but later on you will see the pattern begin to emerge. Each time you visit your psychic room you will be able to build on your prior experiences. Have faith and trust in the process.

Now I do not really expect (and you shouldn't either) that as you first start visiting your psychic room you will blow yourself away with amazing predictions and prophetic accuracy. What I do believe is that by working with this meditation you're opening up your subconscious mind and raising your personal awareness level. It will take some time and lots of practice, but you may be able to use this room to read the energy of other people and project on a line of probability the directions that the energy is flowing in their lives. Be patient with the pace of your development, remain ethically responsible at all times, and always work from a place of humility and love.

15

How to CONDUCT A PSYCHIC SESSION

THERE'S A BIG DIFFERENCE between being psychic

and being spiritual. Make a conscious choice to be both.

My mind is very analytical and logical. That is how I like to learn and also how I like to teach. But applying a methodical approach to psychic development is somewhat oxymoronic, because the subject in its nature is amorphous and intangible. I am attempting to wrap logic and theory around an irrational and magical process. So please be aware of this paradox during this last chapter in which I will share some guidelines and suggestions that you can work with to give your readings structure. Let me repeat once more that I am hoping your main goal in reading *Infinite Quest* is not about doing readings, but about becoming a more spiritual version of You. I do not think most of you should even concern yourself with doing readings when your own spiritual development should be your top priority. But I am also realistic and know that many of you want to give readings, even if just to your friends and family members, so I need to make sure I cover the basics for you as well as give all my readers more food for thought regarding their own psychic growth.

If you are reading this book, you most likely have also read a number of other books on psychic development. Many of the books on awakening your sixth sense only have enthusiastic formulas for development. What I'm offering you in this book are the realities of my experiences. So please keep an open mind as I discuss with you some of my basic theories and applications about conducting a psychic session.

I will reiterate a great deal of what we have already discussed in previous chapters because if and when you attempt to do a reading, I want you to be armed with as much knowledge as possible.

You should always do the best job you can to objectively interpret the information that your Guides give you and must never forget that your words can have a profound impact on the life of the person you are reading. You need to deliver all the messages that you receive in a clear and honest manner. You must strive to inspire and help your clients during your sessions. **My goal is always to leave people**

energetically better off than when I found them, which is a good motto to adopt for doing this work.

JUST A VESSEL

When you set out to do a reading, you must do so with the realization that you are just a conduit, a vessel for the information to flow through. You are not there to editorialize—the message is not about you. The session has nothing to do with you being right or wrong . . . it is about the process. You are the instrument, but your Guides provide the music. Keep in mind that there will be individuals who at times attempt to manipulate you and what you are feeling. They will try to get you to tell them only what they want to hear. It is very important that you listen to your Team and focus on the impressions that you receive and not acquiesce to the client. I constantly remind people that this work and my office are not like McDonald's. There are no golden arches over the door when you walk in, and clients can't just step up to the counter and place an order, expecting to get exactly what they want. I can only share whatever is given to me by my Guides and ask that my clients have faith in the process.

I See Something Bad Is Going to Happen

Turn on the news and you will usually see almost nothing but bad news. Bad news sells and it has a way of immediately grabbing the attention of viewers and sucking them in. The same thing seems to happen with intuition, especially in the beginning of development. You will receive negative impressions during your readings, but it shouldn't always be negative information that you are discussing. Please always remember it is about the process and your delivery. This does not mean that if you see or feel that the person you're reading is possibly going to have a negative experience you keep quiet about it. Not at all. It is important to pass on the impressions that you have, good or bad, but you must choose your words wisely and not embellish or exaggerate when describing what you sense. We discussed this several times before in the book and I admit that it is one of the trickiest parts of doing readings. It takes practice and humility to understand that you could be wrong about how you are interpreting the images or feelings. This is where you must learn how to carefully deliver the information that you are receiving. Let's say you pick up something regarding an automobile, similar to the example I used in Chapter 13. That doesn't mean that you should blurt out *"I see a car accident."* That would be terribly wrong. What if you were totally incorrect in the interpretation of what you were feeling? You might cause the person to become so nervous when driving that they do have an accident. You definitely don't want that kind of karma coming back to haunt you.

A negative feeling regarding an automobile might also mean that the person needs to be careful where they park their car in case it is stolen or vandalized. It could also indicate that they should just show extra caution while driving to avoid a potential problem like a flat tire. Or maybe the car needs mechanical repair, or they are late on a payment. Not to mention the timing question. Maybe there is an event in the past that you picked up upon instead! You need to always be aware that there are many scenarios at play when you just have a negative feeling or image to go on. You can't assume too much or just say whatever you want without thinking about the impact of your words. Has it sunk in yet why I keep saying there is enormous responsibility in doing this work? I certainly hope so.

DELICATE DELIVERY

When dealing with energy and information for other people, just imagine that you are a delivery person for a fine art gallery. You must transport precious items in boxes, the contents of which you don't always fully understand. Nonetheless, you must deliver each box safely. The box may contain glass so you treat it with great care. However, you don't have the right to open the box and tell the owners where the object must be placed in their house.

We have spent a great deal of time together on our journey discussing the serious ethical responsibility that is necessary when working with other people's energy. You should also be aware that your contact with the person you're reading affects your own personal awareness. By this I mean that how you react and handle the situations in your own life will change as a result of your readings for others. **Remember that there are no accidents in this amazing Universe—things happen for a reason.** The people that are put in your path for you to read and help are sent to you on purpose so that you can learn more about your own life. The lessons are waiting for you with each new experience.

ALL SESSIONS ARE NOT CREATED EQUAL

Every reading you do will be unique because every session will be with a different person. You are the constant. In addition, there are many variables that occur during every reading as a result of where your clients are in their life, what lessons they are learning, and what emotions they bring to the table when they are sitting in front of you.

TURNING BACK

During my teenage years I went from mocking psychics and wanting to debunk their abilities to diving headfirst into developing my intuition and expanding my knowledge on parapsychology. Once I started exploring the spiritual realms, I didn't look back. You can't look back, really. It's like being on a roller coaster and deciding that you want to get off in the middle, right before the drop. In metaphysical terms, once you learn a lesson you don't just selectively delete it from your mind. You become accountable for that knowledge. Your actions and your life as a whole seem to be measured against a higher standard. Remember the red pill–blue pill analogy from *The Matrix?* I love that movie because it is an action film laced with true metaphysical lessons. Once you make a conscious commitment to live a spiritual life, there's no turning back.

Trust me—you cannot control any of it, except for one element, and that is the programming of the session by your Energy. Just go with it. You can read three people in a row and I promise you, dare I say predict, that you will have three distinctively different readings. You are the same person, and not much would have changed for you over the course of three hours, but these sessions will be vastly different in tone and content.

YOUR PERSONAL NETWORK

Your Team of Spirit Guides knows that you're interested in strengthening your abilities and most likely they directed you to discover this book. The same way my Guides led me on my spiritual path, so will yours if you let them. As your earthly guide during this experience, I hope to assist you in defining your psychic potential as well as building a strong foundation in the philosophy of metaphysics. The bottom line is that you really need to be conscious of your intentions and actions concerning your spiritual development. You must always appreciate and respect your Guides and the energetic Force that is all around you. Know that your Team is there to help you and will have your best interests in mind as long as you honor and accept their role in your life.

Let me give you an example of why I feel that this sense of reverence and respect is so important. One night a friend stopped over to visit because she was in the neighborhood. I had just finished a phone session for a client and had left my tarot cards out on the table. My friend sat down, noticed the cards, and immediately picked them up—for some psychic readers that is prohibited, but I didn't stop her at first. My friend began shuffling the cards just as she has watched me do so many times. She started to place the cards down in a way that was similar to the layout that I use while she mocked the entire process. I shook my head and warned her not to play with things that she didn't understand. She laughed, threw down a few cards, and wanted to know what they meant pertaining to her. I believe she even sarcastically called me "swami" in an attempt to push my buttons.

Anyway, I looked at how the cards fell, glanced up at her, and asked, *"Do you really want me to tell you?"* She smirked and then, noticing my grave expression, nervously nodded. I simply interpreted the meaning of what I saw, which indicated that she would possibly be having surgery in the reproductive region of her body. Obviously, this bit of news didn't thrill her and she quickly tried to shrug off the whole experience. Again I cautioned her that she shouldn't mock something that she didn't understand, as she may have received more information than she was ready to handle. Tarot and any other divination tools are not games to be taken lightly.

She thought I was just trying to scare or intimidate her. But I would never do that. I only interpreted what the cards said. A few short months later she had an unscheduled surgery to remove a growth from her ovary. Of course she developed a profound new respect for my work, but I wish I had been wrong for her sake. I can't stress it enough: **I want you to understand and respect the unseen world of energy.** This is not about fortune-telling or being able to gaze into a crystal ball and foresee winning lottery numbers. This is about *Universal Energy* and learning how to work with it. And just for the record, when it comes to the lottery, let me save you the time and trouble of trying . . . divination isn't meant for that. Trust me— I tried many years ago with no success. But if you feel the need to find out for yourself, go ahead, and good luck.

RECOGNITION—PERMISSION— ACCEPTANCE REVISITED

As I have stated previously, daily meditation is essential if you wish to proceed on your spiritual journey. During the early years of my development, my Guides gave me exercises and ideas for enhancing my psychic abilities during meditation. I was also shown answers and explanations to a large number of issues, both personally and professionally. My Guides taught me by analogy. I have an amazing and healthy relationship with my Team and communicate with them daily. Now, please don't think that I have coffee and bagels with them every morning. They are of the nonphysical realm, so they do not require food and drink! For now, let me act as your earthly guide and just trust me enough to believe me when I say that your Team is really there for you, ready to jump in to assist you if you ask. Their role and responsibility as Guides is to accomplish just that ... to guide you. To be clear, they are not interested in trivial issues, and they don't work for you. **Your Team is there to love, protect, and inspire you.** Allow your Guides to do their job and have faith in their presence. The more you attempt to listen to them, the more connected to them you will feel. It might start off slowly at first, but the connection will grow if you trust in the process and nurture your relationship with them with reverence and gratitude.

SYMBOLOGY

The symbols that I now use in my readings came to me over a period of time, with a lot of practice and meditation. If you put in the effort, you will develop an understanding of the language of energy that your Guides speak and it will be in your frame of reference based on your life experiences. I will say it once more: *Be patient.* In retrospect, I wish one of the books that I read when I was a teenager had taught me this simple lesson. They all made it seem like paint-by-numbers art; do this and that and then you too can predict the future in five easy steps! Yeah, sure. If I hadn't studied with Sandy and truly learned how to listen to my Guides, I might still be sitting there waiting for some big sign to hit me over the head. I would never have realized how subtle this Energy actually is and how much dedication, trust, and time it takes to develop.

You must learn how to recognize the messages that you receive; over time you will develop a *knowing,* a sense of what it feels like when your

Guides are coming through with information. Everyone is unique, and things manifest differently as a result, so I can't tell you exactly how it will work for you. For instance, if I am not planning on doing readings, but my Guides want me to pay attention, my ears will get bright red, and I will feel a buzz on the back of my neck. *"Incoming"* is the word that I immediately think of when that feeling hits me. It grabs my attention so that I stop what I am doing, settle down, and listen.

My Guides always explain everything in parallels, metaphors, and great analogies. It's simple algebra: If A=B and B=C, then A and C are equal as well. It has been one of the best and easiest ways for people to be able to comprehend the meaning of the messages, especially when doing a psychic reading. Once I understand what my Guides are trying to tell me, then they help me to be more specific and build on it for my client. But I want to stress that your Team will speak to you in a language that is meant for you and your frame of reference. It is not something that I can teach you; the language will be explained over time by working with your Guides. Please hear this point loudly: **The way that you receive the information is inside of you; it is not outside of your body.** When you are thinking about seeing, hearing, and feeling messages from your Guides, it is within you; it doesn't happen outside of you. Don't wait for the billboard in the sky, for the deep booming voice, or for your Guides to pat you on the back for a job well done. **Remember that this spiritual journey takes time, practice, and faith.**

WRITE IT DOWN

Always ask your client to write down the symbolism that you mention during a session. Even though you may misinterpret the message, it doesn't mean that the impression is incorrect. I always feel that the information coming through is 100 percent valid; it is the psychic who, more than likely, is screwing up the interpretation. I don't care if your dearly departed Aunt Susie appears in front of you wearing a huge sign that tells you tomorrow's headlines: you won't know that you are accurate until the events happen and you won't be able to validate the message unless the information is already written down. Often the message may not be clear until sometime later in the future, or after your client has had a chance to think about it further or share it with someone else. Once the session is over and your client has left, you should also take time to journal about your experience, just as you might take notes if you were a counselor or doctor. You can learn more about the ways your Team communicates with you if you keep a written record of your readings. Over time you will see patterns and symbols as you do when writing about your meditations. All this information adds to your understanding of your abilities and is crucial to your development.

RIGHT OR WRONG

For your sake (and your clients'), I am stressing one more time how important it is for you to believe that you definitely have the capability to be wrong. Take the pressure off yourself right from the beginning—not to mention answering the line of people who will most happily remind you when you're wrong anyway. As soon as you start to think that your abilities are about you, you've failed, and you might as well brace yourself for the inevitable crash and fall. By allowing yourself to be wrong, you no longer have to worry about being right every time, and you can completely focus on being accurate, helpful, and responsible.

WHAT'S YOUR TOOL?

Right from the beginning of my metaphysical studies, my Guides directed me to focus on learning how to use one tool of divination so that I would be able to use it to help me develop my abilities (see Chapter 11). I decided to use tarot cards as my psychic tool for no other reason than perhaps I was predisposed to them since Lydia did my first reading with cards. I read several books on psychic development and how to use cards for readings so I thought I knew what was supposed to happen. Guess what? Things never played out the way the books said they would. Naturally, I thought Lydia was wrong about me and my potential. I did exactly what the books were telling me to do and there were no instant results, at least not in the way I expected. It seemed like I achieved nothing; I felt like a big psychic zero. Then I started to recount the readings that I had already done and I noticed something significant. Every person I read had called back to request another session and asked if they could bring a friend. They all told me how eerily accurate their reading was in a short period of time. Following the step-by-step psychic book too literally was causing me to completely doubt my abilities. My epiphany was in my realizing that the client callbacks were the real results . . . they wouldn't be happening unless I was doing something right.

So what was the difference? The answer is simple. When I had no weird formula to focus on regarding development, I had no choice but to pay attention to myself and the messages I was receiving from my Guides. **Remember, ultimately it all happens within you.** I found that when I just talked about what I was seeing and how it made me feel I was able to really get the clients that I was reading to understand the energy that I was sensing about them. Whether it's the past that I was seeing or something that I felt was future-oriented, my clients seemed to feel connected to me. But it was really the opposite: I was connected to them.

Please don't misinterpret what I am saying and throw down this book thinking you didn't need to read it after all. I needed to study (and still do), and every book and class that my Guides pointed out to me helped me to be the student that I am today. It was important for me to expand my understanding of metaphysics in the same way you are doing now. Trust me—I have read lots of books and continue to build my knowledge base so that I develop an understanding of many different perspectives and teachings. I let my Guides choose what I should study, as they are always looking for ways to teach me new information. But the information in the books are only guide-lines, recommendations, and advice—just like in this book. There is no one method of learning. You have to trust that voice within you to point you in the right direction. Same goes for choosing your psychic tool. Take your time in exploring your options by studying books and enrolling in classes, either in your local community or online. Pick the oracle that resonates with you. You can always learn a second one later on, but choose one for now and run with it. Whatever form of divination you decide to use, learn it thoroughly so that it becomes like a second language to you. It must feel comfortable and easy to access whenever you need it. Only you can determine what will work best for you.

ALWAYS A STUDENT, NEVER A TEACHER

If you were to interview me in another twenty-five years, I would say the same thing as I am saying now: **I am still a student of the work.** We must always continue to develop our abilities and further our knowledge. Once we stop studying, become stagnant in our growth, or believe that we can no longer learn, we will begin to fail in our work and our spiritual progress will be hindered. I love to learn about this work as well as many other subjects and always feel that I can learn something new from everyone I meet. Even if it is just a different per-spective on the same topic, it gives your Guides another opportunity to share their messages with you. Additionally, you might discover a new approach to explaining things to your clients that may come in handy one day when you least expect it. As long as you always see yourself as a student of the Universe, eager to learn and willing to listen, you will continue to grow mentally and spiritually. Be hungry for knowledge and keep your mind open to whatever lessons you are meant to receive.

PSYCHIC DOESN'T EQUAL SPIRITUAL!

My wife Sandra has repeatedly threatened that she is going to write a tell-all book one day titled *The Unspiritual Spiritualists.* She claims it would be a best-seller, and she's probably right. She has witnessed a grotesque amount of the Inner Monster running rampant over the years while observing the professional metaphysical world I work in and as a result of our being around so many larger-than-life personalities. (Clearly she is not speaking of me!) She and I have often discussed the unfortunate incongruity of an individual who is amazingly talented psychically but doesn't seem to have a clue about how to be ethical, moral, responsible, or spiritual. Just because a psychic is famous and says all the right things doesn't mean their heart and intentions are pure. The Inner Monster will take over the best of us if we are not constantly keeping our egos in check. The smartest way to avoid the ego trap is by starting on your journey of development with a strong foundation of humility and respect for your Guides and this work. **I want you to consciously pledge to be ethically responsible and spiritual in all that you do.**

PSYCHIC FRIENDS NETWORK

No, I am not referring to Ms. Cleo or any other 1–900 psychic phone hotlines. In my opinion, if all these "psychics" were so talented, they wouldn't be sitting around 24/7, waiting for someone to call them, and charging folks by the minute. They would have a more legitimate business practice where their clients call to schedule an appointment. I personally believe that most of these phone services are a scam, preying on the vulnerability of people who feel lost and confused and who are easily motivated by the fear principle. Anyway, I digress. The psychic friends network I want to discuss is the one you start to build by seeking out a psychic buddy or creating some camaraderie with other students of the Universe. You might find yourself being drawn to people who are on the same quest for knowledge as you—like attracts like. You may decide to work on development exercises with a friend to encourage each other's growth. You could try meeting people through a class or group in your area, or even an online connection could work out well. It would be really helpful to have a friendly support system to practice reading tarot with or to talk over your impressions and dreams. Just remember that others may develop at a different speed than you. One person may be more accurate than the other in a particular area of discerning information or using a certain type of divination tool. Be acutely aware of any competitive energy cropping up, and squash the Inner Monster before it gets a chance to hurt your newfound friendship or hinder your growth. Just enjoy the fact that you have someone in your life who understands a metaphysical language that most of the people around you do not speak.

> **Ego Uninterrupted:** We have spent this entire book trying to keep your Inner Monster in check, but now when dealing with the idea of doing an actual session, I want you to memorize the following: **You need to have enough ego to give you the courage and confidence to allow you to do a reading and work with the information that you are receiving.** Anything in excess of that is too much and will hinder your progress and your future success.

HOW TO DO A READING

There are no simple and easy formulas to speed along your psychic development, just as there is no one way to go about giving a reading. I have shared with you the methods that have worked for me, described the building blocks of Energy, and discussed the ethical responsibility involved in doing this work. How you put it all together will really be up to you. I have read a great number of books that profess to teach intuitive development, but what they often forget to explain is how to manage your expectations in the process. **Be patient.** Learning a new set of skills takes dedication and practice. It doesn't happen overnight. You will always be learning as you go, no matter how much you think you already know.

Schedule All Readings

You must always treat your work with the respect it deserves, which includes scheduling your readings just as any other professional would do. Your intuition is not a party trick, and if someone asks you to launch into a reading and you do, you have allowed them to lessen the value of your work and take advantage of your time and energy. It is also extremely important that you properly prepare for a reading, which may be difficult to do if you are so spontaneous about it. You must always schedule your readings, even for friends. It sets the stage for them to take you and the process more seriously. After you have scheduled this appointment, even if it will occur in the next hour, you need to instruct the person you are reading to bring a list of questions written down on paper. This is to ensure that they are not wasting your time as well. It forces them to really think about what is about to happen for them as special and unique. These questions should be in areas of interest to them, things that they want to know about. Don't allow clients to ask these questions until the very end of the session. I want you to allow the reading to happen as organically as possible, without any preconceived agenda or outcome.

Using Your Tool as Your Key

Okay, now that you have set your appointment, you need to take the time to plan how you will use your psychic key to assist in your reading. Whether you have chosen tarot, astrology, numerology, or another oracle as your primary tool, it comes with its own set of rules to abide by. Make sure to take care of all the logistics ahead of time. For instance, you might need your client's birth data prior to the reading so you can run a chart or calculate the client's numbers. You do not want to experiment with a new tarot card layout for the first time during a session. You need to feel comfortable and confident with the tool you are using so that your client can relax and trust the process. Think all the details through before you sit down to do your reading so that the Energy can just flow naturally once you are in session. When you are using your psychic key during the reading, whether it's a card layout or talking about the client's chart, this exchange will be a profound way to create a good bond with the person you are reading. Ultimately your psychic tool will allow your Spirit Guides to symbolically tell their story throughout the session.

Meditation · Psychic Self-Defense · Using a Psychic Tool · Trusting Yourself to Allow It to Happen

Remember that the first step of any reading is always meditation. This will work on relaxing your physical body and allowing your mind to join in. Once you have that process under way, you can prepare your mind to be able to receive and perceive information. If you are still not completely comfortable with meditation, you are not ready— I repeat, not ready—to do readings.

Step two is to practice psychic self-defense, no matter what and for as long as it takes until you feel the white light of protection all around you. Any time you are attempting to help another person, you must protect yourself first. You have to practice psychic self-defense if you are going to open yourself up to other energies from this world and beyond. I know I have harped on this point over and over in this book. That is because it is absolutely necessary. **There is**

no cutting corners. Would you want your pilot dozing off at 37,000 feet? Would you want your surgeon and medical team to not wear gloves to protect you from infection during surgery? Of course not. Just because in the work of a psychic you can't see the immediate physical ramifications due to the lack of protection doesn't mean it's not energetically lethal. Here's a quick analogy for why you need protection while conducting readings: when a flight attendant on a plane discusses the oxygen mask safety procedures before taking off, you are instructed that if you are traveling with a small child to secure your mask first, then the child's. There's a very important reason to follow those instructions—if you can't breathe, you certainly will not be able to assist in getting the child's mask on. Obviously, that's not a scenario you would ever want to have happen, let alone consider the same thing in regard to your client.

Third, use the primary psychic tool you chose to begin the reading. Whichever tool you are most comfortable with is your best option as it is the one that is most likely to open your abilities so that you can receive your Guides' messages with clarity.

Finally, you will need to let go and allow it to happen.

I want you to begin every session the same way by going to your psychic room (see Chapter 14). Allow yourself to meditate for at least fifteen minutes and make sure to include the white light for psychic protection. As always, you will need to drop off all negative energy into the Negativity Box to get the key to your psychic room. Once inside, flip your psychic center switch to On, open your third eye window, and begin to do prayers of protection to fill you and your room with the white light. Once you are surrounded in the white light, imagine that the area that you are going to use for your session is also enveloped in this light. This is one of the most essential steps in beginning any type of reading.

When you are conducting a reading, you are entering into someone's energy field, and all that person's life's issues are included. Using the white light protection allows you to not take on those issues and treat them as if they were your own.

LET YOUR MIND GO

As you are sitting with your client at the appointed time, you have protected yourself and meditated and are ready to utilize the psychic tool of your choice. Now what? *You must completely submit to the process.* You need to surrender your ego and serve the process and disseminate the information bestowed upon you. Initially, it might feel like free association or a stream of consciousness type of babbling—just go with it. In the beginning, you will have to fight the urge to be "right" since the person that you are reading is staring directly at you and will be waiting for you to "wow" him with information about his life. Be careful not to get caught into the "repeating yourself remix" when you get a positive reaction. Cynical critics say that a psychic will get one "lucky guess" and then paint a bull's eye around it for the rest of the session. Make sure not to fall into that ego trap and move on to give a different message.

Allow yourself to say whatever comes to you; just go with it, whether it makes perfect sense to you or not. Tell the story that your mind is unfolding. Do not look at your client while you are speaking. Treat your client like the mythological Medusa—one look and you can turn to stone. Many times a client's facial expressions will distract you from trusting what you are receiving. Focus on the cards, wall, floor, or just keep your eyes closed. In addition, try not to let your client speak too much or assist you, as it is your job to deliver the information.

(NOT) QUESTIONING YOUR CLIENT

Never ask questions! Instead, you need to make statements and only ask for confirmation. If you are constantly asking for information from your client, then you will lack credibility and it will be hard to gain the person's trust. It will seem like you are guessing or fishing for answers when you should be asking your Guides the questions instead. What you *are* allowed to do is to ask for confirmation from your client. There's a big difference. Once you share your message, the validation you receive will let you know that what you're saying is accurate and that you should proceed on the same track. If you are giving information and the client is saying "no, that doesn't fit" or "I don't understand the message," say that you're not certain and that you could be wrong, but that the message should still be written down in case it makes more sense in the future. Remember you have the ability to be wrong and it's okay if you are misinterpreting the information. It happens to the most experienced psychics, so shake it off and don't let it interrupt your rhythm. There is no reason to continue repeating the same message, so move on to another subject or impression to keep the energy flowing and so you don't fall into the trap of doubting yourself or the process. Ultimately you have to go with what your Guides are relaying to you, so stay true to what you're receiving and keep asking for more clarity from your Team.

PSYCHOMETRY

If you want to do a session without using tarot cards or numerology as your psychic tool, try a psychometry reading instead to unlock the client's energy and quickly connect with them (see Chapter 11). When you begin the session, ask if you can hold a piece of your client's jewelry. Remember, it should be an item that belongs solely to the client and not a borrowed or vintage item. Place it in your left hand. Shut your eyes and react to what you are seeing, hearing, and feeling. Now, it is quite possible that the first twenty or so times that you attempt to do psychometry, you'll get nothing at all or maybe just one simple rush of feeling. Remember that whatever you get will work for that session and that there is a reason that you're receiving it. Make sure to share all your impressions with your client no matter how insignificant or odd they seem, and trust in the process. You might be surprised at how something that sounds strange to you resonates deeply with your client. Psychometry is worth practicing until it starts to work for you. It is one of the fastest ways to connect with the energy of another person, and it can really open up your abilities. Let yourself flow with the energy you receive and see where it takes you.

ASK FOR DIRECTIONS FROM YOUR GUIDES

When relaying messages about what is happening in a person's life, it is important to make sure that you can trust the information that is coming through during the session. You want to ask your Guides for validation of the client's past situation to know that you are tuned in appropriately. You can share what you receive with your client and ask for confirmation to be certain that you're connecting accurately with your Guides.

I think that all readings should discuss where the clients are coming from, where they are at now, and where they are headed. Once you are comfortable with the past, you will be able to ascertain where your client is at in the current situation and read what's on the line of potential probabilities for the future. Don't forget that you are not telling your client what to do or even what is going to happen per se; your client always has free will to operate from so you are only giving possible outcomes, not fated ones.

QUICK RECAP

First, you must always go to your psychic room to meditate and practice psychic self-defense. Second, use a psychic tool and/or perform psychometry to help you unlock the doors to the client's energy. The next step in conducting a session is to become a journalist; be as nosy as you possibly can by interviewing your Guides about the person you're reading and pay close attention to all the information they are sending you.

THE NOW

The first thing is to ask your Guides if there is a situation that is occurring right now in your client's life that they can help shed some light on. I begin here for two reasons. One, it helps the clients in their process of understanding that situation, and two, it will give you immediate validation. If you are able to bring up a past situation or a current event in their life, it will grab their attention, gain their trust, and make them more willing to listen to what you have to say about the future.

What you want to do is peel away at the situation, layer by layer, providing as much detail as possible. Remember, the more details you deliver, the better. The more specific information you can relay to your clients, the easier it will be for them to understand what it is that you are receiving and perceiving. Keep asking your Guides to fill in the missing pieces so that you can offer a complete picture. Once you have worked on it for a bit, switch to the next issue in the person's life and start coloring in the details. Continue to put more questions to your Guides while you are doing the reading. One of the most important issues to discuss is personal relationships, both romantic and family. Ask your Guides if there is something about love that needs to covered, and then fine-tune the information. Each area that you work with should start out as a big picture and then zoom in to get more and more specific before you move on. Make sure that your client writes down what you are saying because much of it may not make sense until sometime after the session, and the client will want a record of everything, especially the future events.

THE FUTURE

More than likely in the beginning you will receive messages about situations that will occur rather soon in the sitter's life. The reason that you will have more impressions about the immediate future is to give you the confidence to keep honing your skills. Your client may even be able to validate some of the information during the actual reading, or perhaps later on with a follow-up call.

Here are basic areas of future interest for you to work on during the session: love and relationships, career and money, family matters, friends, travel, basic life lessons, and, of course, health. A client's health is an important topic but also can be dangerous territory, as discussed in Chapter 14. Remember that your job is to act as a facilitator for the information. **You are not a diagnostician.** It is unethical to formally diagnose people when you are not a doctor. I know I am repeating myself, but for the record it is important. If you do receive a message about something that is health-related—perhaps when you are using your detection screen in the healing center of your psychic room—just acknowledge the location of the stressed part and suggest that your client pay more attention to that area of the body. If you feel a negative energy around it, make sure to suggest that the client make an appointment to see a medical professional to have it checked out.

CLIENT'S QUESTIONS

When you feel that you have amply provided the clients with all the information that you are receiving, you should allow them to break out the list of questions they brought with them to the session. You will find that often some, if not all, of these questions will have already been addressed during the course of the actual reading. Remember, it is imperative that clients prepare a list of questions before they sit down with you as it allows them to focus on the areas and issues that they really want more information on, which your Guides will then pick up on during the session. Also it is good idea to have the clients ask any questions about the reading if they need clarification on a particular issue. You can always use your psychic tool to help you to answer the questions, whether you add another layer of cards to your previous layout or spend more time looking at the client's natal chart with a certain issue in mind. Your Team will stay with you throughout the reading so you can always ask them for more assistance. You are the vessel; let your Guides tell the story.

Wrap It Up

Once you have covered all these different topics, answered any questions that your clients might have about the reading, and also handled the questions that they had brought with them, you're basically done. Once again, don't forget to encourage clients to remember everything you said by writing it down. This advice is as much for you as it is for them. As mentioned earlier, it is always wise to journal after your client leaves for your own records. You might not recall everything you said, but go ahead and jot down what you do remember as well as a few notes about the overall experience. This will help you to track any patterns or insights that may not be clear or mean much at the time, but might make perfect sense in the future.

The session will probably last about an hour or so. It may take you more time if you allow the client to talk with you during the process. I don't usually allow people to say much at all during the actual reading, usually only to validate that they understand what I'm telling them and to make sure that I am on the right track.

Now please remember that you will probably be staring at the back of your eyelids for a number of attempts before you get anything at all; just be patient. This is why working with a psychic buddy, or at least some very tolerant and supportive friends and family members, would be very useful. **When the information is there you will know it, you will feel it.** It is like the smell of a certain flower or spice; once you know it, it is hard to miss. Eventually you will understand the language that your Guides use to communicate with you, so have faith and trust in the process.

* * * * * * * *

MEDIUMSHIP

If you are born to be a medium, you will not wonder if you are: you will know it. It is like saying you have blue eyes. You either do or you don't; there isn't much to question. You may have been brought to this book because you are a medium, and I hope you find the support and encouragement you need to take your development to the next level. However, many more of you might think you have the ability to be a medium, but the odds are highly unlikely. Perhaps you have been fortunate enough to communicate with your loved ones in the Afterlife from time to time. That is a very different experience, one that I wish for everyone. In fact, I encourage all my clients and students to reach out to their friends and family who have passed over. The love never dies and they are around you. But the reason you are connecting with them is the bond of love you share. This does not mean you can do it for others on a professional basis. I can't tell you how frustrating it is to see people make this mistake time and time again. I am thrilled when my work is validated to the point that my clients' experiences in a session allow them to open up and continue to be able to communicate with someone special on their own afterward. But my joy sours quickly when those same people then begin to claim that they can commune with everyone's relatives and they now want to go professional. It just doesn't work like that. You already know how I feel about this topic since I have brought it up numerous times in this book. The general rule is don't go messing with the dead people if you don't know what you are doing. Leave it to those who specialize in mediumship and who are trained to be deeply aware of the responsibilities and ramifications of this work. A lot of irreparable damage can be done if you play around with something so serious, and you don't want that kind of karmic build-up in your life.

I have to tell you that most psychics are not mediums, but every medium is definitely psychic. But there might be a special occasion when you are doing a reading with a client and some other type of entity comes through that doesn't feel like one of your Guides. If you are receiving messages in a very different manner from the way you normally do, then pay very close attention. Once you see that you're making the connection, and you will know immediately, keep sharing your impressions with the person you are reading. The client may state that what you're saying doesn't fit them but it sounds like one of their deceased relatives or loved ones. Now more than ever it is important to validate the information. The Spirit is showing up because of its strong bond with your client and it might see the reading as its only chance to connect. This is a bonus for you and your client, but you must be strict and draw some boundaries with the Ones that are coming through from the Other Side. Stay in the moment and do not use this experience as a way to convince yourself that you are now a medium. You are a psychic receiving a special message that you must relay to your client. It's critical that you focus on setting some ground rules to keep you and your client emotionally safe.

BE FIRM WITH THE DEAD

If you are making a connection with the Afterlife during a psychic session, you might notice that the biggest difference is the location that you feel the information originating from. Although it is a bit tricky to explain unless it's happening to you, the message will feel, sound, or appear slightly different from the normal type of information that you receive from your Guides. The impressions will not come from within so much as from the other person's energy field. Acknowledge to your client that although you are not a medium and were only planning on giving a psychic reading, you are receiving a different kind of energy which you believe to be from the Other Side. Gently explain that you feel the loved one's presence and that it is out of love for your client that the Spirit is making its presence known. Don't feel that you need to attempt a connection to communicate. Also don't allow the client to tell you what the dead person is saying—it will always be based on the client's own issues and emotional needs. This is where the session can get dangerously uncomfortable. Many times a client will burst out with some sort of exclamation like *"They are trying to tell me that something is wrong!"* But that is rarely the case. When Spirits come through from the Other Side, they are usually trying to let their loved ones know that they are okay, that they love them, and that they are still connected. But some clients, because of their overwhelming desire for drama, will attempt to read more out of the message than that. I know, it sounds pretty special as is, but sometimes humans get in the way of the beauty of the message of love.

One simple way that you may be able to discern who is coming through is by using the method that works for me. I have found that if the information feels like it is falling all around me, I know it is coming from my Guides. But if the information appears to be coming from around the client, I know it is the client's loved ones, or someone connected directly to them, who has crossed over trying to make contact during the reading.

At this point, you cannot lose control of the session. **You have to remain in balance.** Some clients get very emotional when you start to bring through their loved ones, and that may cause one of two things to happen to you. It can either make you uncomfortable or distract you from the process. Or, for many psychics, the intensity feeds the Inner Monster. *Don't go there!* I have seen too many mediums create an emotional issue while doing their readings and the elicited response makes everyone feel the energy of the loss, instead of the love of the reconnection.

Your job is to pass on information from a balanced and centered position. You are like the lifeguard sitting in the high seat watching everyone in the pool. As soon as you jump off your perch and into the pool of emotion, you can no longer do your job effectively. Remaining a compassionate but detached observer will allow for the least amount of harm and the best outcome.

When you are feeling the energies from the Other Side, I would suggest taking the following steps. Immediately ask if there are Spirits from the Other Side who want to connect with your client. Tell them to give you their messages in a way that you'll receive them best. This basically means that you are asking them to give you the information in your frame of reference. Ask them to show you how they died so that you can describe that to your client, and ask them to show you or tell you their name and give you an identifying piece of information that you can offer to the person you are reading.

You will need to always validate the presence of the loved ones from the Other Side who just decided to drop in unannounced at the start of your session. Be certain to pass on the messages they wish to have relayed to your client before you proceed any further with the reading. Let me just say this: If Spirits stop in for a visit, they will not allow you to continue your reading of the client's future until you acknowledge that they are there with you. They didn't come all this way for nothing, and they will not easily be deterred. Tell them that they have your attention only for the first part of the session and be specific about your abilities and what you need from them so that you can understand what they want to communicate. **Their main message is always one of love.** It is to allow their friends and relatives here in the physical world to know that they are still with them even while on the Other Side—that we are all still connected. It can be a very rewarding, comforting, and extremely healing experience. However, keep in mind that you are not a therapist or grief counselor, so proceed as carefully and compassionately as possible. On the other hand, it might also turn into a difficult time for you. Many clients want you to essentially become that deceased relative before they can actually accept that you are talking to a loved one. So be patient, remain centered, and keep the white light of protection all around you.

Conduct the same type of interview process with those from the Other Side as you do when communicating with your Guides. But this time you are asking about *them* versus the client. Inquire who they are, how they crossed over, and when they departed. Relay this information as you receive it to your client so that you do not leave any detail unsaid. Ask the Spirits to identify specific events either from the past or that might be happening soon. Pay special attention to any pictures, smells, sounds, and physical responses that you may experience. The messages with mediumship that you pick up can be very surprising and unique. Do not try to interpret or embellish any of your impressions; just pass them on. These validations are imperative for your clients to receive, as they will likely understand them more than you do. If your clients are unsure about what something means, tell them to write it down because it might make more sense to another relative or friend than it does to them. Also, sometimes something might not click for the client until later on. Usually people are in a bit of shock or an emotional space while their loved one is there, so it is understandable that they might not be able to think clearly. Do not insist that you are right, but at the same time do not doubt what you are receiving. You must never lose sight of the fact that you are just the vessel transmitting the message. **Be humble and reverent, and always work from a place of love.** Remember your ultimate goal for any type of reading should be to leave your client in a better emotional place than when you started.

AFTERWORD
THE END OF THE ROAD

We have officially come to the end of our journey with each other. Now pull over and let me out of the car! Just kidding—this has been a great ride and I hope that I was not too annoying along the way by reiterating some of the most important and valuable lessons that I felt needed to be repeated. I feel confident that you will never forget them! Make sure that you continue to grow by questing for knowledge and aspiring to be both student and teacher.

Thank you for the time you have spent with me. Thank you for allowing me to assist you in your development by sharing my insights and experiences. Thank you for giving me the respect of listening. I discussed in detail the importance of ethical responsibility when doing readings for others, and I truly hope that you now fully understand the profound impact that you can have on those around you, your clients, the work, and your own growth. Above all, strive always to be ethical, honest, and spiritual. My hope is that after you pull the car over to the side of the road and allow me to exit, you will continue to evolve and grow far beyond the pages of this book. There are many adventures for you to experience and learn on your spiritual journey, so buckle up with the white light to keep you safe, make sure to bring your Team along for the ride . . . and let's see where this life takes you!

All the best,
JOHN EDWARD
Your fellow student of the Universe

INDEX

*For more information about John Edward
and his online community, go to*
WWW.JOHNEDWARD.NET